Advance Praise for Steve Hanna's
A Home Called Your Own

"Steve Hanna has taken up the standard of his family's quest for permanence. His story is one of responsibility, resistance, humility, and honor."

— Kim Barnes, Pulitzer Prize finalist and author of
A Country Called Home and *In the Kingdom of Men*

"When Steve returned from his journey, he told me the incredible story you're about to read. I told him that he should write a book about what he encountered, and two years later, here it is. Prepare to be surprised."

— Dan Bukvich, composer of *Symphony No. 1*
(In Memoriam, Dresden, 1945).
Dresden is a major location in *A Home Called Your Own*.

"Inspiring."

— Kellen Moore, NCAA record holder in career football wins

"The University of Idaho prides itself on producing a legacy of leaders. Behind every leader, however, is a pressing dream and an equally powerful believer. Steve and his father, the two main characters, are two such believers whose vision of home constantly eludes them. *A Home Called Your Own* isn't just fine writing, it's fine storytelling that speaks to the heart of who and what we call home."

— M. Duane Nellis, President, University of Idaho

"A riveting and engaging story about our own lives and how we individually and collectively seek to rediscover a home called our own."

— Dr. Vincent Kituku, CSP, author of *Overcoming Buffaloes*
and international motivational speaker

"*A Home Called Your Own* with its search for ancestors reminds us that no matter how forgettable our lives may seem at the time, they're anything but forgettable."

— Mark Olson, US Army, Iraq veteran

A Home Called Your Own

ABOUT THE AUTHOR

Photo © Karthik Ram

Steve Hanna is the sixth-generation descendant of a small but determined band of Bohemian immigrants. He lives in Boise.

A HOME CALLED YOUR OWN
A Journey Across Six Generations

STEVE HANNA

RIVERVIEW

Boise

RIVERVIEW PRESS
1710 N. 12th Street
Boise, ID 83702
www.riverviewpress.net

The names and identifying details of some characters
in this book have been changed.

Visit the author at
www.stevehanna.net

DESIGNED BY STEVE KUNIOKA

Printed in the United States of America

All Scripture quotations from the *Holy Bible*, Revised Standard Version.
Copyright © 1952 by Thomas Nelson.

Publisher's Cataloging-in-Publication Data
Hanna, Steve.
A home called your own : a journey across six generations / Steve Hanna.
p. cm.
ISBN (print): 978-0-9857403-9-9
ISBN (digital): 978-0-9857403-8-2

1. Hanna, Steve—Travel—Spain. 2. Hanna, Steve—Travel—Europe. 3. Hanna, Steve—
Travel—Czech Republic. 4. Foreign study—Spain—Personal narratives. 5. Students—
Travel—Personal narratives. 6. Bohemia (Czech Republic)—Emigration and immigration.
7. United States—Emigration and immigration—History. I. Title.
JV6455 .H36 2012
973/.0992—dc23
Library of Congress Control Number: 2012916373

AUTHOR'S NOTE

The story you are about to read is my best recollection of the events as they occurred. For storytelling purposes, I have changed the order of some minor situations and conversations in the book. Because the story spans six countries and eight languages, I often wasn't able to understand the exact words that someone said in their native tongue, but I did my best to capture the spirit of what I heard, saw, and encountered. This is the story through my eyes.

ACKNOWLEDGMENTS

GENEALOGY

THE BELOHLAVYS

THE HANNAS

Vaclav Belohlavy (1857-1947)
married
Marie Jimel

Josef Hána (1829-1902)
married
Mary Karas

Tillie Belohlavy (1888-1984)
married
Tony Bowers

Josef J. Hána (1858-1934)
married
Barbara Planansky

Sadie Bowers (1912-2006)
married
John Huebert

Joe Hanna (1894-1980)
married
Frances Wagner

Arley Hanna (b. 1933)
married
Bonnie Huebert (b. 1934)

Don Hanna (b. 1956)
married
Janet Rupel (b. 1953)

Adam   Steve   Paul
(b. 1985)   (b. 1988)   (b. 1993)

For the Hannas and the Belohlavys

Departure
Baker City, Oregon

"There's a story I need to tell you," Dad began, and we sat in rapt attention. The room shrouded itself in warm darkness as he left time for us to take it all in. In a valley that most people tended to drive by and forget, here we were, late after dinner, after the sun had set. Frost pressed against the windows, and if you could touch it—the air felt still. Outside it was winter, more than slightly chilly (half a degree above zero), and empty across the hay fields. Inside, the four of us sat hunched around a table, as if we had gathered in secret and someone had said, *shhh, don't tell anyone.* A dark cabinet with one knob was barely visible behind the circular table and all of the lights in the house were out but one. There was nothing on the table.

We usually had long family talks after dinner, but this one was different. It wasn't just the day or the time or the place, but perhaps it was the occasion. By next week I would be leaving for Madrid and other places three thousand miles away, but that still didn't explain the mood. There was a sense of expectation, of viscous cold, and although it was winter, it was also right after Christmas and the air carried a hint of already-burned cedar and of fire on the hearth.

In that light, seconds dripped away in quiet as we sat and waited at the table. Mom had her customary glass of white wine in her right hand. As she held it to her lips to take a sip, a single, low-hanging light cast a reflection on the glass and illuminated worn eyes under red hair. Paul, my younger brother, sat across from her, legs crossed as he sat in his chair, all sixteen years of him ready to bolt when the talk was over. Next to him and five inches shorter, I leaned on my elbows and looked toward Dad's end of the table. Dad leaned back in his chair for the telling and a slight smile crossed his face under dark, lively hair. He was enjoying this, too much, perhaps—it sounded like a lecture was coming. He smiled and looked over at my brother and me before he began. "Do you remember the Belohlavy Story?"

That was always a rhetorical question.

"Well, if you don't, I do."

Paul got up to leave, but Mom motioned him down. "Dad, we've already heard this story too many times."

Dad laughed and his voice filled the air—the room was not so dark then. "Of course you have."

There were three parts to the story. The first part was that my great uncle Leonard had once thought to cross France and enter the country that used to be called Bohemia—Czechoslovakia. "Those Nazis shot old Uncle Leonard in the foot, but if they hadn't, he might have reached Bohemia. He wanted to find them, but he never got the chance." Dad readjusted his glasses on his nose and leaned forward. "That's why we're here tonight."

The center light cast a glow and a shadow under our eyes. I looked across the table and saw lines run across Dad's forehead. "Those people—the ones Leonard was looking for, are your ancestors." Leonard survived, of course, but his plan to enter Bohemia had failed. There was something about the Bohemians.

Dad's words hung in the air, swallowed by darkness and veiled in myth. It was as if dust was being scattered from old volumes that had sat in the back corner of the library, waiting to be read. Dad was, after all, the family historian.

The cupboard behind the table began to fade from sight, until all that I could see were three other sets of eyes looking toward the light in the middle of the table, each of us looking inward, but our eye paths never crossing. It was a soft yellow light, warm like Christmas, yet a reminder of winter all the same.

"There's a reason Leonard wanted to find them, even if he did get shot," Dad said. "And the reason we're here tonight," Dad paused and looked directly at me, "is because you might have the chance to find them."

He disconnected his snap-on glasses at the nosepiece, and hung them on his neck before he turned to look at me again. His blue eyes shone through and settled comfortably over a graying beard.

Silence.

My brothers and I had heard the Belohlavy Story many times. Not a when-I-was-your-age sort of thing. An *if I were you* sort of thing, lecture format, of course.

"You could be the first one to go back and try to find them," he said.

What Dad wanted me to do was finish the story. "One hundred and twenty-five years ago, your ancestors sat at a table just like we are now," Dad continued, except gathered around the table weren't just the immediate family like us, it was aunts, uncles, cousins, grandmas, cats, dogs, everyone. In that year, they were miserably poor, but determined to change their fate and their future. "They knew that not everyone would be able to escape the lives they had been born into, but they also knew that if they could get one person out, well, then that was at least a start," Dad said. "They had to change something." We'd heard the Belohlavy Story in parts and pieces over the years, but basically it all boiled down to this: things were pretty bad for a lot of years. It was a true story, but it felt more like a campfire muse because it was so distant.

As Dad told the story, I imagined all of the Belohlavys meeting at night, in the middle of winter, around a circular table and a single candle, almost like us. The story goes that at the original meeting, all of the relatives pooled all of their money to send one person to America in search of a better life. They had exactly enough money for a single one-way ticket, and whomever they decided to send, they knew they would never see again. "How's that for really going for it?" Dad said with excitement as he leaned onto his elbows over the table. "They were willing to put everything on the line, the only problem was, no one wanted to leave Bohemia. They wanted out, but they didn't want *out*."

Eventually one man volunteered to go to America. A few days before he was supposed to board the train and leave Bohemia forever, he got cold feet and realized that he couldn't do it—he couldn't strike out on his own. "Only one man had the guts to volunteer to take his place, and that was your already-married ancestor, Vaclav," Dad said. "Not a one of them had the courage to do it, so they sent the married guy."

Never to return, Vaclav Belohlavy got on the train, boarded the ship, and sailed to America. He left his pregnant wife behind and many unanswered questions. Months later, he sent money for her to join him in America. "We don't have much more information than that," Dad said. "A lot of it has been lost, but we already know the name of the town he was from. *Nepomuk*. You could do it. You could go back and find the ones who sent him here and see what became of them."

Dad leaned forward and rested his hands in front of him, his eyes shining in anticipation. It was a quest to be sure.

I tilted my head down as I peered into the center of the table. In the shadow of the hanging light, I briefly caught Dad's eyes before looking away.

I was already nervous about leaving home. As it was, I was about to be the first one in the family to return to Europe when there wasn't a war going on. Other than my uncle who had been stationed in Germany following the Cold War, none of us had been back since. Before that my other uncle, Leonard, took a bullet to the foot and the Army sent him back to America.

"So what it all really boils down to," Dad began before he paused, "is that you should go and find the family."

As far as we knew, no one had ever successfully gone back and found the original family who had pooled their money to send Vaclav to America. We had braved odds before, getting shot at by Nazis, and doing some shooting ourselves in both World Wars, but we'd never been able to actually find them and I suspected there was a reason for it. Maybe they didn't want to be found.

One hundred and twenty-five years and six generations later, I would be the next Belohlavy to return to Europe since my uncle was stationed in Germany. My role was to unite the family across continents … by studying abroad. Was it even possible? And if I could, how? We didn't know anything other than the name of our ancestor and the name of the town he'd left long ago. In the wake of two world wars, a lot had been destroyed and a lot had been forgotten. They had probably even forgotten about us.

I turned my gaze to the wall behind Dad and watched shadows flicker. Mom looked over at me, and Paul glanced over his shoulder as if he wanted to get up and do something else. Dad remained with his head resting on his arms, waiting. He required an answer.

I thought about it for a moment, but I had already made up my mind. "I'm not going to Europe to find the Bohemians," I told Dad. It was an intriguing idea, but finding the Bohemians had never been part of my plan—it had been his.

Dad looked at me expressionless for a moment, and then looked down. As he held his eyes on the table, there was a bittersweet pause of hopes from years ago, opening and closing, appearing forth and vanishing. It was a pause of yearning.

I held my ground. There were other things in Europe that I wanted to do, like learn Spanish and see Poland. I would be busy, too, studying and spending most of my time visiting different parts of Spain. Mom reached behind her and turned the overhead lights on, and went to put her glass in the sink. We all got up from the table. The moment was gone.

One Week and Counting

I was originally going to study abroad in Costa Rica. That plan, like many others, began with a promise. My freshman year of college, my best friend Curtis and I sat in his room and talked about the future—what we were going to do tomorrow. Curtis sat on his bed and I sat on the bed across from him, about four feet away. He was a boyish sort of tall—a six foot blond with a third grade face and a mind full of girls and first dates.

We talked about the homework we hadn't done for our Spanish class, then about starting a painting business that summer, then about the distant future. It was a long, luscious conversation between two friends that quickly turned to the tropics.

"We should study abroad," Curtis suggested. "Maybe Costa Rica." He tilted his eyes up toward the ceiling as he adjusted his neck on the brown pillow he was leaning against. "We could talk Spanish all day, maybe surf and stuff."

For two small town guys, that sounded pretty exotic. "Let's do it," I said.

And that was that. From that day on, we began making plans.

Two years into our planning, I told one of my uncles what we were going to do, and he pulled me into a different room so my parents couldn't hear him.

"I remember driving on a dirt road in Costa Rica," he told me. "It was a lonely road in the mountains, forested, like the jungle. As I stopped to admire the view on my way up the mountain, a Jeep crept around the road behind me and began to crawl forward. Out of the open windows, two men in their forties ran their eyes across my car as if they were studying it for sale. I thought to myself, 'Why aren't they at work? It's ten in the morning.' They had scars cut across their faces, but I couldn't see much more before they rounded the next corner and disappeared. I had to cross the mountain, too, so several minutes later I followed them up the road."

My uncle continued driving normally, swerving up the mountain and around a series of blind corners. When he rounded the final corner, he slowed to a stop. The Jeep he had seen earlier was now parked sideways, blocking the road ahead. The men stood next to it with their forearms strapped across their chests. I pictured them standing there expressionless, a cigarette tucked between their lips, a gash running down their foreheads. My uncle flipped a U-turn as fast as he could, and tore back down the mountain. "That's why you don't want to go to Costa Rica," he said. "They'll rob you."

I heard this story when I was nineteen, and he had a certain look in his eyes that I now understand. "Europe isn't like that."

He was only telling me part of the truth; I paid attention to his eyes.

There was an excitement about the road ahead, but it was veiled in a clouded warning. He'd been to Europe before, but I could tell that he was leaving out several details.

"So I'm thinking about it," Curtis began again. It was a year later and we were in his truck, out driving somewhere after dark. Gritty headlights lit up the road and the windshield betrayed hints of falling raindrops on the road in front of us. In the dim interior of the car, all I could see was the side of his face looking straight ahead at the dotted yellow passing strip on the road. We had gotten away from campus for a bit to shoot the breeze, a heart to heart if you will, and after several moments of looking forward, he turned to look at me. The boyish look in his eyes was gone, replaced by a blonde goatee and something on his mind. "So I'm thinking about it," he said again, "thinking about our plan."

"Thinking about what?"

"Well, I'm thinking about getting married."

"Really?"

"Yeah—I can't explain it. I just get this feeling, and I know." He stopped talking and turned his gaze back to the road. I'd asked him about popping the question to his girlfriend for the last year or so, ever since they started dating our freshman year, because something like marriage or a relationship could really change our plans. The headlights glanced across an indiscernible road sign that disappeared behind us in the rain. I couldn't see much of his face as he squinted and turned his head to follow the sign. "Sometimes you just know."

I'd never had a serious girlfriend up till then, so I didn't really know what he was getting at. Other than the fact that it spelled bad news for me. "What do you mean?" I asked.

Whether we turned left, right, or kept going straight at that sign, I don't remember. Plans changed.

Curtis came to visit the day before I left. He knew he couldn't go with me; after all, he was now married, but he could at least climb a mountain with me the day before I left and we could say goodbye properly. "You'll have to see Spain for both of us," he said as he looked behind me into the distance. "You know how much I wanted to be there." His voice trailed off, lost in the morning fog that surrounded the mountain.

We talked it over that evening. It wasn't going to work out, really, both of us going to Europe together. He wanted to go, he said, but he needed to spend time with his new wife. I understood.

The next morning we stood next to our trucks, hugged and said goodbye. Then Curtis drove back home and I threw Dad's old hiking backpack from the seventies into the diesel, and Dad and I drove to Seattle. Snow fell around us on the side of the road as we made steady progress behind a semi truck. White flakes dangled, turned and attached themselves to the windshield. It wasn't worth it to turn on the wipers. That would only really ruin the beauty of the snow anyway. "I don't know how and I don't know why, but somehow I get the feeling that this trip is exactly what you're supposed to be doing," Dad said. He mentioned other things, but that was what I remembered the most. It was just after Christmas time.

Twenty years ago, Dad wrote a letter to the last of the original Bohemian ancestors. Of course, I imagined him sitting at an old mahogany desk, writing by candlelight on a dark and stormy night. But whether that's what actually happened or not, I don't know, but I do know that he asked our ancestor one very important question. She wrote back to him with the answer right before she died, but he can't remember what she said. Dad doesn't remember where he put the letter, either, but it's hidden somewhere, waiting to be rediscovered. He wrote the letter just after Christmas time.

DAY OF DEPARTURE

Overhead panel lights flooded the terminal with a stale mono-white that artificially turned the night into day. Madrid 8:00 p.m., ON TIME, the sign emphasized above the American Airlines desk in red electronic letters. I checked my watch and it was six o'clock—two more hours to go. On the Philadelphia airport's black leather seats, people were speaking in three different languages. In between Italian and Arabic, I caught a few words of Spanish, and in between sentences I hardly understood—*es una lastima que todo los americanos no hablen otras lenguas*—my mind wandered back to the ranch, and to Dad, Mom, and Paul. I remembered seeing my older brother Adam, too, before he left home and joined the Navy. This was what it must have felt like. I put on headphones and left the waiting area.

After a while, I walked down the hall and found an unused phone booth, then dialed home. Mom answered the phone.

The day before, I had called the study abroad office with a list of forty questions about Spain and talked to them for two hours. They reassured me that I would be fine and in that moment, I thought so too. Keep your expectations low, they said. Drop your head, and when things turned out better than you expected, you'd come out on the heads side of the coin. It was like cliff jumping—you pulled in a deep breath, tried to erase your fears, then jumped.

I walked over to the counter and handed the woman my ticket. "Let's go."

I

THE DREAM

ARRIVAL
MADRID, SPAIN

"HOW'S YOUR SPANISH?" a girl wearing a form-fitting shirt asked as I sat down next to her on the plane. Not wanting to sound stupid, I set a copy of *Don Quixote* on my seat while I stood up and placed my coat in the overhead bin. Outside the plane it was dark, but inside the cabin, overhead lights cast a soft glare on tired eyes and leather seats. *"¿Cómo es tu español?"* she asked again.

She was beautiful. Dark hair was brushed to one side of a smooth, olive-skinned face that was decorated with black diamond eyes and a button nose. Her question would be a tough one to answer. When you don't know enough Spanish to talk to them, the Spanish girls become especially irresistible.

"*Estoy embarazado,*" I said. What I meant to say was, *I'm embarrassed.* What she heard was, *I'm pregnant!* She couldn't hold her breath for more than a second before she burst out laughing.

"So how about I just talk to you in English, then?" she said.

I'm sure she meant well, but that was an insult. I removed *Don Quixote* from my lap and hid it under the seat. After studying Spanish for four and a half years, all I could manage was an "I'm pregnant." It was slightly embarrassing. I fiddled with the airline magazine in the seat pocket in front of me, pulling it out and then replacing it.

"So what's Spain like?" I finally asked her.

"Well, it's not like America," she replied before turning to look out the window as the plane began to move forward onto the runway. "In Spain, we work to live, not live to work."

I looked over her shoulder and out the window. It was mostly dark, but the runway in front of us was lit with little bulbs every twenty yards or so, casting just enough light to reveal an American Airlines worker who was pushing an empty baggage cart toward the terminal. "See? In America, people are always working."

Her accent was barely noticeable, but in the back of her voice was the slight Spanish lisp that I'd heard about in Spanish class. "In Spain, you'll get to *botellon* and drink in the street, take a *siesta* in the middle of work and sleep next to your boss, then go party all night."

She sighed and rested her head against the window as the overhead lights shut off and the plane began moving faster down the runway for takeoff. "I want to go home," she said.

"*Bueno*," I responded. "That sounds good."

The plane was moving faster now, and I was pushed into my seat as we launched into the air. For a moment, we saw all of the city lights until they disappeared into clouds and conversation. The air in the cabin drew tighter with the increased altitude.

"So why are you going to Spain?" she asked as she stretched her feet in front of her in the dark.

"To study abroad mostly. To do something new, the usual reasons I guess."

"But why Spain?"

That was a good question. "My Uncle told me it would be better than Costa Rica."

"Well, he's right about that."

She reached under the seat in front of her and pulled out a round container of sleeping pills. "Do you want one? It's a long flight."

Over the next several hours I learned a lot about her home in Madrid.

As her sleeping pill began to lull her to sleep, our conversation loosened to reveal several things. The first: "I grew up in a small town in Kansas," she said. Lola was her name. She was originally born in Spain, but when she was eleven, her mom had moved her and her sister to America in search of a better life. "How old are you?" she asked me.

"Twenty-one," I said.

"When I was twenty-one, I went and studied abroad and everything changed—including my home. I went to Spain to live with my relatives and then I never came back." After her study abroad term had ended in Madrid, she had become an English teacher and taught formal English to Spanish businessmen.

The second thing I learned was that her mom had remarried in Kansas and never wanted to return to Spain, except to visit family for two weeks every other year. "Life is hard in Europe, and it's especially hard in Spain," Lola began again. "Well, now that I think about it, it's hard everywhere." She turned toward the window and pulled a pillow from beneath her seat and rested it on the window frame.

As she began to fall sleep, I couldn't shake the sense that Lola was the kind of person I'd never met before. I'd never met a girl who'd jumped ship and left the country she was born in. In Baker City, Oregon, population ten thousand people and one hundred thousand cows, folks tended to stay put. Our closest neighbors were ninety-nine year-old Nellie and a ranching couple whose family had been farming since the Oregon Trail. Nellie, for instance, had lived in the Baker Valley her entire life and although she'd been a widow for nearly thirty years, she still shot her shotgun, played her fiddle, and mowed her lawn. Just last week she had helped some forty year-old men push a riding lawnmower into the back of their pickup. The word around town was that she'd dusted off her hands and bid them a nice day. "You've got to put some work into life," she said. Nellie tended her own flower patch and put her own logs on the fire—she didn't need any help with that.

Our other neighbors, Fred and Barbara Warner, were still running their ranch that dated back to the 1862 wagon train. Since most people in Baker had seniority based on what year their wagon train had arrived, I always thought most folks tended to stay put. My family hadn't necessarily done that, and while we'd lived in two different states and five different houses, we'd always been known as the traveling ones. "You guys move a lot," people in Baker told us. "It's better to set down roots."

Given all of this, then, I was more than a little surprised to be sitting next to a girl who had lived in two countries and who had left a small town and her real family in Kansas to live in Spain with her ancestral family. I flipped on the overhead light and a sterile beam filtered between us, as if we were in a laboratory. She was intriguing.

Before she fell asleep, I asked her what it was like to go back to her family in Spain, but she didn't say anything more. We changed topics to the metro system, and she gave me a crumpled foldout in Spanish with a map of the metro. "If you're pregnant when you arrive," she said, "you're going to need this."

Bright red signs plastered with *¡Bienvenidos!* welcomed me to the Madrid Barajas *aeropuerto*. I didn't have anything to carry except *Don Quixote* as I stepped off the plane in a sleek black coat that I'd bought to look more European. Newsstands bore headlines that I couldn't read in *El Mundo*, *El País*, or *otros periódicos* and *televisiones* blared *las noticias* in foreign words. It was all too much to suddenly take in, as if in one breath I'd scratched and sniffed ten different stickers and lost all distinguishing characteristics. What remained, however, was a vapor of olive oil and the crackling of rising Spanish inflections, of murmured greetings and *suavecitas* that carried more lubrication than a can of WD-40. *"Preciosa suavecita,"* a man told his girlfriend while she wrapped her legs around him and he put his tongue halfway down her throat. It was foreign and familiar all at once, and when the customs agent stamped my passport with la *empresa de España*, it finally hit. I was where no Hanna had gone before. *¡Bienvenidos a España!* The customs clerk said, before brushing me away to talk to the next person in line. I moved forward a bit, and just inside the customs gate, I stood still in the middle of the hallway, trying to take it all in as people passed on either side of me.

Instead of getting used to Spain and trying to decipher the Spanish on the signs, I read the English translations and found my way to the baggage pickup. As I was waiting for my bag, I saw a dark-haired guy nearby wearing a USAC study abroad t-shirt. His hair was spiked in the front and gelled firmly into place, and he wore a pair of Nikes. I walked over to talk to him.

"*David*," he said, throwing in a Spanish accent as we shook hands.

"Steve," I said. "Good to meet you."

"*Con mucho gusto.*"

"Is it *David* or David?" I asked.

"*David*." He motioned around us at the people and the signs. "If we're both studying abroad in Spain, we might as well get used to it, right? So I'm *David*—with the accent."

Within a few minutes, we learned that we were in similar study abroad programs, and although our programs weren't exactly the same (he was going to Bilbao and I was going to Alicante), we had to find the same hotel. "My family is from Ecuador originally," he said. "So in a way, I'm coming back to my roots, back to the *conquista*." He'd grown up speaking Spanish at home, and he worked at a Mexican restaurant to pay his way through school. "That's a better way of saying that I'm a hard worker— with my boss' daughter," he added. "With her, I've been studying international business. In more ways than one."

"So it's fair to say that you're good at international relations?"

"Bro, I'm a pro."

We grabbed our travel gear from the revolving baggage claim and prepared to navigate the metro system. On my back was Dad's old hiking pack from the seventies that he had used when he was my age. An American-made label on the front pocket said Ponderosa Camp Trails, and the pack had faded from a deep sierra to a dusty russet. Other than the pack, I carried a laptop case from Wal-Mart in my right hand. Next to me, David stood between two seventy-five pound rolling suitcases. He had pulled the plastic handle up on one of the rollers and stacked a bulging green duffle bag and another bag that weighed fifty pounds. He stood dwarfed between his suitcases and blinked several times. "I don't remember why I decided to bring all these accounting books," he said before examining his pile on either side of him. He looked hard at his rollers and furrowed his brow. "Should we call a cab?"

*　*　*

Our breath wisped out of our lungs like ghosts as we walked down Avenida Álcala under a frosted, sparkled sky. Usually when I'd heard about Madrid, I'd heard about plazas and wandering streets, sunlit cafes and charming corner shops, but the real thing was a festive version of that stuck in fast-forward. Windows lined the streets with red signs of winter bargains and *rebajas*. Unlit Christmas light frames in the shape of wreaths and *¡Feliz Navidad!* stretched across streets, tied to eight-story buildings by buoyant wires. People walked briskly and talked fast. The men wore winter sport coats and pointy dress shoes, the women high heels and heavy makeup. Twenty-something street promoters approached us and told us about their friend's store across town that sold something we didn't need, and tried to convince us that we needed it. *Discothèques* and nightclubs opened their doors to the daylight and people spilled in and out of bars where they stood instead of sat, clutching San Miguels and Maus to their chests while on siestas from work. Lined with cars, people crossing crosswalks, lights blinking and flashing, and tall buildings with elaborately carved statues and balconies under every window, Madrid was a sight to behold.

"Wow," I said, blinking frosted sunlight out of my eyes as we stood beneath what appeared to be the Spanish National Bank. Featuring marble columns, a black dome on top, and several golden angels, it was the kind of bank that neither of us had seen before.

"Wow," Davíd said. We both stood silent for a moment and looked up as a slight breeze set in behind us, both of us in our black coats. "We need our Bank of America to look more like this."

We lowered our heads and continued down the same street. Five minutes later, after passing a Starbucks, we came within sight of a palace on a corner block, but it was gated. Behind the palace walls, we saw a world that was ours for the taking if only we could unlock it.

As we continued wandering the city, a certain character began to unfold. A marimba band played in a round plaza where a man had painted himself as the Tin Man, while in a square plaza several blocks away, a brass band entertained a crowd of men with mullets and women with straight-cut bangs. In a different plaza, a man stood on a pedestal dressed as an angel, and across from him in protest, another *madrileño* stood on a pedestal dressed as the devil. We discovered, among other things, a fifty foot-tall Christmas tree in the center of Plaza del Sol topped with a big red bow, a museum of *jamón* decorated floor to ceiling with hanging pig legs where you could buy ham spreading to put on bread. Next to the museum, a souvenir store sold the exact same stuffed bulls and bullfight shirts as the souvenir store next to it. We discovered a series of shops ending in *ía*: a *calcetinería* that sold the same socks you could get anywhere else, a *carnicería* that sold only the best meat you could get anywhere else, a *pastelería* that sold only the same kinds of pastries found anywhere else, a *cafetería* that sold only the same two kinds of coffee available anywhere else *("¿Con leche o sin leche?")*, and an *heladería* that sold the same flavors of ice cream you could get anywhere else—at all of the other *heladerías*. Spain was highly specialized and uniform, but not without personality. The Spaniards' willingness to attempt to sell the same thing as something different was admirable, and we fell right into step with homogeneity. We would be our same selves and hang out with the same people, but somehow, we would be different.

When the other sixty American students arrived that night, we took the Spanish lifestyle to heart. In a city we knew nothing about and surrounded by people we knew nothing about, we were eager to get to know each other. On our first night, we discovered a country that never sleeps, and a city that could become blonde or brunette in an instant, if those were the sort of people you surrounded yourself with. Seven-story nightclubs blasted music for locals and foreigners until sunup when the Spaniards would forsake sleep and go to work while the foreigners would sleep and forsake work. By day, our study abroad program had a full itinerary planned that included visiting art museums and that sort of thing, but most of us showed up on the dregs of last night's beer can. We knew that in Spain you were supposed to live a twenty-four hour day, and we were eager to get started on that, which usually meant that we were drunk or hung over.

At first, maybe, the partying seemed like the right thing to do. I originally went to Europe to get away for a semester, to *escápate hoy* and escape today. I was tired of usual life. Studying abroad was supposed to be about living an adventure. In my freshman year of college, I remember seeing a picture of people riding camels through Morocco and the words, "you can do this" on a study abroad poster. I wanted an adventure, a quest, like riding camels through Morocco or something like that. Something grand, something out of the ordinary, and something not many people had ever done before. And since no one I knew had ever been to Spain, foreign bars were enough of an adventure to suffice.

Our group was wild with excitement. We could have been anywhere really, because most of us had never been outside the States. On the first night, I stumbled into my hotel room at three in the morning, my shirt sticking to my chest from nightclub sweat. My roommate from New Jersey had ripped his shirt off and was sitting cross-legged in front of his laptop watching the NFL playoffs as the Cowboys lost 7-45. "Dammit!" he yelled. A girl from Maryland called down the hall to ask what we were up to and a group of Californians staggered in to say hello. The hallway was filled with raucous noise for a four-star hotel, and the glass doors and solid wood floors in our rooms were a stark contrast to the boxed wine and grocery store lunches that we brought home. People quickly got lost in all the chaos, and when I went looking for David on the final day, he was nowhere to be found.

As I left my hotel room to move Dad's hiking backpack into the bus that would take me to my new home in Alicante, I heard a scraping crash. A large hand-painted vase came tumbling onto the tile in front of me as a drunken study abroader staggered up from the ground.

"That was such a great night," Jeff said as he picked himself up from the fall and wiped his mouth with his shirt, exposing part of his beer stomach that spilled over his belt. He started to laugh, but his voice echoed off the walls of the stairwell landing, unable to settle anywhere. "That was such a good time!"

The hallway was silent. All around us, the hotel styling was immaculate. A gold-trimmed mirror stood across from a vintage painting in the landing. Crushed into a thousand pieces, the black vase laid on the white-tiled floor. Beyond the tile, a cold hallway of red carpet and silver door handles stared back at us. "Shit!" He laughed again. "Spain, *tío*, holy shit, they party till seven in the morning!"

I had just woken up from three hours of sleep and his voice sounded like it had been worn out at the club. He put his hands in his pockets; he wasn't going to pick up the mess. "You should have been there," he said. "The girls were unbelievable."

I dropped to my knees to begin picking up the pieces of the vase when footsteps echoed up the stairs. He took off running down the hallway and dove into his room. I stood up and looked around frantically, but didn't move fast enough. A man in a black suit and tie came up the stairway. When he saw the vase, his eyes fell to the floor. It was the hotel manager.

He bent over and touched several pieces of the vase, running his hand over the cracks and sharp points. It was hopelessly broken. He had picked this vase out years ago, he said, did I know what that meant? He pointed at me and looked me in the eyes, digging for an answer. "Do you know what these words mean? *Te jodes*."

He turned to me in a fury. *Joder* and all the other Spanish swear words came out in force while he alternated between pointing at the vase and the frame it had once stood on. In the moment of accusation, all of my Spanish suddenly disappeared, and I was left standing in front of the angry manager, speaking a language I was learning but didn't fully understand, in front of a man who was pointing a finger and ready to fine me a thousand euros for something I didn't do.

I threw my arms up and pointed my right hand at the vase. "I didn't break it. I was just walking down the hall when someone else broke it."

"Right." The vacant hallway echoed as the manager turned and threw his weight into the stairwell. He was going to tell my study abroad director about the vase.

I dropped to my knees and began scraping up the remnants of the vase. Jeff returned, but never offered to help. As I was about to finish cleaning the floor, he passed by on his way out, carrying his duffle bag. He nodded. "S'up."

As Jeff was leaving the landing, Davíd came up the stairs and stopped him. Dressed in black pointed shoes, tight embroidered jeans, and a black designer shirt, Davíd looked a little different than before. "Jeff, you drunk," Davíd said, as he slapped Jeff on the back and laughed. "Did you do this?"

"Shut up—I was drunk!" Jeff fell against the wall and slipped down several stairs before some of his spit gargled out of his mouth and onto his shirt.

Davíd laughed. "¡Viva la vida! That's how we do it in Spain, tío!" He walked by as I knelt over the floor, picking up the last pieces of the vase. He didn't look down or offer to help. "S'up."

Davíd calmly walked down the hall and into a girl's room where I heard laughter and a door being shut. Jeff walked down the stairs and left. I stood alone on the landing, then, between a silver mirror and a trashcan full of someone else's broken vase. In the quietness I could hear people packing and gathering their things, but the hallway remained still.

WEEK 1
ALICANTE, SPAIN

SIX HOURS—THE BUS. The ride to Alicante featured plains at first: open wheat fields under a partially clouded sky. Cows were staggered across some of the rolling ground, but most of the land was empty and lonely. There was the occasional stone building, but it was usually crumbling next to lines of strung fence. For a while, the road was straight. Then one bend in the road led to two, then finally toward mountains. Intermittent with yawns from still-awake study abroaders in going-out clothes, the crunch of gas station snacks in mouths, and the crinkle of plastic wrappers and several conversations—the bus wandered on in nervous delay. We were about to meet our host families.

The girl next to me, Sarah, leaned over and asked to practice introductions, so we rehearsed back and forth. "*Soy Sarah*," she said, her knees scrunched against the seat in front of her, her posture in a ball.

"*Encantado*," I said. "*¿Otra vez?*"

"*Sí.*" Behind her and out the window, I watched stone houses and seventy-degree air begin to infiltrate my senses—all of it gorgeous, unable to be tipped from frames and broken.

With another bend, we rounded our way into Alicante and the sparkle of the Mediterranean met us eye-level across the windows like a silver screen. All of the sudden it was a bit much and everyone woke up. "The beach!" we shouted.

The bus wound its way through wide, uneven streets, weaving through stoplights at roundabouts and braking for frequent pedestrians. "*A la izquierda, Castillo de Santa Barbara,*" the bus driver announced over the intercom as we drove by a mountain in the middle of the city with a castle on top of it.

The Alicante that unfolded was tall; a consistent five stories with lots of palm trees on the street. Apartments and stores blurred by in tones of off-white as balconies hung above us, strung with clotheslines and colors. "*Prepárate,*" our study abroad director Luis said. "They're waiting—the people you're going to live with."

In the heart of Alicante, a wet ball of sun settled over four statues and a fountain as our study abroad bus pulled up to the curb. All around the circular plaza, people walked and talked, moving in between tables and street vendors, but one group remained static with their arms crossed. Standing on one side of the Plaza de Luceros, a group of forty middle-aged women was waiting.

"When you step off this bus," our program director Luis said, "something is about to happen to you." He clapped his hands in front of him and held them there, suspended. "Well," he paused and looked into each one of our eyes, "you probably won't realize what this means until much later."

We crowded the aisle and shuffled into place. I looked out the window, away from the curb, and saw a fountain surrounded by palm trees in the center of the plaza. I watched the trees bend slightly in the breeze, kicked about by a gimp of wind, but someone said *shhhhh* next to me and I turned my gaze back to the interior.

When the bus doors swung open, fifty-nine sets of eyes watched the first girl from Nevada get off the bus, flanked by Luis. When they reached the curb, Luis waved at the crowd. "*¿Maria está?*" A woman with a drooping perm and red heels ran over and threw her arms around the girl and kissed her. Before I could watch how the girl from Nevada reacted to the kiss, Luis had already called the next student off the bus.

"Alec!" A blond guy from Maryland walked off the bus and Luis threw his arm around his shoulder. Together they walked over to a woman with tangled hair who pinched Alec's cheek and said *hola guapo*. "Hi good-looking." She laughed and he looked at the ground. She wore big gold earrings.

As I got closer and closer to the front of the line, I watched one woman in particular walk back and forth along the side of the bus, gazing into each window one by one. Her arms were crossed as she studied each American face before moving on to the next. She knew exactly who she was looking for.

As Luis called my name and I stepped off the bus that had carried sixty of us from Madrid, her gaze fell upon me. She had pale skin and black clothes, blue eyeliner and lots of eye shadow. With five mismatched plastic bracelets jingling on her right wrist, she looked a little bit like a witch. She bounded over, reached across my backpack, and devoured me in her arms. After the hug I tried to step away, but she pulled me into her again, this time closer to her face. Her lips began gliding across my cheek before they settled and puckered, then she grabbed my shoulders and turned to kiss my other cheek. It happened so fast, I didn't know what to do but kiss her back. She liked that!

The woman partially released her grip around my shoulders, but kept a loose touch with outstretched hands. "*¡Hola Estif!*" she said. "*Soy Carmen.*" She held me at a distance as she studied my face and drank in the moment.

¡Jajajajaja! She began to laugh, a bursting, high-pitched sound that seemed better fit for birthday parties than first-time introductions. My immediate assessment of Carmen, then, was that she was the sort of woman you'd never be able to lose in a crowd. She'd clearly been looking forward to this. "*¡Qué bien!*" she exclaimed. "How wonderful!"

I didn't understand everything she said next (after all, my Spanish was still pregnant), but the next thing I caught was, "*Hola mi amor, ¿cómo estás?*" For a first impression, it may have been a little strong. "Hello, my love, how are you?"

Bien.

Like the rest of the Spaniards I'd met, Carmen wanted to make sure we became close friends in five minutes. I'd heard something about culture shock at study abroad orientation, but somehow they'd failed to mention the fact that you'd be kissing fifty year-olds on Week One. I wondered what came after that. Making out with them? Or maybe trying to understand everything they told you?

"*¿Cómo puedo ayudarte con tu mochila?*" Carmen asked, inflecting her voice at the end of the question—something about offering to carry Dad's backpack to her house.

"*Gracias, está bien,*" I managed.

"*Bueno,*" she said. "*¡Vámonos!*" Let's go!

And with that, we were off. Carmen waved goodbye to Luis and we did an about face to leave, setting the sun to our shoulders. Luis waved back. "You're in good hands," he said, before his face disappeared and he led a girl from South Carolina off the bus and into the arms of her host family. They looked happy to see her, but she looked a little bewildered.

As my new host mom attempted to tell me the abbreviated history of Spain, we stepped off the curb and onto the plaza proper—a street filled with people, dogs, beggars, kids in strollers and elderly walkers. In Madrid I'd seen a crowded, narrow-street, hustle and bustle, frosted-over version of Spain, but in Alicante, I saw something else entirely. Yawning sidewalks twice as wide as most Madrid alleyways spilled onto sun-draped main streets. Crowds of walkers in sunglasses and winter coats meandered around hundreds of café tables that stretched into the middle of sidewalks while eighty year-old café goers sipped beer from wine glasses to get an early start on the day. It was the sort of street where conversations were never over, where one thing simply carried over to the next, and where people walked slow and talked fast, but never on their cell phones. No one seemed to wear watches and they seemed to have plenty of time to tell jokes. I heard them laugh a lot.

We passed a paella restaurant and Carmen waved to the waiter standing outside as smells of shrimp and rice wafted over the street and towards the sea. She chatted to the waiter for a bit before introducing me. "*Es m'ijo, Estif,*" she said. She couldn't pronounce the *s* in my name, so she began calling me Estif. "This is Estif, my son."

I shook hands with the waiter and he said something I couldn't understand. Carmen nodded and we kept walking.

As we continued on, we met other shopkeepers who stood outside their doorways. We waved at them and they waved at us. Carmen knew almost all of them and we said a lot of *cómo estás* and *qué tal* as we slowly made our way down the street. As we walked, my eyes followed lines of palm trees on either side of the main avenue that climbed as high as the second story on neighboring *edificios*. "How do you say palm tree?" I asked Carmen in Spanish.

"*Palma*," she pointed out as she grabbed my arm. "*La palma.*"

As we neared the end of the main street and began to veer off down a side street, I looked over my shoulder. A long ways behind us, I saw the statues standing guard around the plaza before they disappeared as we rounded the corner. I turned my head and followed Carmen.

In the next few hours I was introduced to the rest of my Spanish family. If my host mom's five jingling bracelets and blue eyeliner were any preview of eccentricity, they proved correct when she led me into her *apartamento* on the fourth floor.

The front door to the apartment opened into a long hallway draped in shadows. "We don't turn on the lights during the day," Carmen said. I imagined myself walking through the hallway at night, gliding my fingertips through moisture on the walls that had been absorbed from the sea breeze. There was a low-built dresser on the left side of the hallway covered in fake flowers, plastic hair clips, a Catholic Cross ("*la cruz*") and other trinkets she'd bought at a Chinese store.

She walked me down the hall and showed me her room on the right. Two dressers were covered in kitsch mementos from Santiago, along with other old souvenirs. A book on non-traditional herbal medicine techniques and a book of adult sexual jokes sat on the nightstand. Above and on the walls, Carmen had printed out pictures of family members on sheets of paper and taped them across worn picture frames. A pair of workout pants was on the bed in the center of the room. "*Es de Asis papi*," she said.

We turned around and met my host dad, Asis, in the kitchen. "*Hola Estif, ¿qué tal?*" he said as he gave me a firm handshake. He had a large body, thick across the torso and chest, with curls of chest hair that peeked above the neckline of his shirt and gave the sense of enlarging his already large frame. He was the sort of man who used his size to make you feel bigger in the room.

"Asis *papi* is from France," Carmen said, as if this was the most important thing to know about him.

Asis was wearing a blue polo; he told me this was important. Welcome Day was a Blue Polo Day, he said, because he only wore blue or pink polos. Like Carmen, there was a larger-than-life feel to the whole encounter, except he didn't look like a witch—he looked like a bodybuilder.

Two more men about my age entered the room. The taller of the two (six-four) had obvious triceps, the whimsical face of a Spanish redneck-turned-jock, and the look of a circling hawk. "*Soy Adán,*" he said. From what I gathered, he liked to ride dirt bikes and *motocicletas* around in the mountains and go camping. Adán worked as a physical trainer, but was studying to become a policeman.

I turned to meet my other host brother standing next to Adán. At six foot one, he was the shorter, but older of the two ("by only two years," Adán corrected). He had obvious biceps, an inviting look, and a softness in his voice and bearing that seemed unusual for a guy his size. "*Asis hijo,*" he said, clarifying that he was Asis junior. Like his brother, Asis junior was also studying to be a police officer. "You want to see my room?" he asked.

I nodded and he led me into his room adjacent the kitchen where the walls were covered with pictures of himself. A MISTER ESPAÑA 2006 banner hung across the end of his bed and a shirtless picture of himself was taped to the closet. "I was the third runner-up," he said matter-of-factly, as he looked at the picture of himself showing off rippled abs in front of the beach for a GQ-style pose. His stomach didn't look quite as good now as it did several years ago, he conceded, but girls still wanted him. He pointed to a magazine cut-out of a *señorita* with big boobs in a yellow bikini that hung eye level at the foot of his bed. "That's my girlfriend."

He grabbed a muscle shirt and flicked off the light in his room, but left the door open. "*Mami* will come and clean it later," he said, as we walked back into the kitchen to find her. Carmen was scrunched over a gas-powered stove in the dark, making a pan of the same shrimp and rice mix that we'd smelled earlier in the street restaurants. "*Paella*," she said, pointing to the pan. "*¡Buenísima!*"

All things considered, the Bujans were quite the family. While Carmen was now a full-time trinket collector and host mom, she used to work abroad with the Spanish consulate. She'd left home at eighteen, gotten married to Asis at twenty, and lived in four countries on two continents.

Asis padre, I learned, was a former Spanish fencing champion who used to compete across the Mediterranean. He also used to manage the Hotel Melia down by the beach, but now was the director of a chain of European gyms. In his spare time, he taught nine year-olds how to fence. "I'm addicted to working out," he said, "whether that's teaching or playing sports." A peek of dark hair curled over the top of his shirt and stretched across his pecs. He reached down and tucked it beneath his shirt.

"Go see the rest of the house before we eat," he said. He pointed to my triceps bearing the load of Dad's backpack and laughed. "You're strong, but you've got to set that down and get settled in at home."

Before I could set my backpack down, Carmen led me back down the shadowy hallway to see the rest of the house. Our first stop was the bathroom on the left. "The water's always cold because we never turn on the heat," she said. "Besides, you don't really need it anyways."

While most of the other study abroaders had heating with their host families, Carmen and Asis had decided that they didn't want to pay for it. They had a Mercedes sitting in the open-air parking garage below us, along with another car and a motorcycle, but heating was *muy caro*, really expensive, Carmen said. It cost them fifteen Euros per month to fill the propane tank—also *muy caro*.

She tapped me on the shoulder and pointed out the bathroom and down the hall. "*Eso es*," Carmen said. A propane tank sat against the wall at the far end. "You just light it with a match, but be careful that you don't blow up the whole house!"

Carmen directed my attention back to the bathroom—there was more to explain. "The most important thing is that you can't flush your toilet paper," she said. "The plumbing here is so old that it gets clogged and it won't fit through. Then we'd have a real mess in here," she said, wiping her forehead while turning to fumble with the showerhead. One bathroom (six-feet by six-feet) "is more than enough for all five of us," Carmen proclaimed, while pointing out that movement in the bathroom consisted of turning your torso. "The water in the shower is always cold," she added, "but if you want a hot shower, there's another gas tank in the other room." She paused to test the cold water. "You get one shower per day, just don't get sand in it."

A box of dollar store make-up products and used toothbrushes sat on top of the toilet that bore a Winnie the Pooh sticker. Her sons had grown up years ago, but Carmen had recently decided to put the sticker on the toilet seat. "Isn't he cute?" she said, pointing to the sticker. "Every time I look at him, I laugh." Her bracelets slid along her wrist and jammed up at the front, clinking together until the sound dulled.

We proceeded to my room at the end of the hall. A closet said UNLV and UNIVERSITY OF ARIZONA in mismatched stickers, and the bed-spread had a picture of a watermelon on it. An old picture of Asis junior and Adán in elementary school was on the wall, and Carmen confessed that she sometimes snuck into the room to look at it. "I'll try not to sneak in while you're sleeping," she said, "but I'll probably forget and do it any-way."

From the watermelon bedspread to the fading UNLV sticker on the closet, there was a lived-in sense to the room. The desk was scratched and worn, but it had endured with a ragged sense of love. Like Carmen and her five plastic bracelets, there was something so quaint about the room that it felt welcoming. I took a moment to stretch and sit down on the bed before taking off Dad's backpack and setting it down in the corner.

"*Ven*," Carmen said, as she turned to walk back down the hall. "It's time for lunch."

I checked my watch. It was 4:30 p.m.

* * *

"There aren't enough police officers in Spain," Asis padre said while we were eating.

He was really talking about why his sons had decided to become police officers, but it also happened to be one of the first things he said, so I assumed it would be important. "In Alicante, you have to be careful at night."

That night John, a fellow study abroader who was living with one of Carmen's friends, called our house and asked if I wanted to get away for an hour or two and "speak American." I said yes.

Asis got up from the kitchen table. "Take this," he said, and reached into his pocket before handing me a silver key ring with a brand new *llave* for the house. "You're going to need it."

When I met John on the street corner below Carmen's apartment, he had his hands in his pockets. Standing in front of a car repair shop that had closed hours ago and that had been locked up behind a wall of iron bars, I saw him take several glances over his shoulder. The alleys on either side of him were dark. Strewn across the street, trash and clumps of animal feces marked space on the concrete. Dumpsters were nowhere to be seen, but apartment buildings five stories high lined every street, hunching over the sidewalks; the lower stories were completely covered in graffiti. Every hundred feet or so, a streetlight was burrowed into the sidewalk, but the light was swallowed in an eerie glow. "*Hola*," I said.

"Shit," John said. He took another look over his shoulder and started walking before I had time to catch up with him. I looked over my shoulder but didn't see anyone following us. It was just dark.

"S'up," he finally said. We walked silently with our hands in our pockets as we navigated a maze of alleys to find the main street.

"S'up," I said.

"My head hurts."

"*¿Qué?*"

"From talking all that Spanish. Twenty-four hours a day, one day in a row. My name is Juan now, by the way, according to my host mom. This shit's hard."

I had to agree with him.

Juan glanced over his shoulder again, then swung his head around to face forward. "So I talked to my ex tonight," he said, "and she wants to get back together with me. Problem is, since we've been in Spain, I've already cheated on her."

Streetlights began to appear more frequently as we got closer to Avenida Maisonnaive. Lit up billboards began to appear and we passed Lizarrán and several other bars as we moved out of the side streets and into the downtown. The shadows and lights began to change.

Alicante was different at night. In between Juan telling me stories about his Mormon girlfriend and why he had dated her in the first place—he was the first guy she'd ever slept with, so she wasn't going to cheat on him—in between that talk and another, the talk of the city, Alicante showed a new side at night. At night, flamenco avenues filled with midnight walkers and tricycles replaced sun-draped main streets. Three year-olds wheeled around in front of thirty year-old parents who walked small dogs, all while Juan talked about cheating on his girlfriend.

As we talked, a twenty-something *guapa* walked in front of us in heels, her butt sculpted by a thong and a black mini skirt. "I'd put my hands all over her," Juan said, "if only I could talk enough Spanish to get her clothes off."

The night was young, I told him. Elderly couples held hands and drank beers on park benches, young people stood in groups and none of the Spaniards looked over their shoulders like we had in the alley. The action was here, on a Tuesday night or any night, in the exuberance and the pink neon lights and the music, as crowds of people our age sat on park benches holding Coke bottles in their right hands and wine bottles in their left. *Calimochos*, we heard them say as they mixed the two and passed them back and forth. We passed El Corte Inglés ("The English Court"), a six-story superstore with its doors wide open and streaming with Spaniards. The same street cafes that bustled during the day seemed even livelier at night, and there was a zest for living, an excitement for the moment, that even though unemployment hovered over twenty percent, life was still for the taking. Maybe it was Spain, or maybe it was Alicante, but it was something I had never seen before, not even fully in Madrid.

When we caught a glimpse of the ocean in the distance, we turned onto Avenida del Doctor Gadea and followed it for a mile or so. Our conversation quickly turned from girls to what life was like in Iowa and Idaho, then dropped off entirely as we tried to inhale as much of Alicante as we could. The air had a gritty sweetness to it that tasted like a salted lime. It wasn't like the limes you put in margaritas, but in Alicante you'd never know the difference. "Right or left?" Juan asked.

"Right," I said. "That's closer to where the beach is supposed to be."

We walked for another mile or so, until we found a shopping center on the edge of a wharf that jutted into the ocean. Orange signs and the word *Panoramis* flashed and reflected over rippled water, bending the light into rays of deep purple and auburn. We were standing in front of a waterfront mall, but since it was closed and we couldn't access the beach, we continued on.

Further ahead, the road darkened. We were still on a main road, but now cars shot by us, bearing their headlights straight into our eyes. We shielded our foreheads and turned our heads to the sidewalk as we continued walking for another mile, unaware of where we were. In between oncoming cars, I squinted up. Buildings had suddenly become dilapidated, roofs had caven in, graffiti covered the walls, and torn sheet metal hung in scraps and parts, huddled to the sides of exposed buildings. "Do you think we should turn back?" Juan asked.

"Let's go a little farther," I said. "We don't know if this is normal yet."

We kept walking on the sidewalk next to the main road. As we neared a street corner, a woman stepped out from under the shadows of a concealed overhang and stood directly in front of us in high heels. Her shirt was undone and her breasts hung freely in the night air, her nipples taut in anticipation. She said something in Spanish and began clicking forward, moving her hips and tongue in unison. I'd never seen a hooker before, but I immediately knew that she wanted us. She wanted us to pay her, preferably together. What I remember most, however, was that she had a hard look that was different from the other Spaniards, almost a glare of contempt, a look of brutal honesty. She wanted nothing to do with us, yet she wanted us. The static light of the streetlight above us cast a dirty glow across her chest as she continued her advance. Behind her, shadows threatened and figures detached themselves from the ruins of a crumbled building plastered in government warnings. "Let's go," Juan whispered. "Now."

We made an abrupt turn and pounded in the other direction. Juan looked behind us and saw a car flash its headlights at the bare-chested woman. She didn't give chase.

"There are only a few police officers on duty at night," Asis padre reassured me when I got back. The Bujans had just finished dinner, and Asis, Adán, and Carmen were gathered in the living room watching the ten o'clock news. Asis and Carmen were in their pajamas on the couch, while Adán leaned his arm against the living room table. I sat down next to him and my host dad lowered the volume on the TV. "Alicante is lawless at night, especially in the barrio."

I told them about the woman on the street. It turned out that Juan and I hadn't been in the barrio, but we'd been in one of the bad parts of town and in serious danger. "That's where most of the cocaine deals take place," Adán said before adding, "down by the port." He swung his legs over both sides of his chair. "That's where the *putas* are!" He humped his chair for emphasis as his legs hung on either side of it.

We all laughed, but I was struck by the seriousness of the encounter with the *puta*. "Is there anywhere else I shouldn't go?" I asked, taking out a city map that Carmen had given me.

"*Juan Veintitres*," Asis said. "It's one of *those* neighborhoods. We have a friend who lives there. She sleeps during the day and cowers behind her door at night because she can't go to sleep with all the shooting."

"They'll rob you and maybe kill you," Adán added. "They'll even kill you on the bus ride into Juan Veintitres. Cops don't go there. The gangs— they'll shoot you." He did a gun imitation, holding it sideways like a rapper on a music video. "*Cincuenta Centavos*," he said. "Like 50 Cent."

The conversation moved from barrios, gangs, and drugs to how I should protect myself from thieves, to what I thought about Spain's recession ("*la crisis*," they called it). It was a lot of conversation for our first night, but I loved it. They asked questions and wanted to listen, even if I could barely speak Spanish. "The only way for you to get better is if we talk, right?" Asis said. "We love talking."

There was something about the living room as we sat in conversation. A low-hanging light illuminated the room where the four of us sat talking: father, mother, son, would-be son. Eventually the night wore on and gradually we spoke less and less until we began to fall asleep on the couches. If silence can become a sort of glow, it did that night, and in a bout of homesickness and closeness, I remembered words from conversations and letters long ago, letters from a father to his sons on January nights, that when the world gets the best of us, that when the world gets darker and stranger around us, what matters most is having all of us together, safe and warm in our home. Dad wrote that in a letter to my brothers and me many years ago when we were out wandering, and I had copied it down and put it in a safe place. I've never forgotten it.

Weeks 2-3

Alicante, Spain

Morning comes. The first week is gone and a lazy Saturday morning ushers itself into my room through an open window. Light bursts and my head hurts. It's been a lot of Spanish for one week, but habits have begun to set in.

Life with the Bujans is curious and unusual. We don't flush the toilet, but we do put our toilet paper in a little basket by the door. The bathroom smells. We take showers in the dark and heat our water by lighting a propane tank attached to the outside of the house. Next to the propane tank, Carmen washes our clothes in a washing machine that *gracias a Dios* we're fortunate enough to have. Our washed clothes hang outside the kitchen window, fastened to white wires by Chinese-store wooden clips. There aren't many dollar stores ("euro stores") in Spain, but Carmen thinks it's better that way. She doesn't like the Chinese ("they're taking over our country!"), but she loves the cheap stuff they sell; our house is covered in little trinkets—figurines on top of desks and good luck charms hidden inside closets. I've been to several other houses in Spain, and none of them are covered in plastic toys. Our dog Dior pees on the floor and

Carmen smiles at him before telling him to become a better dog or else *¡se va!* and go away.

As for our individual routines, the siesta shapes our day and every store in the city of 350,000 is closed from two to five in the afternoon. Asis leaves at seven in the morning and comes home from work to take a nap at three, then goes back to work managing the gym and teaching fencing lessons. Carmen sleeps in late and complains about constant housework. She works for three hours in the morning, makes lunch, then sleeps or watches TV for the rest of the day. "It's too much work to fix both lunch and dinner," she says, so whatever we eat for lunch is what we're going to eat for dinner. Adán and Asis junior are in and out. Adán is usually home between classes in the afternoon. He comes home for lunch at two and sometimes we watch *Los Simpsons* while eating. Asis junior spends most nights with his bikini-model girlfriend, but occasionally drops by to say hi. Life ebbs, moves, and flows and is becoming a constant sort of unpredictable, a rhythm, something like home.

It began with a bag of chips taped to my desk with a note. *Estif—de Carmen. Besos.* To Estif, from Carmen. Kisses. Sometimes I would return from school to find a note and a fresh snack on my desk. "I went out shopping today," Carmen would write. Underneath the note were things she thought I might like, and she became a good guesser pretty quick— Coke, Cheetos, Alhambra beer.

Weeks down the road I would arrive home to find my favorite cans of soda in my room, our dog Dior lying on the bed waiting for me, and a newly cleaned room. "You wouldn't want to have to clean that all by yourself, would you?" she said.

Almost every afternoon I went into her room to talk. "*Hola Carmen, ¿qué tal?*" I said, and sat down on the bed next to where she was lying down. Since we didn't heat the house during the day, Carmen was buried under a pile of five blankets, and I was double-layered in a sweatshirt and a coat.

"*Estif, tengo algo mostrarte,*" she said. She had something to show me. Carmen stuck her hands out from under her blankets and slowly pushed herself up, then reached across her cluttered nightstand. Trinkets rattled as she moved her hand blindly across the surface until she clasped her fingers around a small four-by-six photo. "*Es Mitch*," she said, pointing at a balding blond wearing a University of Idaho t-shirt. He was from my university and the picture looked recent.

"Where'd you get that?"

"From Mitch. He lived here last semester." Carmen stood up from the bed and walked over to her dresser by the door. On top was a picture of her and Asis twenty-five years ago, in front of an altar in a bare church. "So many memories," she mumbled, before opening the bottom drawer. Dust wisped out of a dresser filled with stacks of old files. Yellowed paper cracked as Carmen pulled out several manila folders and set them down on the linoleum floor. "*¿Dónde está?*"

She dug out more files and then looked up at me, her brown eyes outlined in blue eyeshadow, her long hair tucked behind her forehead in a plastic headband. "Take a look," she said, and began pulling out old black and white passport photocopies of former students, "*hijos*," Carmen called them, sons. "This is Jacob (Carmen pronounced it HAH-cub), Jake ("Djake"), Stephen ("Esteefen"), Michael ("Mykel"), and Mitch ("Meetch")," she said as she flipped through the stack of photos. They had all lived here.

"So many *hijos*," Carmen said, and sighed. "I love all of my sons." She closed the file she was holding and pulled out another from the stack. She reached inside for a ten-page letter and held it in the air, flipping through it in front of me. "This is what Hah-cub wrote me. I get so many letters, but I will never see any of my sons again."

Every year, Carmen and Asis would open their home to two students, one in the fall and one in the spring. Within five months the students would become sons, and after five months they'd never be seen again, except in memories and once-a-year Christmas letters.

Carmen slipped the letter back into the file and ran her hand along it to crease out the wrinkles. She put the stack of files and crusted papers back in the lower drawer and closed it. Her head dropped and her eyes glazed over the floor. "I'm think I'm going to go back to sleep."

*   *   *

For the first few weeks I was hardly ever at home. In between figuring out how to work the bus system, taking salsa dance lessons from a fiery Cuban, and taking a Spanish cooking class, regular schoolwork had begun to set in. Classes were getting started, and after I finished up at noon, I would usually hang out with the other study abroaders and occasionally I would get the chance to meet their host families. One night, my friend Ashley from Nevada invited me over to meet her host family. Ashley had short, bleached-blonde hair that tended to attract Spanish men, but she tried to keep them at bay by getting a silver nose piercing.

In the living room of her host family's apartment, two auburn-haired kids sat watching TV. We waved and said hello. They turned their heads briefly, then turned back to the screen. They didn't say anything, so we walked by them to reach the kitchen. "*¡Hola!*" Ashley called into the kitchen where her host parents were making dinner. Ashley introduced me, and I reached to shake their hands and do cheek kisses like the Spaniards do, but my hand wasn't received and it hung limp in the air. "*Bienvenidos,*" they said, before leaving the kitchen to join their kids in front of the TV. "Welcome."

We walked straight into Ashley's room at the end of a trinket-less hallway and shut the door. "They're always watching TV," she muttered, before reaching into her closet and pulling out two beers and a box of cigarettes that she had hidden under a pile of clothes. "The beers aren't exactly cold, but they're alcohol."

Ashley's room was bare. There were no UNLV stickers, no taped-to-the-closet American postcards from students come and gone. Her desk was new and bore no noticeable scratch marks; it looked mostly unused. Ashley sat on top of her crinkled blue bedspread and leaned against the wall in a plain black shirt. I sat on the other end of the bed and opened my Cruzcampo.

As we began talking, Ashley began to unwind. Every day, she would come home from school and her host parents would say one, maybe two words before leaving her in silence. Their kids were allowed to watch as much TV as they wanted. "They're spoiled," she said, "and crazy." In her first two weeks with the family, she had tried to play with the kids and watch TV with them, but when they had refused, she left them alone and decided to start smoking.

We finished our beers and went out to the balcony for a smoke break. Ashley pulled out a cigarette. I leaned forward against the black steel railing and my toes hung over the edge. In alternating motions, I moved them up and down. Underneath the outline of my shoes, I saw people appear and disappear as they walked on the street five stories below. Beneath us, bright lights flashed and glittered as crowds of people sat talking and eating at street cafes and the chorus of their inflected voices rose to the balcony in a low murmur. Confined by the railing, I turned and looked over at Ashley. A slight draft of wind pulled her hair away from her eyes, and I saw that her forehead was drawn tight.

She took a long drag on her cigarette. "I hear that a lot of people don't like their host families here." She paused and puffed a ring of smoke over the city. "But I don't know if I like my own family back home either."

There was only one light on in the apartment when I got back. I couldn't see anything down the hall except a warm light at the end coming from the living room. From the faint light at the end of the hallway, I could discern a tiny space heater that sat in front of the door to the living room. A small orange light glowed steadily on the machine ("we only use the heater two hours a day," Carmen had boasted). From the distant sound of the nine o'clock news that carried down the hall, I assumed that Carmen and Asis were in the living room, eating dinner in their pajamas.

"*¡Hola Estif!*" they both called down the hallway, one right after the other. "Your food is in the kitchen," Carmen added, "but you might want to change into your pajamas first."

I readjusted my eyes in the darkness. Other than the outline of the heater, I couldn't see anything but a thin film of moisture and sea-cold that had formed on the walls. A humid chill had blown off the Mediterranean earlier in the day and clung to the walls, choking any heat contained in the fifty year-old building. Carmen always kept the windows open during the day ("the house would smell like sweat and dog piss piss if I didn't," she said when I asked her why the house was always so cold). It wasn't insulated, either, and sea breeze often bottled itself into droplets that you could collect on the walls. I ran my fingers along the mist, leaving a thin line in the wall as I made my way to my room.

The room looked different now. Carmen had given me some of Adán's beach toys to use, including a paddleball racket that proudly featured a cartoon of people having sex on the beach. "*Jajajaja*," she laughed when she gave it to me. "*¡Tienes que refrescar tus ojos!*" You have to relax your eyes when you go to the beach!

I reached into my dresser and pulled out a fresh shirt. I had always heard that you were supposed to pack light when you traveled, so I had packed accordingly: seven shirts, two pairs of pants, two pairs of shorts, one swimsuit, one pair of slacks for special events (but no dress shoes), ten pairs of socks and underwear, my camera and computer, an American football (for my cultural exchange item), Paul's copy of *Don Quixote* (which I never read), postcards from home, and a $2 Oregon Trail coin from Baker. Other than these items, my dresser was mostly empty.

I put on one of my shirts. "We need to go to the store and get you more clothes and some pajamas," Carmen told me yesterday. "I know a good Chinese store that I think you'll like."

To help tide me over until we could go shopping, Asis had loaned me his old orange and black pajamas from the eighties, which meant that I looked pretty cool around the house. Well, not really, but I didn't mind though. While Asis' extra-large pajama pants swallowed me whole and his button-up top covered me like a bag from the grocery store, the pajamas were warmer than the white t-shirt I'd worn before. I tucked an extra shirt underneath for some added girth.

After changing, I threw my dirty clothes in the hamper next to Dad's old backpack. He'd called earlier in the week, "just to see how I was doing," and we had decided that we would talk every week on Sunday at two o'clock, or, if I happened to be gone on the weekend, sometime before I left. It was a mutual agreement, really, because hanging above my desk was the final thing I'd brought from home—a picture of home. A five by seven of Mom, Dad, Paul, and me was taped above the desk. It was a picture of us on the farm, next to the old rope swing that Paul and I had built in front of the Powder River, where all of us stood in our winter coats. The picture was several years out of date, but it was the last family picture we had taken and I looked at it often. Several feet away from the family picture was a postcard of the wheat fields near my university. That was from Mitch.

I started walking out of my room when I heard Carmen yell, "*¡Apaga la luz!*" I reached inside and turned off the light.

I paused in the now completely dark hallway and waited for my eyes to readjust again before walking to the kitchen to grab my dinner tray. "When you're in the kitchen, it's okay to turn on the light," Carmen had told me earlier in the week, "just as long as you only have one light on at a time, you can use the lights." I stumbled down the hall, feeling my way blind with the help of the moisture on the walls. When I made it to the kitchen, my hand was completely wet, but I turned on the light and found a bright blue plastic tray that Carmen had prepared for me. *Estif—cena*, said a napkin note on top of it. *Adán will eat your food if I don't label it.*

I shut off the kitchen light and began walking back down the dark hallway. With each step, an orange rolled back and forth across my tray, shifting the weight with its movement. I gripped the tray with both hands. As I tried to feel my way forward with my feet, I smashed my toe against the dresser of Carmen's trinkets. With a crash, plastic knickknacks tumbled to the floor and the tea mug that Carmen had placed on my tray fell to the ground, shattering and flinging pieces of porcelain across the hall.

At the same time, Carmen and Asis burst out laughing at something they'd seen on TV. They didn't hear the mug break. I didn't know how they would react to the broken mug, but I did know that if a propane tank for the heater in the house cost fifteen euros a month and was *muy caro*, then a tea mug was probably expensive, too. I set my tray on the ground and collected the broken pieces, then went to my room and tucked them in the back corner of my closet. I walked back into the kitchen and filled a new mug with tap water.

I entered the living room for dinner. The flatscreen TV was playing the tail end of the nine o'clock news, while Carmen and Asis sat on the couch peeling oranges on top of crumpled napkins and worn plastic trays.

Asis lowered the volume with the remote and Carmen looked oddly content in red pajamas decorated with sporadic white poinsettias. She didn't seem to notice that I had swiped a new mug.

"*Mira*," Carmen said, pointing to a polished oak china cabinet against the wall. Large *copas* and *trofeos* covered the top of it, nearly touching the ceiling, and I could read Asis' name on most of the trophies that bore fencing insignias. Inside the china cabinet, shelves were intermixed with wine glasses, French dictionaries and other cultural items, and next to a Moroccan tea set, an Arabic mask, and pictures of the family in younger days was a book called *Idaho*. "Eee-daho." Carmen said. "*Es de Mitch*."

"*Mitch fue militar*," Asis began, and swung his arms up as if he was about to shoot a rifle. "*¡Pow pow!* He was a soldier."

More importantly, Mitch was the last *hijo* to live with them before I'd arrived, and they were eager to talk about him. "It's very strange that he went to the same university as you," Carmen said. "That's never happened before. Usually our students are from Iowa and then Nevada, not Idaho and then Idaho."

Other than when Carmen had shown me the picture of Mitch earlier in the week, I'd never heard them talk about their former students.

"Mitch left in December," she said.

"He was very disciplined," Asis added. "He would wake up at six in the morning before anyone else in Spain and go running." Asis ripped off a section of the orange in his hand and put it into his mouth, swallowing it in one bite. "But Mitch was also very sad."

Every day Mitch would get on his computer and Skype his dad back home. He was always on his computer, Carmen said, always typing away, *¡chuk-chuk-chuk!*, always writing to people far away. He was *militar*—an ROTC Air Force officer candidate, and it became obvious when Carmen mentioned the names of some of Mitch's friends that we'd had several mutual friends in college.

He used to bring his friends Leah and Hannah over to the house all the time, Carmen said. "We really liked them, but Mitch was always sad or in his room, even when they were around. I asked him why he didn't have a girlfriend, but he didn't say anything. He was just on that computer with his dad all the time, sometimes even while his friends were here. One day though, his dad came to visit, and Mitch was finally happy. I never forgot that."

Carmen tilted her head towards Asis and then lifted her feet onto his lap. *"Jefe,"* she said to Asis. "Boss, a foot massage please."

Asis looked at me and winked. "The thing about women is that they always want you to do something for them."

"Well, what I wanted was for Mitch to feel like he belonged," Carmen said, changing the subject back to Mitch as she sunk back into the couch and closed her eyes. "Maybe he knew someone you might have known—and maybe that's why you're here."

I was still figuring out that part. At first, there was nothing to figure out. The first weeks of class were just plain fun. My professor Paloma, a short, stylish *señora*, was forty and recently divorced. Because of that, she liked to work out, correct poorly written papers, and wear tight jeans and low-cut shirts to class because she was ready to get over her ex-husband. My other professor, Juan (also in his forties), came to class dressed like he was going to the nightclub. His usual attire consisted of chic leather jackets, embroidered jeans that provided some lift, and pointed black shoes with little steel buckles. He liked speaking with a thick lisp (his *c*'s became *th*'s) and he would correct us if we pronounced words without "the lisp." Juan also liked Lady Gaga's "Bad Romance," and while he never explicitly mentioned a romance, he did ask all of the guys in class if we were gay.

Other than my professors, my classes had ten to fifteen students in them—all Americans—many of whom like me had never really been on their own outside the US. At the Universidad de Alicante, we sat at normal-sized tables, and instead of the computerized learning and online homework that we were used to back home, we were immersed in old-fashioned chalk and blackboard instruction.

A certain camaraderie began to form as we sat through lectures that none of us were really able to understand. What did she mean by that? Could you even understand him? Most of the study abroaders in my class section didn't live with host families, so once they discovered that I lived with Carmen and Asis and that I actually had to speak Spanish, they began to take all of the seats in the back of the classroom and I was forced to sit up front and answer every question the professor asked. I've never been a front row kind of guy—I've always preferred the middle, where all of the talking was to be had. The first week of sitting up front was good though, because I got to practice more Spanish, but it quickly became a nightmare. As my Spanish continued to improve, the other study abroaders began to get jealous, until one day I was left out of the group almost entirely.

It happened like this. At first, I went to the beach almost every day with the other study abroaders. On our second week in Alicante we had a surprise burst of twenty-two degree Celsius weather, and while we didn't know how to convert that number into Fahrenheit, it was hot enough to get in our swimsuits and splash around with soccer balls in salty Mediterranean water. Casting a shadow over the beach, an old Moorish castle stood watch over Alicante, sitting atop a dusty hill in the middle of the city, the color of yellow dirt. Behind Castillo de Santa Barbara, mountains roamed the distance and it felt like Southern California, only livelier and more exotic. And just like California, as soon as we figured out how to get European cell phones, we were constantly talking and texting. Any day of the week, you could spot us walking down the *passeo* underneath the palm trees, pressing orange phones to our ears (made by a French company called *Orange*).

The trouble with cell phones, however, was that they set you apart. The Spaniards only used cell phones to call and hang up on you, a *toque* that told you they were ready to meet up somewhere, usually a street cafe. I hardly ever saw the Spaniards on their phones, but I talked to another study abroader on mine as I walked to the beach.

To meet the other study abroaders at the beach, I took the *explanada*, a marble walkway of tiles set in red and blue waves. Large palm trees grew on either side of the explanada, and beneath them, people in bright-colored booths peddled handicrafts while Moroccans and Algerians sat on pink rugs in the middle and sold counterfeit Dolce & Gabbana purses to local women. Along the way, restaurants displayed signs in English, French, and German to attract tourists to their *menús turísticos*, even though they catered to local meal times and opened at 8:00 p.m. for dinner. Roughly thirty percent of Alicante's economy was based on tourism, but throughout the city the locals were determined to only speak Spanish and the local *valenciano* dialect in order to give visitors "a more authentic experience." Getting around town was also an issue. There was an extensive bus system, but you had to know Spanish in order to figure out how to use it. Alicante was a tourist town in search of a tourist.

I reached the end of the explanada where it opened up to Playa Postiguet. One hundred feet in front of me, I saw crusted sand set before rippled waves. In the distance, our study abroad group huddled in a circle to sing songs with my guitar-playing friend Mike, who since we had arrived in Spain, had now become Miguel. As a sign of his new identity, he wore sunglasses emblazoned with sparkling dollar signs while strumming Michael Jackson.

I began walking toward the group. Along the edge of the water, I watched a Spanish couple hold hands and skirt the bubbling foam of oncoming waves. When a wave would recede, they would run into the sand and dig their toes into it, flinging up little bits and pieces as they laughed.

I looked around, and other than the Spanish couple and our group of study abroaders, there was hardly anyone else at the beach. "*Hola guapos,*" I told the group.

They must not have heard me at first because they didn't look up. "I'm on a boat!" someone began singing. "I'm on a boat—on the beach!" Shirts and shoes were off as they spread across towels in bikinis and board shorts, holding cigarettes and cheap forties in their hands. I sat down at the edge of the circle.

"This guy needs a beer!" someone said and threw a bottle my direction.

I twisted the top, pulled my shirt off, and began unpacking my backpack that contained two important things: a towel and a football.

"Alright!" one of the blond guys from California said when he saw what I'd brought. "Let's play some real *fútbol*—American football!" He flicked off his sandals and took off running as I stood up and tossed him a pass like I was the star quarterback. "Touchdown!" He threw his hands above his head and made a field goal in the air, then ran back and high fived the group as if we were the home team. Why not throw our hands up? This was our beach as much as anyone else's.

We spent the rest of the afternoon lazing around, drinking, and being loud and generally obnoxious. The girl sitting next to me, I learned, was from South Carolina and her name was Rachel. We talked a bit. She had long blonde hair and was as thin as a stick. That was my first impression anyway—I didn't know much else about her. While we were talking, I found myself wanting to ask about her host family and what they were like. Were they like Carmen and Asis? Were they a little eccentric? But when I asked her about it, she said she only lived with other Americans.

"It's fun, though," she said.

I asked the same question to a guy with a buzz cut sitting next to her, but he didn't live with a family, either.

"My host mom is nice," a girl from Virginia chimed in when she heard what we were talking about, "but she's never around. She's divorced and works two jobs."

I had met the girl from Virginia once before; that was the thing about studying abroad. At first, there seemed to be so many of you, so much that it was hard to keep track of everyone. We only knew each other by where we were from, or if you happened to do something out of the ordinary.

"When I'm home at my host family's apartment," the girl from Virginia said, "I'm either online and watching movies, or sitting around and getting bored. What about you?" she asked.

I filled her in on Carmen and Asis, and apparently what I was said became interesting, because soon enough, the other study abroaders turned to listen. Guitar strumming quieted down, and after awhile I realized that I was the only one talking. I didn't quite understand it. What was so interesting about Carmen and Asis? I told them how we didn't flush our toilets at home and how Carmen made my lunch every day; how my host brother Asis junior was a runner-up for Mister Spain 2006, and how Asis padre taught fencing lessons and used to be a Spanish champion.

When I finished telling them about life with the Bujans, Rachel tossed her head back to tell a joke.

"There's something wrong with your host family," she said. "Your host parents aren't old lonely people, and they're still married. What's wrong with this picture?"

We all laughed, and some of the other study abroaders began talking about their host families. Danny from Maryland told us how he was living with a sixty year-old lady about to die of a heart attack the next time she stepped into a Burger King. "God, she loves that place." Since his host mom didn't have anyone to talk to, and since both of her sons had left the house years ago, she'd signed up for a host student to keep her company. But since she wanted to talk to him all the time, he usually ended up leaving the house.

Following Danny's story, a girl from Chicago told us about her host dad and how he was confined to a wheelchair. She felt sorry for him, she said, he always had a remote in his hand and he was so quiet. From what she could tell, he spent his days and the rest of his government pension in front of the TV while his wife puttered in and out of the picture; she would come home late with other men. We also learned that another girl's host mom was divorced and worked the night shift; she was never home. And a curvy girl in the group, this one from California, had a family that constantly told her she was fat and that she needed to stop eating so much—did she know that she was costing the family a lot of money? Girls were supposed to be skinny, they told her.

"Host families are more like a temp home," the curvy girl said. "Well, that's what my family has always been. A temp home." She turned away and began talking to a shirtless guy sitting next to her, so I looked elsewhere for a new conversation.

Across the group I spotted a corn-stalk blonde from Iowa in a dripping black bikini. I immediately thought of Davíd from Madrid and what he would have thought of her, what he would have wanted to do with her, and I subconsciously began talking to her in Spanish.

"*Guapa, he oido que—*"

She cut me off. "Just say it in English. I don't speak Spanish."

"You *what*?" As soon as the rest of the group realized that I was startled, they stopped talking.

"I don't speak Spanish," she said. "I drink." She took a swig from her bottle of Mau that was crusted in sand, and looked at me through her sunglasses. The group laughed.

"But we're in Spain," I said. "They speak Spanish here. Don't you speak a little Spanish?"

"Wait." She held up one of her hands like a stop sign. "You actually think I'm in Spain to learn Spanish?" The group laughed again and toasted to that, sloshing out a loud *¡salud!* as they clinked bottles all around. "I'll cheers to that," she said and raised her glass into the middle of the group where they clinked bottles again. "*Salud*. That's my Spanish for you."

I hadn't clinked bottles with anyone and my Mau hung loose in my hand; I didn't know what to say. Weren't we in Spain to learn Spanish? The girl from Iowa swung her hair behind her back and smirked. I reached into my backpack, pulled out my crumpled shirt, and put it back on.

Guitar strumming started up again, the group started talking to each other, and one by one, small conversations pushed me away until I was on the outer circle of the group. I stood up, put my football in my backpack, and left.

The next day in class, the other study abroaders started talking about me when our professor asked who had done their homework. "Ask him," they said and pointed to me. "He lives with a Real Family." The other kids would stall to answer when Paloma asked a question, so she started calling on me all the time, and since they took the seats at the back of the room, I was stuck with the Front Seat in a row all to myself. I was the only person in my section living with a host family.

After class, I went into the *cafetería* where everyone usually went to talk and eat lunch. Maybe we could work this out. I made two laps around the circular cafeteria, but the other study abroaders were nowhere to be found; I was the only foreigner. Surrounded by tables of Spaniards, I took a seat at an empty table and began reading an insert on the napkin dispenser: a student group was putting on an event and everyone was invited. That made me feel even more isolated. While I didn't particularly like the other study abroaders, I liked them well enough—they were the only people I could actually talk to.

I dug into the lunch that Carmen had prepared for me. *Estif—besos,* she'd written on a napkin. I unwrapped a handful of chips that Carmen had packed in a ball of tin foil and munched them one at a time, smiling and hoping that someone would stop by and say hello. What I didn't realize at the time, though, was that the Spaniards knew any conversation with a foreigner was likely to be strained and jolted with infinitives and pieced-together sentences. I watched them walk by and sit at tables with other Spaniards, guys with girls, girls with guys. I tried my best to ignore it, so I finished my lunch in a hurry and left.

At the end of the week when our professor handed back our tests, I ended up getting the same grade as the corn-stalk Iowa girl, the only difference was that I was now speaking Spanish twenty-four hours a day and she wasn't.

I approached Paloma after class to explain how hard I was trying. I wanted to learn, even though my grade didn't reflect it.

"You might not think I know who's trying to learn, but I do," Paloma said after all of the other students had left the room. "You think no one is watching, but someone is always watching."

It was supposed to have been a normal day. I went to class, sat up front and answered all of the questions, got my homework assignments, then left to sit under a palm tree while I ate a *salchichan* sandwich that Carmen had slathered in olive oil. Other than a slight breeze that blew by with the scent of oranges, the day was fairly normal. On days like this, I usually went to talk to Luis in the study abroad office. When I peeked inside his office, however, he wasn't at his desk. Sitting above his empty chair, a large poster of a lonely dirt road stared back at me. Revealing nothing more than a brown path winding through the countryside, *El Camino de Santiago* was inscribed in white script. The road in the picture looked familiar. I couldn't quite place the feeling, but I had heard of it before.

As I turned to leave, Luis' secretary, Veronica, poked her head around a computer monitor in the corner of the office. "*¿Estif?*"

I jumped. The poster of the road began to come alive, and I saw myself walking on it.

"Do you need something?" Veronica asked.

"No—I just liked the poster." My eyes glazed over and I continued to stare at it.

"Do you know what it is?" she asked.

"What?"

"The road."

"No." I took my eyes off the poster and looked toward the back corner of the room where Veronica sat at an empty desk behind a keyboard and her monitor.

"Well, if life's a long dirt road where you forget most of the things that happen, you at least try to remember the landmarks."

Veronica drew her hand across her desk to dust it off, but a sliver of wood caught her thumb mid-motion. "Ouch," she said and jerked her thumb toward her body.

She pulled the sliver out, then held her thumb to her mouth and sucked the blood out. "You remember Mitch?"

I nodded.

Veronica leaned back in her chair and crossed her arms. "I do too," she said, before crossing her arms and sucking more blood out of her thumb. "One day Mitch came in here with a friend, then the next day his friend came in and asked me to place you with Carmen and Asis. I don't know why I remembered that just now, but I did. Mitch's friend said she knew you. Our home placements—they're supposed to be random, even though they're not."

"What was the friend's name?" I asked.

"Leah," she said. "But she's gone now. It happened just like that."

"Let's watch a game show," Carmen suggested. "Instead of the news."

We were back in front of the TV, eating dinner from twenty year-old pink plastic trays. Tonight it was Spanish spaghetti with red sauce and chorizo, coupled with lettuce and carrot salad wilted by olive oil and vinegar. "*Es muy fresca*," Asis commented to Carmen about the salad—very fresh.

Carmen grabbed the remote and started flipping through channels, and ended up stumbling across a program on Chinese dating habits. "*Los chinos*," Carmen said and shook her head.

On the flatscreen TV, we watched a group of Chinese men tape pictures of themselves to a wall. "*Es muy interesante*," the Spanish announcer said while pointing at the wall. "Since there aren't enough women to go around in China, the men post pictures of themselves on the dating wall and the women call the men they want to date."

"Do you have dating walls in America?" Asis asked.

"No, but we have Las Vegas." I did a steering wheel motion and kissed the air beside me. "You can get married at a drive-thru window. You just pull up, tell them you want to get married, and they do it right there. It's like McDonald's, except you get married."

Carmen laughed. "*¿Ventanas de bodas?* Asis, we should have gotten married in one of those!"

Asis laughed. "We were so young when we got married," he said. "Too young maybe, but at least we didn't need a wall or a window to do it."

"America is a strange place," Carmen added. She set her plastic dinner tray on the floor next to the only heater as Dior started to pee on the floor. "No piss piss!"

It was time to replace the mug I'd broken earlier in the week. The following weekend I took the train up the Costa Blanca to Barcelona for a weekend trip, and brought back a Gaudi mug for Carmen and Asis. They had never been to Barcelona, but they'd always wanted to visit, especially since it was only five hours away.

"This is for you," I said, and presented a package wrapped in white paper. I was about to say something more when I stopped myself and ran back to my room to grab the shards of the mug I'd broken earlier in the week. "I got you this because I broke one of your mugs earlier in the week."

Asis smiled when he unwrapped the package in his hand. The new mug was a modern collage of colors, a mosaic mish-mash of orange, blue, yellow, and red on clear glass—a gift offering. "This is beautiful," he said. "If you break a mug, so what? You break a mug. We can buy another one. But this … this is going to stay with us forever."

"No, I want you to use it," I said. "Drink out of it, because I broke the other one." I grabbed it and did a swigging motion.

"This isn't for using," Carmen said, and pointed around the room to

Iowa State mugs, University of Nevada picture frames, and Switzerland fridge magnets. I handed her the mug and she reached above her head to place it on one of the shelves above the sink. "We have lots of mementos because students are happy here. When you live here, you're family, and when you leave here, you'll still be family." She brushed my shoulder with her hand as she left the kitchen to go do laundry. Implicit in her touch was a message. *We won't leave you, but please don't leave us.*

It was a Friday night and for some reason or other, I'd been invited to a house party with the other study abroaders. I was surprised that they had invited me, and I knew that I had to take them up on their offer; it felt good to be included once again. At the party, shots went down quickly, and since wine was only one euro at the *supermercado*, there was plenty to go around. With enough *calimochos* (wine mixed with Coke), I could be anyone and hang around anyone. "Give me another shot!" I yelled.

"Look, Steve's getting crazy!"

We left the house party and headed into the barrio to continue drinking, but I didn't make it very far down the street. Sickened by the alcohol, my stomach began to heave and I threw up in the middle of a crowded street. I quickly moved to the side and grasped an alley wall for support, then hung my head as the Spaniards glared at me while I continued to throw up.

A few minutes later I began to shake, and two of the study abroaders offered to carry me to a nearby bench. "You don't look so good," they said.

After awhile they helped me stand up straight, but I told them I felt nauseated and wanted to go. They put their arms around my shoulders, nodded, and began walking me home.

We took the elevator to the fourth floor. Outside Carmen and Asis' apartment, one of the study abroaders dug around in my pocket for my key, and I threw up again. Then they opened the door to the apartment, and Dior ran to greet me and I threw up in front of him. He disappeared down the hallway and I don't remember anything else.

When I woke up the following afternoon, sunlight bled through the open blinds of my room. Clothes from the night before littered the floor, and my shoes were overturned in the corner next to Dad's old backpack; my belt was still attached to pants that had been pulled off in a hurry. I rolled across my watermelon bedspread and into a pool of my own vomit. It clung to my skin, wet and disgusting, and I lay there in the midst of it.

Bit by bit, my memory came back and I remembered that I'd thrown up all over the house and hadn't cleaned it up. It was time to do that. I got out of bed and opened my door.

At the far end of the hallway, Carmen's back was turned to me and her head was down. A mop was in her hands and I watched her slide it slowly across the floor, applying pressure, soaking up the dirty stuff. In the dim light of the shadowy hall, she looked like a silhouette and she hadn't heard me yet. Before she could turn around and see me with vomit still clinging to my chest, I slipped into the bathroom and closed the door.

Inside, I looked at myself in the mirror. My hair was greased and stuck every which way and my stomach was bloated. All of it—the fool I'd been, the mess I'd left, the vomit—it reminded me of the vase incident in Madrid, except now I was the culprit. I was an embarrassment.

When I got out of the bathroom, however, Asis pulled me aside and told me that every study abroader made the same mistake their first weekend or two abroad. "The question," he said, "is whether you'll learn from it, or if you'll keep doing the same thing."

He stopped with that thought. "I'll leave you to think about it."

By the end of the third week, I was mostly done hanging out with the other study abroaders. Other than in class or at salsa lessons every Monday night, I hardly ever saw them. I didn't get invited to go to the beach or to travel around Europe with them, but I didn't really care either. Actually, I did care a little bit. It was hard to be in a foreign country all by yourself. I made a few friends with kids from other sections, but I began to spend more of my time with Carmen and Asis.

While I enjoyed being at home with them, I realized that I needed to get out of the house for a bit. I was itching for travel, and one of my friends from Idaho happened to be studying abroad in Germany. I called Aaron and bought a plane ticket. "It's cold and there's two feet of snow up here," he said. "Get ready for it."

I told him that I knew what it meant to be cold. I had a lot of trust to regain, and even if Carmen and Asis were used to their American sons throwing up all over their house, that wasn't the kind of son I wanted to be.

Dad called for our weekly phone call and we talked the situation over. He hounded me about the drinking, but told me that he thought it would be wise to get away from things and get some fresh air, no matter where that was. "Where are you going?" he asked.

When I told him I was going to Northern Germany, he became excited. "Grandma Frances' family was from a little town not far from there!"

Hamburg would be a fresh start, and coincidence or not, my friend happened to be living close to where my non-Bohemian ancestors were from. The opportunity was mine for the taking.

Week 4
Hamburg, Germany

The search for the long-lost family had officially begun. At least Dad thought so anyway.

"How about finding those Germans?" he called and asked the night before I left for Hamburg.

It was a cross-legged moment. I was sitting on my bed with my legs crossed, pressing an orange European cell phone to my ear, while wearing Asis' matching orange and black flannel pajamas. They were two sizes too big, and when I breathed out, my stomach barely touched the fabric. Of course I didn't have a heater in my room, so it was colder than usual, too. But despite the chill, there was a certain warmth pulsing from the phone in my hand, almost as if I was holding one of the old fat Nokias from back home.

Dad had been excited ever since I told him I would be visiting Germany. "You start throwing out our name in the right places, and they'll come find you," he said. "Those Germans don't see many Americans up there."

Ever since we were little, my brothers and I had grown up with stories of the Germans and the Bohemians. Through Dad, we'd been there when they came over in 1870 from Bohemia to Sioux Indian Country, Nebraska. We could speak intimately of Manifest Destiny and its imprint on our soul. We knew what it meant to leave the trail and carve your own path, to trade chickens to the Indians for harvest seed and live to tell of it. On road trips that were almost always designed to visit other family members, we'd hear of their exploits.

"You don't do what they did and go to Sioux Indian Country unless someone is out to kill you back home," he would tell us as he looked over the wheel at my brothers and me in the back seat. His blue eyes shone with anticipation and Mom reached over to touch his shoulder in the front seat. "I don't know why they came to America, but they were running from something."

That got my brothers and me excited. Were our ancestors criminals, outlaws, or something in between? I wanted to be related to dangerous and daring men. We'd grown up with adventure stories, and the next best thing to being in a book about romping around somewhere was having a family that had already done that.

We loved hearing Dad's stories, but for some reason I never remember asking more questions about our ancestors—he just laid it all out for us. Stories of our family were never told in terms of this-is-who-you-are, this-is-where-you-come-from. Stories for us were an adventure, about the Bohemians saying *jak se máte*, and about the Germans and how they were so big that they couldn't fit through the doors of other people's houses. We heard about the time when Great Grandpa taught Dad how to pick cherries ("Grandpa was going to make darn sure we knew how to work!"), and we heard about Great Grandma and how at nineteen she rode the train all by herself to the Middle of Nowhere, Nebraska to teach kids how to read ("Now that's a brave woman!").

Whenever Dad told us the stories, it always felt like we were looking at Christmas lights. There was a reverent sort of silence to them, a sense of awe amidst darkness, an improbable sense of wonder, something like new snow falling over muddy paths. We stopped putting up Christmas lights at our house when I was about ten years old, and ever since, I've dreamed of putting up my own lights one day.

Sometimes we'd hear of one adventure, then a year later on a different drive we'd hear of another exploit. Time passed though, and the link between the Bohemians and us became more than six generations. It was something like being forgotten.

For whatever reason, the Bohemians wanted to disappear. One day during the Depression when he was just a boy, Grandpa Hanna was walking down the street in Nebraska and was run over by a woman who was rich enough to have car insurance. Grandpa broke his leg, but he survived all right; he was a tough six year-old. With the money the family received from the insurance settlement, the Hannas left Sioux Indian Country for a small farm in Emmett, Idaho. The settlement money ended up providing just enough to make it through the Depression.

Idaho was alright, but we encountered a similar problem: we didn't have any better luck with car crashes. Great Grandpa was eighty-six and walking to the grocery store when a teenage driver ran a red light and killed him. One minute he was walking to the store, and the next—he was dead. I never met Great Grandpa, but everyone said it happened just like that. One moment you were living with the Indians, and the next, you were dead. That was Joe Hanna. He died about thirty years ago. He was one of the last people in the family to speak Czech and a farmer straight through.

The trouble though, Dad told us, was that Great Grandpa Joe Hanna had married a German. "Oh, you didn't marry Germans in those days if you were Bohemian," Dad said. "That was *intermixing*, but those two were one happy couple. They used to make me feel so special! I thought I was the only one who felt that way around them, but years later all of the cousins said the same thing: 'Grandma made me feel like the most special person in the whole world.' One thing was for certain—they made sure that there were a lot of special people in the world," Dad said. "That's all I knew about them when I was little, that they made you feel really special."

On Great Grandma's side of the family were the Germans Dad wanted me to find. Following Great Grandpa's death, Dad began collecting stories and letters from the Bohemian and German sides of the family. The Bohemian side naturally carried more weight since both of Dad's parents were Bohemian, but the German strand was important nonetheless. They were family, so we had to find them, too. The Germans just didn't get as much storytelling attention because there wasn't a common credence like the Pact to rally around—like when the Bohemians had gathered together one night and made a pact to pool all of their money to send one person to America while sentencing the rest of them to poverty.

"I wanted to pass those stories onto you boys someday," he told my brothers and me, "because I didn't want you to lose them. I always felt a sense of indebtedness for what they did for us—maybe someday you'll understand the sacrifices they had to make."

Dad wasn't the only historian working on collecting memories from the second generation before they disappeared. Working alongside him, Cousin Bentz began an exhaustive history of the German ancestry that spanned five trips to Germany and forty years of work. There had always been at least two historians in the family, but Cousin Bentz had died several years ago. In the years since, Dad became the unofficial genealogist and sent letters and gathered the stories of distant aunts and relatives to try to get some idea of where we were from. "I was always just interested in their stories," he said. "Ever since I was little I wanted to find them."

In the seventh grade I did a report on the German-Danish roots of our family. The German ancestors were from the North, somewhere near Hamburg in Northern Germany, and I say German-Danish because in the seventh grade I wanted to believe they were Vikings and that they went around killing people. "That's a bit of a stretch," Dad tried to tell me back then, "but yes, they were from close to the Danish border."

The kind of details I wanted to know then weren't going to help me now—how many fights they used to get in, whether or not they wore horns on their helmets like in the movies, and how they were able to sail their boats around the world. Other than these essential details, I knew only what Dad had told me. They were a big, strong people ("Your Great Grandma was built like a horse!"), and they were from Northern Germany about two hours north of Hamburg where I was about to go. I didn't think twice about visiting them.

"I'm going to visit a friend," I told Dad before the visit. "Not to find the family."

"Well, you can do both."

"In three days—no."

My orange phone pulsed silently in my hand, waiting for Dad's response. He was slow to answer. "Someday you'll think back on what you just said and be sorry you did what you're about to do. Someday you'll be my age and wish you'd done what you didn't do."

What he didn't understand was that I would only be in Germany for three days. I wasn't going to find the family, in fact, I was already discovering a family in the making in Spain. Why would I want to find another one? I was going to visit a friend. That's what I thought, anyway. But somewhere tucked far away and out of sight, somewhere buried deep within me, I held on to Dad's words. Maybe there was a chance, a small one, and I wasn't going to count it out just yet.

I used to think that expectations produced results. That when you woke up expecting one thing and did everything in your power to find it, that you'd find it. I wasn't so sure now. Sometimes things just happened.

Dad told me a story of happenings. "I once heard a story of a man who went to Germany to find his family. He went back to the small town where his family was from and walked around the streets saying his last name. Just that. That's all he had to do, just say his last name. He didn't speak German so he couldn't say anything else anyway. That'd be like you going to Germany." Dad paused before continuing. "After the man proclaimed his name in the streets, he went into the village stores to look for his family. When he didn't find them there, he walked up main avenues and back alleys once more, and *a strange thing began to happen*," Dad said, with a pastoral sense of emphasis.

"When he went looking for his family, people came to help him." There was a faint urgency in his voice. "It's not really the sort of thing you can do on your own. The village people knew something special was happening, and they wanted to be a part of it. People came out of their houses and swarmed around him when he kept saying his name, because everyone in the town knew a family that went by the same last name. The townspeople didn't really know what to do but get involved. They brought the man to the local English schoolteacher, who promptly cancelled class to help figure out who this American was. Isn't that crazy? You don't see that in a lot of places. People don't do that anymore, yet they do. Schoolteachers don't just walk out of their classes. Something was going on, and that teacher knew it. He translated the American's story, and for the rest of the day that lucky guy got to sit down and talk to his family through the help of the townspeople and that one English teacher. All you have to do is find one person," Dad said, "and you could be on your way to finding our family."

Dad had heard the story a long time ago, and for some reason it had stayed with him. "That man later told me, 'of all of the things I did in Europe, finding my family produced the most wonderful feeling.'" Dad's voice hung in the air like a whispered song. I could see him looking up to the ceiling as we talked on the phone, praying. "If you did something like that, they would come running for you."

I wanted to believe him, but it was hard. "It can't be that easy."

"Oh yes it can—they're all over there. I've even emailed some of them."

Dad had never heard back from the family he'd tried to email in Europe, but nevertheless, he wasn't deterred. He was going to find them, and it would be nice if I would assist in the endeavor. Dad's belief was that the world operated much like it had in the man's story, that families were reunited after hundreds of years, and that deliverance was indeed the most important part of our existence. Some miracles were on the road waiting for you to run into them, he said.

And some roads happened to be deterred.

The diversion started with Carmen's suitcase.

Every day before I went to school at the Universidad de Alicante, I would load my school supplies into a backpack the size of a keychain. It was a keychain backpack made of plastic so thin that you could fold it into a square in your palm, yet flexible enough so that it could expand to hold one or two textbooks. That seemed like enough space to pack my things for Germany. The night before I was about to leave, I tried to load my stuff into it when Carmen came into my room and saw what I was doing.

"*Estif,*" Carmen said. "*¿Qué es esto?*" You can't pack all your clothes in this!

"I'll have to—it's all I have." I looked up at her from where I was kneeling on the floor. Other than Dad's old hiking pack, this keychain bag was all I had. After packing just two shirts and a travel towel, however, it was already bulging.

"Come with me," Carmen said.

I followed her down the hall and into her room. By now I was used to coming into Carmen's room to talk every afternoon when she was resting during siesta time. When she was lying down, she liked to pull the blankets over her body until they rested just below her chin. Then she would wrap the end of the blanket around her feet and tuck the sides under her body, like a mummy. I took a picture of her like that once. "If I'm a *momia*" she said, "then you're paparazzi."

Every time I went into her room, I noticed something new. The clutter of trinkets on top of desks and dressers was a barrage on the senses—it was hard to take it all in. Even if you breathed slow and inhaled, the essence of Carmen and Asis would somehow escape to other parts of the room. They weren't going to be confined to one or two objects. They were going to spread themselves everywhere, including America, because each trinket represented a memory from one of their former students and they had lots of memories.

When I was in their room this time, I didn't notice a specific trinket, but instead, a picture frame. The picture sat on top of Carmen's desk at an angle, turned away from the room's entrance and barely noticeable in its plain wooden frame. It was Carmen and Asis on their wedding day. Unlike their room, the picture was memorable for its stark emptiness. There was no altar, no decorations, no cross, no church mantel, and no special background in their wedding picture, nothing but them standing in front of a blank wall in plain dress clothes. I don't even think Carmen wore a wedding dress. In the picture, Carmen's cheeks swelled like roses as she stood next to a younger Asis in a gray suit. "We were young then and we didn't have any money," Carmen said. Weeks later I asked again about their wedding, but she didn't say anything more.

Carmen moved deeper into her room and opened her closet. She began digging for something, and several moments later she stepped back to reveal a brand new suitcase in her hands. She motioned for me to take it. The suitcase was carry-on size, suede in deep blue, and it smelled of newness, too; the metal zippers collected the imprint of my fingerprints. The suitcase had never been used. "I want you to have this," Carmen said.

If there had been music, a shimmer would have been audible in the distance. But other than a rustle of wind that blew past the open window and stirred the curtains, there was no sound in the room. Host moms weren't supposed to do this and Carmen whispered into my ear. "Don't tell Luis that I gave you this." She raised her eyebrows and winked. "I won't tell if you won't."

I smiled and drew a zipper across my lips.

"Promise me you'll call when you're gone," she said.

"I will," I said, not really knowing where to begin. "I'll call, but I don't think we'll have any problems in Germany."

There's no better way to start off a visit to the land of your ancestors than by getting lost. Aaron met me at the airport with red hair and a shamrock-green jacket that could have helped him find his ancestors in Ireland. Even in the crowd of Germany's second largest city, I could easily spot his signature gap-toothed smile and ear-to-ear freckled grin a mile away. By default, we slapped high fives, gave each other half-hugs and said *hey man*. Before our introductions could get much further though, Aaron informed me that we only had an hour to find our way back to his house in Lüneburg. "We've got to hurry to make it back."

At nine o'clock, the Lüneburg bus system shut down, so we skipped the rest of our introductions and took off. Aaron lived an hour outside of Hamburg, he said, but he was confident we would arrive on time. It was dark and snowy.

I checked my watch. It was eight o'clock and he was still learning German. "I'm feeling pretty good about my German though," he said.

We caught the train on time, then arrived at the bus junction. A white bus pulled up. "I think this is it," Aaron said.

Fifteen minutes later at exactly nine o'clock, the bus driver pulled over to the side of the street and kicked us off the bus and into the middle of an abandoned road. We had taken the right number—in the wrong direction. As soon as our feet crunched the sidewalk, the driver pulled away without a word. We were miles outside of town.

Nighttime had fallen, and snow had begun to turn to ice. At our landing site was a bus bench, a murky streetlight, an industrial-sized dumpster, and a forest. And there was us.

The air was completely still. I listened to myself breathe as we stood and faced each other without saying anything, puffing out clouds of restless air that dissipated in front of us.

Silence.

We began walking around the abandoned bus stop, trying to figure out where we were. When we realized that we had no idea, Aaron started to laugh. "Well, welcome to Germany!" Aaron was always a believer in life against the odds. He was a small town kid who thought a lot about big towns and big possibilities, and who believed that Germany was going to be the best thing that ever happened to him, if only he could figure out how to script it. He was the sort of person who liked to talk about politics and policy, but he was also the sort of person who understood that the most important politic was personal. He was a natural talker, an adapter, an adventurer, and he was the sort of guy who had landed at my house last summer with nothing more than a gap-toothed grin and a bag of potato chips while taking a road trip across the western United States. He didn't have a job or any means of paying for the trip other than student loans, but that wasn't going to stop him from driving across the Great State of Idaho to visit. In the three years since our first week of freshman year, we'd gone camping and cliff jumping, stayed up late at night talking, broken several school rules, and now we'd gotten lost in Germany. He'd left Idaho Falls for Lüneburg Germany, and dammit, he was going to tell of it.

We picked a direction and began walking. There was no sidewalk. After the forest, we passed hedges, neighborhoods, and country fields under a cloudless night with distant stars to guide us. It had stopped snowing, and there was a chilled haze to the night that huddled against a dangerous sense of homely beauty.

"So what do you want to do while you're in Germany?" Aaron asked. We had decided before I arrived that it was better to make plans on the fly and not be bound to things like rigidity or expectation. "We can do whatever you want," he said.

The hot breath from his words rolled across my face and clung to my exposed cheeks. It was an open invitation. All I had to do was give the word and we would embark on a quest to find "the Germans." This was the moment to chart the course, fill in the map, and find the family we'd lost so many years ago. Aaron was the sort of guy who'd be up for that kind of adventure. And unlike the man in Dad's story who'd found his long-lost family without knowing a word of German, I would have the benefit of a close friend who could guide the search to the ancient village. All I had to do was give the word.

"What do you want to do?" I answered.

Dad wanted to show me a picture. It was several days before I was about to leave for Europe, and just like in Germany, it was snowing. The houses in our neighborhood looked the same as where I was now: big and covered in snow. Streetlights outside became pools of invitation on wreathed doorsteps, and house lights from within became beacons to lost strangers wandering in the night. Home was somewhere warm and safe, and there was a fire behind the hearth.

"I want you to see this picture," he said. He was wearing a red flannel shirt that I remember him wearing on Christmas a year ago when we opened presents. His glasses made his blue eyes stand out as we walked down the hall and over to his dresser. "Paul!" he called. "Your younger brother needs to see this too. You guys both need to see this."

Paul walked into the room. At nearly six feet he was about five inches taller than me. Unlike me, he had darker hair ("Adam is our redhead, you are our blonde, and Paul is our dark-headed one," Dad was fond of saying). Mom was lying on the bed, so all of us were together in the room. If Mom were talking to us, she'd just talk to us one on one; it didn't need to be a family lesson, just a personal one. For Dad, a family story meant a family story—and we all had to be there to hear it.

"Tall Paul," Dad called to my brother as he entered the room.

"*What?*" A sharp-tongued reply rushed out of Paul's mouth. It was his signature, long-haired, are-you-kidding-me reaction to being summoned to one of Dad's usual talks. You could bet your money on it, Don Hanna's sons were not going to grow up and wonder where they came from.

"I want you guys to see this picture of your family," Dad said. He took down an old black and white eight by ten off his desk and held it in his hands. It had been copied and recopied, but the essential parts remained unchanged. A group of probably twelve Germans sat with serious faces, their mouths blind, their eyes mute, staring straight ahead. I didn't recognize any of them or see any resemblance; they didn't have square chins or bumped noses. "These are your ancestors," Dad said. He pointed out minor facial resemblances and other defining characteristics, but that's not what I remembered now as the scene and the house began to fade and disappear. What I remembered was all of us being together in a warm house, together for the last time.

Houses glowed from the side of the road as Aaron and I kept walking. Lights beckoned us inward on a windless night, but we didn't know anyone. As we struggled on, lugging Carmen's suitcase between us, the temperature continued to drop. Time stopped like water dripping from an outside faucet, frozen at the mid-drip point, even as the night drew later with each second in passing. Wearing nothing more than my thin black coat designed for the warmth of the Mediterranean, Germany felt more arctic than homely. But even though we were alone in this cold new world, we were friends, and we were able to share the load of Carmen's suitcase by handing it off to each other every few minutes when our arms got tired. In Alicante, I would have been scared walking around after dark with a suitcase because of the constant thievery (just a few weeks ago Carmen's purse had been cut off her shoulder by a thief when she was out shopping). In Germany, however, there was something calming, almost reassuring, and Aaron and I stopped more than once during our travels to flag down cars and ask for directions. Every time, each person we asked pointed us closer to home.

"You know what we need to do while we're in Europe?" Aaron said. "We need to go to Prague."

"What's in Prague?"

"Haven't you heard about Prague? That's where everyone goes when they go to Europe."

"No—where's it at?"

"The Czech Republic."

"Oh."

Since I didn't know much about Prague, Aaron changed topics and mentioned a local fact: there were three tall towers in Lüneburg. "The three spires are there so that you always know where you are in relation to the others."

The spires were supposed to be visible from miles away, so we kept a steady watch on the white horizon that appeared and disappeared behind occasional fog. We kept walking, but we'd been given enough direction to know where we were supposed to be heading.

We passed through rolling country fields, and in the absence of additional scenery, something changed. We lightened up. It was good to be around an old friend again, and we had plenty of time to catch up.

Aaron told me that when he first arrived, he had spent a lot of time with the other study abroaders, going out to bars and stuff. Then he started reading a lot. Then he started doing anything he could to meet actual Germans. While he didn't live with a German host family, he did live in a host house ("It's really quite normal in Germany," he said about not having a host family). As it was, he lived right across the street from his landlords, an old German couple who would invite him over for dinner and help him practice his German. "Things are getting better," he said, "but the first few weeks were pretty hard."

I told him what had happened in Alicante and the trouble I was having with the other study abroaders.

"You know what? Those kids don't know anything. They don't know you like I do, so they can forget about the rest."

I certainly forgot about the rest when I saw one of the spires he had been talking about earlier. A long way off, I could barely discern the outline of a cross through the haze of orange streetlights, but it was there.

"Lüneburg," Aaron whispered. We were on the home stretch.

Germany was beautiful, but certainly not exotic by any means. As we walked through Aaron's neighborhood to his house, it felt like wandering through the old part of Baker back home. Tall, aged trees bordered and shaded wide streets that held at least a foot of snow on the ground. Brick houses with triangular red roofs dotted the side of the road, spaced out every so often. Smoke wasn't coming from the chimneys of the houses, but the feeling of hearth and home was present.

The word *house* is significant, because in Spain only *los ricos*, the rich people, get to live in houses. "Houses are for people that move to Spain from rich countries like England or Germany," Asis told me before I left. In Alicante, I'd never seen a house before, so I was surprised to see them here. In Spain, houses were built on the outskirts, beyond the suburbs, while regular people like us lived in uninsulated apartments that rose five or six stories high and blotted out the sun. Germany, however, didn't need to block out the heat, since it was cold enough as it was. "They're cold blooded in more ways than one," Asis had warned me, "*Gente con sangre fría. Ten cuidado.*" In other words, be careful. He didn't like them.

I could see why Asis didn't like the Germans. From the few that we had met on the road, I gathered that they were like ovens—people who were cold at first, but who gradually became warmer—if you stuck around long enough to give them time to heat up. Aaron told me that once they had invited you into their house and out of the snow, then you knew that you had crossed the threshold. While I hadn't seen that happen yet, Germany seemed like the sort of country where you would walk into someone's home and expect to smell fresh-baked bread coming out of the oven and a nice family sitting down to dinner; the dinner would probably be polite and formal. I imagined them sitting down for dinner at an old, polished table that had been in the family for generations, yet that somehow still managed to look new. People like Dad called that waiting. "They're just waiting for us to find them," he might have said.

There was just one problem. In our long talk on the way over, I never told Aaron about the family in Germany. Why ruin a good vacation with that obtrusive piece of information? Some things change everything. And sometimes not saying anything at all changes everything in more ways than you were expecting.

"Do you want to go to the red light district?" Aaron asked when we got back. "Prostitution is legal in Germany."

Instead of going to find my long-lost family in one of the local villages, we went to find some hookers. On my last night in Germany we went to see a hockey game with some of Aaron's friends from his study abroad program, and afterwards some of the study abroaders started talking about the Reeperbahn and the Red Gate. I didn't know what either of those things were, but it sounded like an adventure to me. When someone said, "let's go see some strippers!" I quickly learned what the trip might entail. I'd never been to a strip club before, and I never really wanted to go, either.

My only experience with strip clubs came about a year ago at a friend's bachelor party. The night before the wedding, the whole group of us went out to dinner at a burger joint with his family. Brian was sitting next to his wife-to-be, his black hair nearly enveloped in an ear-to-ear smile as he looked at her and giggled. I sat next to Brian, and across the table from him was his older sister. Mid-dinner, Brian's sister waved me and the other groomsmen away from the table and disappeared around a corner in the restaurant.

I followed her around the corner and she held a finger to her lips. "I want you to do something special for me tonight," she said. "I want you to take my brother to a titty bar and get him a lap dance. That girl he's about to marry is way too uptight to give him one!"

"But your brother's not that kind of guy," I said.

"That's because he's never let himself be that kind of guy."

"What about his fiancée, then? Do you want him to do that to her?"

"Look, they don't understand that this is what you do at bachelor parties. You have to get stuff off your chest before you get married."

"No, you—"

The other guys in the wedding party cut me off. "We'll do it."

"What?" I said. I couldn't believe it. They were corroborating with something Brian never would've wanted to do.

"What do you mean *what*?" one of the guys said. "Of course we're going to do it. I want me some titties."

"Good," she said. "Then it's settled."

At the party later that night, Brian's sister sent her husband along to make sure we followed through on the plan. After an innocent round of bowling, it was getting to be about that time, and some of the guys started talking about hiring some girls.

"Pole dancing is kind of degrading to women," I remembered saying. That was a party killer.

"What's wrong with you?" a guy at the party asked me. "Don't you want some girl grinding her ass all over you?"

I didn't respond, but instead threw my bowling ball down the alley where it probably landed in the gutter. I shook hands with Brian and wished him well.

Brian nodded, his eyes silent, his forehead tight. A communion passed between us in understanding. While he didn't know what was going to happen next, I think he had a suspicion. As I walked away, his face began to droop, as if a sudden realization had passed before his eyes and knocked him down a notch. He knew right then why I was leaving. Somehow, the party he'd always wanted had gotten sidetracked.

I didn't have a ride home since I'd carpooled with one of the other guys to the party, so I walked two miles in the dark to get home. My hands went in and out of my pockets, and my shoulders were locked and tense. I don't know what my eyes looked like that night, but they must have registered some sign of defeat. Was I really just a boy for not wanting girls like that? The lesson I learned was never to speak up when guys were talking about "bitches and hoes." You were going to feel like a loser every time.

Memories of the bachelor party replayed over and over in my mind as I stood with Aaron and the study abroaders on the train platform, waiting for the ride that would take us to the Reeperbahn and the Red Gate. I felt like a loser next to them.

"When was the first time you saw some hookers?" one guy from Iowa asked the group while we waited. One by one, the question was answered and handed off, and passed person to person around the circle. I tightened my stomach muscles and braced myself for the question, but I didn't know what I would say. The group laughed as the question made its way closer and closer towards me. When the person next to me was answering the question, I left the group and went to check the train schedule.

"Are we even going to make it to the Reeperbahn?" I asked when it was my turn. "The train's not here."

The question halted in place and the study abroaders looked over at Aaron. "Why don't you go ask somebody?"

Aaron ran off to figure out what was going on, and the question disappeared as the group began talking about something else. Without my friend, I remained in front of the sign, trying to read German words about places I had no frame of reference for.

Aaron went to talk to a German couple standing a few feet away and returned several minutes later. "The train should be here any minute."

A howling sound echoed down the tunnel and I suddenly felt the urge to run away. Were we really going to look for hookers?

"Come on," Aaron said, and jumped on the train with the rest of the group. "This'll be fun!"

I followed him onto the train. While I didn't want to go, it wasn't really my choice. The train took off as quickly as it had come, carrying us closer to the Herbertstrabe and the Red Gate.

Neon lights, strip clubs, and sex shops lined the street in greeting as we emerged out of the metro tunnel. Ice slicked the pavement and we slid around and tried to balance ourselves as we began walking down Europe's second-most famous party street, and I began to tense up. *The Reeperbahn*. It reminded me of everything I'd ever heard about Amsterdam, with only two exceptions. There were no canals and there were no special brownies at cafes (but you could still buy them from people on the street). The dominatrix, the girls, the lights, the hard drugs, they were all here. I zipped up my coat and put my hands in my pockets.

The Herbertstrabe (the "Red Gate" in German) is the entrance to one of Europe's most famous red light districts. Aaron had never been through it, and he didn't want to brave it alone. To get to the Red Gate, you had to wander your way up the main drag through a half-mile of bars and sex shows until you reached a certain side street. Where there were no longer any street lights and when alleys turned into abandoned street blocks—that's when you knew you were getting close.

We began working our way down the main drag. Almost immediately we stumbled upon steel cutout frames of the Beatles in front of the club where they'd played their first show, and after taking a picture and posing as two of the Beatles (I was Ringo Starr and Aaron was Paul McCartney), we continued down the street, stopping at occasional bars and clubs to check out the scene. Aaron made a joke about a strip club as we passed, but I took it literally; I tend to tense up around some topics. And some-where along the way, I don't remember exactly where, we lost the other Americans on a street lined with bars and peep shows. "It's better that we don't have a big group because the Red Gate is the kind of thing we should do in a small group. We don't really know what's going to happen," Aaron said. "The hookers might swarm us."

He explained that in Germany, being a prostitute was an esteemed position. "You get free healthcare," he said. "It's just another profession, really, like being a doctor or a lawyer. Except you're more skilled." From the way Aaron talked about prostitution, it sounded like it was a career-track job. Since I didn't know much about Germany, I imagined little girls sitting in school and talking about what they wanted to do someday. Was it a big deal to say that you wanted to be a hooker? A sign on the Red Gate said it was. If you were a prostitute, you were able to go places no other women could go—into the Herbertstrabe. To other women, the Herbert-strabe was forbidden.

"I'm going to teach you some basic German before we get there," Aar-on said as we neared the end of the main drag and closed in on the Red Gate. "*Nein bitte*—no thanks. If a hooker approaches you, say nein bitte. These girls are trained to fight—some even have blackbelts—so you have to say your German right."

"Nein bitte," I repeated.

"That's not forceful enough."

"Nein bitte!"

"Still not good enough. Look, what do you say when a woman grabs you by the arm and begins dragging you off the street and into the room of some abandoned building? She wants you … bad!"

"NEIN BITTE!"

"That'll keep their hands off you. But don't scare them. They might just kill you."

As we made our way closer to the street that would lead us to the Red Gate, we passed neon light-ups of boobs, dildos, and beer bottles, and sex shops appeared with increasing frequency as we advanced further down the Reeperbahn. One of the doors to a sex club had a picture of a woman's legs spread open and you were supposed to enter through the dark hole in the middle. Blonde girls in bursting shirts and thigh skirts followed men through the door and into the club. I kept my hands in my pockets.

We talked through the plan again. "It's going to be an adventure," Aaron said.

"I'm still not sure about this."

"But isn't this exactly why you told me you wanted to go to Europe—to have an adventure?"

Part of me wanted to forget about the whole adventure thing and go home, but part of me didn't. A dark sense of excitement rushed through me. *Think of the stories you'll be able to tell!* This was an adventure, yes, but a different sort of adventure than I was used to. I took a step forward and nodded at Aaron to continue walking.

We turned down a certain side street and neon lights disappeared. It got darker. A single streetlight at the end of the alley cast an eerie glow on brick buildings that had fallen into disuse. In the silence, moldy bricks and a hushed scent of violence replaced the glamour and noise of the Reeperbahn. Underneath the shadow of a crumbling building, a hooded group garbed in black coats stood in a circle, clinging to a wall of cracked windows. I couldn't see their eyes from underneath their hoods, but I imagined eyes like cess pools, following our every movement, studying our every intent.

I drew my mouth tight and pointed my eyes straight ahead. As we passed the circled group, two hooded figures detached themselves and swung behind us from the side of the building. One moment they were behind us, and the next, they were upon us. A hooded figure jammed an arm between mine and began yanking me away from Aaron and toward the other side of the street. A whisper and an abrupt woman's voice broke the snow in a cacophony of tone. They were here. I began to panic and tried to rip away, but she grabbed tighter and began talking in terse German. I did too. "Nein bitte, nein bitte!"

She looked at me and glared. When she turned her hood my direction, I saw a plain face and nothing more. Her hair was lost in shadow, but she kept her arm locked in mine and tightened her grip.

"Nine bitte, nein bitte!"

I repeated my lifeline but she wouldn't let go. We were now halfway across the street, and I realized that I would have to change my tactics. As she continued to drag me across the street, I began to relax my arms and act sluggish, painting my eyes straight ahead in lazy disinterest. She continued to pull me along, but began to loosen her grip and I kept up my act. After a few moments, she let go of my arm and hurled a look of disgust before walking away. The same scenario would replay three more times for three more blocks, with varying levels of aggressiveness. This wasn't what prostitutes were supposed to be like.

I had one image of a prostitute in my head. She was a Size 2 DD blonde, with a devilish smile and a preview of a red push-up bra showing through a partially unbuttoned white blouse. She had dripping red lips, a sliver of eyeliner, heels and a black miniskirt. On the street, the women who had grabbed us were wearing coats, pants, and snow boots, while the regular party girls on the actual Reeperbahn looked more like what I had imagined. And all this made the Red Gate even scarier. If the prostitutes were already here, what was behind the Red Gate?

I imagined that just behind the Red Gate was a crowd of girls ready to mob us. They wouldn't just lead us astray, four of them would drag us into a room in an abandoned building, steal our wallets and rape us. Two thousand girls behind the gate would have been close to the crowd I was imagining, a voracious, ravenous lot. I wasn't the only one, however, who was getting worried. I looked over and saw Aaron trying to stride forward confidently, but his eyes gave him away, and for the first time that night, he looked legitimately scared. Neither one of us had any idea what we were getting ourselves into.

When we turned a corner, the Red Gate was directly in front of us. It wasn't a normal gate. There was no main entrance, but inset side panels formed entrance slits on either side. The Red Gate was about seven feet tall and covered in graffiti and a small sign in German that read "for more foreplay." Aaron and I stopped in front of the gate, looked at each other and nodded. We split off. I took the left entrance and he took the right. I turned my shoulders and slid through the narrow shaft.

It was quiet when we emerged from the opening. A hollow rustle whispered through a long tunnel of neglected buildings, creating more of a suggestion than a sound. The street we had entered was nearly empty. A wide avenue lay open before us, but other than three men walking slowly away from us in the distance, it was mostly abandoned. There were no women in hoods, but there was an eerie red glow coming from the windows on either side of the street.

In the first window sat two girls on stools that looked like they were posing for Playboy: naked, or close to it. They had large, luscious breasts and they swung them in front of them as they leaned forward and put their arms at their sides, exaggerating their features, their faces covered in longing. I felt a sudden urge within myself to jump through the window, scoop up the brunette in my arms and begin working my way down her creamy hourglass figure. When we stopped and stared, the brunette pulled a cord that opened a small window next to her. Next to the window was a door. They began to call to us in German, bending over and dripping their breasts across slender bodies, motioning us toward the door. When one of the girls stood up, Aaron and I began moving away from the window, but we couldn't avert our eyes as we moved into the middle of the street. When we had backed away, I noticed something I hadn't seen before. There was a third stool to the right of the two girls. It was empty.

As we moved farther and farther down the street, we saw more and more empty stools. Some windows were completely empty, but in the absence of the girls there was still that hushed, dirty red glow. It lingered over empty stools and waited in the back of my mind, somewhere hidden in the dark, veiled in a terrible sense of awe. We had seen the most beautiful women in the entire world. We had passed through the Red Gate, but in the process I had traded something very special, without knowing that it had ever been up for the trade.

In the back of my mind, a black and white strip of filmed memory began to play, creaking away silently, the same way that black and white had long ago given way to colored productions. In a moment, I was back to the familiar time in Mom and Dad's room when Dad was showing my brother and me the picture of our ancestors. *This is your family. Don't they mean anything to you?*

No.

Aaron and I stayed up all night partying at one of the German clubs. When dawn turned to day, we collected Carmen's suitcase from a storage locker in the metro and took the train to the airport. As quickly as the opportunity had come to visit Germany, it was gone, and it was time for me to be off. Before I left, we made plans to do a backpacking trip across the Alps. We also decided to abandon a trip to Prague.

The next day, I knew Dad was going to call me. He always seemed to call at these sorts of times. Growing up, I'd always told him everything, even when I'd done something wrong or gotten in big trouble. But this was different. This was Dad's dream, and I had abandoned it for the Herbertstrabe and hockey games. There were some things I wouldn't tell him.

WEEKS 5-6
GRANADA, SPAIN

SEVERAL HOURS LATER I was back on the plane to Alicante. The weekend in Germany had flown by, and now it was time to go back to school in less than twelve hours. I tried to sleep on the flight back, but found that I couldn't. A flight attendant asked me what I wanted to drink, and without thinking, I responded in Spanish. A German lady at the airport asked for help, and *de repente* I answered again in *español* and she looked at me like I was crazy. Someone asked me where I was from and I said España. It just came out like withdrawals, and for the first time, I found myself unconsciously thinking in Spanish. *¿Cuantas horas hasta regreso a Alicante? Quiero regresar otra vez a Alemania, si posible.* The man sitting next to me looked at me funny. Was I talking and thinking at the same time? I looked up and made sure that Carmen's suitcase was still with me.

I returned home around midnight to the usual scene. The front door opened to the long, shadowy hallway with the only light in the house coming from the living room. *"¿Estif?"* I heard Asis say. A little white dog bounded down the hallway in greeting and Dior jumped to lick me, peeing all over the floor in excitement. I lifted Carmen's suitcase over the puddle. There would be plenty of time to clean up the mess.

In the living room, Carmen was sitting on the couch in red pajamas with her feet in a bowl of water and Asis next to her. *"¡Mi amor!"* she said, as I went over to give her a hug. A late night comedy show was on, but they turned away from the TV and leaned forward on the couch. "Tell us about Germany," they asked after introductions, as if they'd never heard about it before. Asis had only been to Germany once when he was twelve, and Carmen had never been there.

"I can't travel in airplanes because I get claustrophibic," she explained with her hair pinned to the top of her head like she was a China doll. "But I do pretty well in a tiny apartment!"

I told part of the story, but I didn't get far before we began to fall asleep. There would be plenty of time for retellings.

Days turned to hours as time slowly began to pass. Over the next few weeks, I replayed and retold stories from Germany, even as new stories began taking shape in the form of afternoons. Usually during our three hours of siesta naptime, I would go into Carmen's room to talk. Asis always came home to nap in the middle of the workday, so when he was sleeping, Carmen and I would move our conversations into the living room.

Some of her stories got me thinking.

"We lived in Morocco for awhile," Carmen said one day. I waited for her to add more, but she left the thought hanging, so I took the opportunity to fill in my own details. I imagined that the Morocco years were something like midday sun stretched across rusted machine parts, a sort of burning nonchalance, Casablanca in black and white. I pictured Carmen and Asis walking my host brothers to school in sandstorms and somehow enjoying it.

"The terrorists were everywhere," Carmen said while we were talking in the living room, "so I wore a burka." I had asked her about a porcelain mask of an Arab hanging on the wall, and she couldn't help but tell me where it came from. "One of our American sons decided to go to Morocco several years ago and he bought us that mask," she said. "Another son bought us a tea set." She pulled a golden platter of teacups out of the cupboard and ran her hand across the surface before putting them away.

"One time, I was in a car with my friend when we got inspected. That's when they take you out of your car, point a gun at you, and ask you a bunch of questions. I wasn't supposed to be in the car with my friend, so I put on a burka and hid on the floor. They found me hiding, so they threw me against the hood of the car and forced me to put my hands up while they pointed their machine gun at me and questioned me. I pretended to be from Morocco, and of course I didn't tell them that I worked for the Spanish consulate. It's Morocco, of course, so some people get killed there, and they rape women right on the spot. Right in front of you. But I was a *gorda* back then, as wide as a *hamburguesa*. I don't know how or why we made it through that inspection, but *madre mía,* I thank God every day that we weren't shot and killed."

There were other stories about Morocco—stories of thieves, friends, and neighbors, all of which were somehow intertwined. It sounded like the sort of adventurous place I wanted to see for myself someday. When I asked Asis about it, he mostly just talked about where they used to live in Rabat and how much Adán and Asis junior hated living there. Since Carmen and Asis both left out a lot of basic details about the North Africa days, I saw them alone in movie-like settings, facing off against the world and carving a place for themselves with Asis' fencing sword and Carmen's dollar-store hair clip. There was a certain grittiness that arose when they would tell stories about Morocco, and I always felt like a single grain of sand had somehow found its way into my boot, grinding against any sense of comfort. Algeria didn't sound too bad either, although Carmen told me they were in the midst of a revolution. "We used to live there too, but I wouldn't go there if I was you. I used to be scared just walking to work."

One afternoon, I asked Carmen how she'd ended up in Morocco. "When I was seventeen I fell from a second-story ladder," she began, as we sat huddled in the kitchen as if it were a World War II bunker. Shadows danced across the ceiling and created slits of light above and below our eyes, while we wrapped our hands around tea mugs as rain slapped the side of the house. We had just eaten lunch and Carmen was already in her pajamas. I thought she'd mention a story about something other than falling from a ladder, perhaps another event, but she wouldn't stop talking about it. That was one of the only concrete events she ever mentioned. She fell from a ladder. I don't know if the fall left one particular mark on her or many, but she said she always remembered what it was like to see herself dangling in midair with nothing to grab on to. When she fell to the ground that day, her body crashed and stilled under her. She couldn't say anything and she began to cry. Her father was there, but instead of helping her up, he beat her and told her to watch her step next time. He didn't take her to the hospital, either. He didn't want to pay for it.

The moment Carmen fell from the ladder seemed to describe the next several years of her life. She had a falling out of sorts with Francoism and Spanish tradition when she left home at eighteen and headed out on her own. Spanish law at the time dictated that women weren't supposed to leave the home alone—they had to be accompanied by a man at all times. Carmen did neither. She would live in many towns over the next several years, but none of them would become home. "When you've never had a home in the first place," she said, "it's hard to know how to find one."

Her parents had lavished attention on her younger brother. That little snot. If that boy asked for anything, he got it. But it wasn't worth saying a lot more about him. After all, they used to be on good terms and she'd tried to mend bridges. While working in the fields growing up, she would look out and watch her brother play soccer with their father. She would leave her gloves in the tomato patch and run to join them, but her father would drive her back into the fields with a switch. Women had to work in the garden. Because if she was ever going to be a good daughter, she'd better do as she was told. If she was ever going to be a good wife, her father said, she had to learn how to obey. Then, God willing, maybe someone would actually want her. But her brother—that little snot didn't have to obey. Oh no, he got whatever he wanted. In all her life, she never saw her father beat her brother. After years of coming home from school to the belt or the switch, she started taking longer and longer to come home, until one day she never returned.

Some time after she left home, Carmen found a job processing visas for the Spanish consulate and was transferred all over Spain and southern France. Every few months or so, she would be moved to a new town where she didn't know anyone and *el ciclo* ("the cycle") would start anew. She would be excited to arrive, then disappointed when no one would return the favor. There were lots of faces over the passing months, but none of them would become people. She was alone in the worst way, in a foreign country with no one to turn to, and the first time she was sent to France she didn't know any French. "The French will never talk to you if you speak Spanish," she said. "So I started to eat a lot and get fat, like a balloon." She puffed her cheeks out like a blowfish. Her eyes grew wide with a wonder as she raised her hands to her side. "I used to be *this* fat. I was such a *gorda*."

Almost every day that I was in Spain, Carmen would make a fat reference ("I used to eat like Adán eats"), but every time she made a fat reference, it was never about what she'd fallen victim to. In those early days, she said, there was no turning back and no regret for running away from her family, but instead a deep sense of emptiness when the realization hit of everything in life she'd missed—birthdays, Christmas, playing with friends, first kisses, a father's love. All she could do was move forward and hope that someday, maybe if things turned out right, she would be able to help people like herself, people across the world who had no one to turn to and nothing to hold on to. She didn't want anyone to ever have to feel like she did, but she had paid a price for it.

"I'm so jealous," Carmen told me one afternoon. "You got to go to Germany. I've never been there."

"But you live in Europe! Can't you and Asis just go and visit any country you want? You get a whole month of vacation in August like everyone else in Spain."

"Well," she sighed. "It's not always that easy."

I didn't really understand what she meant, so I had to ask. "How many countries have you been to?" I had assumed that all Europeans were world travelers, but maybe I was wrong. My Bohemian ancestors had, after all, remained in Bohemia for the entirety of Belohlavy existence, and the American gene strand hadn't ventured very far, either.

"I've been to four countries," Carmen said. "And that's only because I've had to live in four countries." She moved her hand across her forehead to brush a strand of hair. "The long and the short of it is that I grew up in northern Spain, fell off a ladder, moved around, met Asis on a beach and then we got married. That's about it. We lived in France for fourteen years, spent some time in Morocco and Algeria like I was telling you earlier, and now we're here." She stopped talking and went to the fridge to grab chorizo slices and cheese to start making lunch. "But now I'm getting too old to travel. Besides, I get claustrophobic in airplanes."

As she put a baguette on the counter, her face began to brighten. "But do you know how many American sons and daughters I have?" she asked, turning to me. "More than eleven years of them!"

"You're the *madre de América!*" I told her, and gave her a hug. She laughed and grinned. Every year she told me that she received more letters and emails from her American sons and daughters than she could possibly respond to. The other day a letter from Jacob ("Hah-cub") arrived in the mail, and Carmen danced around the house before she and Asis sat on their bed and read it together. After they'd read it, Carmen filed it away in the bottom drawer of her dresser, slipping it into the same crusted manila folders she'd shown me several weeks earlier when she told me about Mitch. In that drawer, she kept a file of every letter she ever received, along with two photo albums of past students and the postcards they'd sent her. She had almost as many pictures of her foreign kids as she did of her own. That posed a serious problem.

Later in the week, I arrived home past my usual time of nine or ten o'clock. It was about dinnertime. Carmen had a pan of lentil soup on the stove and was chopping tomatoes. Asis sat at the kitchen table in his blue pajamas, trying to delay doing the dishes by talking to Carmen. He was good at that. But since she was *la cocinera* and he was *el jefe*, the boss, it meant that he had to wash the dishes, Carmen said.

Asis got up and went to the sink. I watched him turn on the cold water and begin scrubbing as chunks of food fell off plates and spoons, collecting in the bottom of the steel basin. Every so often he would stick his fingers into the drain stopper and gather little pieces of washed-out food between his fingers and flick them into the garbage can, some landing where he intended, others landing on the kitchen walls. He poured a small amount of soap into a dirty wooden bowl, rinsing the rag every so often between swipes, even as the soap he was using became dirtier than the plates he was washing.

Carmen finished the tomatoes that she had been chopping and turned to me. "*Mucho trabajo*," she said, and something released in her bearing. I recalled in her face then the look of Young Carmen that she usually kept sealed away in a small picture frame in the living room, a still-life image of a lively young brunette in a yellow flamenco dress, dancing. "Teach me some salsa," she said, as she set down the knife she had been using. "*Jefe*," she called out to Asis. "Boss, count the beats for us."

Asis turned around to face us from the sink, and began singing and counting a beat from under his dark curls. My right hand found Carmen's shoulder and I took her left hand in mine as we faced each other. I took a step forward and she followed. Then I raised my arm and gave her an *enchufla*, a twirl, and she spun around and giggled. "*Repítela*," Carmen said. We did another enchufla, then a *dile que no*.

As we danced, Carmen threw her head back and laughed. *Jajajajaja*, she hadn't done this since she was young!

There was something about her now, a lovely whirling feeling that glided across the kitchen as we moved in an out of time. We swayed through the kitchen before I gave her a final enchufla and twirled her across the kitchen. "My God, I'm getting old!" she told me before she nearly collided with the counter. "We'll have to do that again sometime."

When we sat down to dinner later that night, a door sounded down the hall; Adán must have arrived home. Before we could say *hola*, Asis told a joke and Carmen and I started laughing. What Adán saw then, when he poked his head into the room, was all three of us laughing and me sitting in the center chair—his chair—with his parents on either side of me. I slapped my hand on the table to emphasize Asis' joke and he burst out laughing again. *¡Dios mio!* Everyone laughed except for Adán.

From across the room he stared at us. There was a lot of space between the door and the table: a low-hanging light, the couch cluttered in pillows, little Dior sprawled across the floor. As it was, the pathway to the table was nearly inaccessible to Adán. I looked up at him and tried to say something, but Asis grabbed my shoulder to tell another joke: I was really going to like this one, he said. I waved to Adán to come in, but his eyes twisted mine with a hard look before he tore away and left the house. He was being replaced. His parents didn't see this little glance between us—they were still laughing at Asis' joke—but I had seen it. The message was clear: when their real sons weren't around, Carmen and Asis would find others to take their place.

We resumed eating, but something was lost then, something that would be hard to get back.

"You're not going to Granada in that thin little coat, are you?" Carmen asked.

It was still cold in February and I was about to go to the Moorish mountain town of Granada on a weekend trip sponsored by my study abroad program. My professors had warned of bitter cold and *los andaluces*, those lazy people in southern Spain, but I hadn't heard much more than that. I was just ready for another adventure, and like the keychain backpack, I figured my thin Mediterranean coat would keep me warm just fine. I'd never been a coat person and was famous back home for braving snow and ten-degree weather in a t-shirt and living to tell of it.

"You're going to need something else to wear," Carmen said the night before I was about to leave. "*Ven.*"

I followed her to the front door where she removed a key from a small box on the wall. We left the apartment and climbed the stairs to the top of the building and Carmen used the key to open a door that led to the rooftop. The city creaked open before us, all white and yellow like a rundown version of Snow White, where some buildings were taller than others and where more balconies were mismatched than matching.

On the roof, a series of doors lined the east end of the building. White and hollowed out, the doorframes looked like tombstones, and I followed Carmen toward them. She inserted the key into one of the unmarked doors in the middle and turned the latch. Inside, a heap of used treasure awaited us. "*Está aquí*," Carmen muttered. "*¿Dónde?*"

Carmen dug through her treasure; she was looking for something.

Several bikes hung on the wall, old rugs and rags covered peaks of furniture, and a layer of dust had settled over a series of black garbage bags that Carmen was digging through. No one had been here in a long time, but this was an important place. The Bujans were the kind of people who never threw anything away.

"Aha!" Carmen sifted through a garbage bag that she'd just torn open and held up a sweater. It was red and white with lines running down the middle and a bold *1968* was embroidered on the left bicep. "This used to be Adán's favorite sweater when he was a little *chico*."

In other words, this was Adán's favorite sweater when he was in the seventh grade and as tall as I was at age twenty-one.

"I don't need to ask Adán in order to give you his sweater," Carmen said. "He'll say yes, he always says yes, so why even bother to ask?"

Like Joseph and his coat of many colors, I was dumb enough to wear Adán's sweater when I returned home to my Spanish brothers.

GRANADA

Blossoming olive and almond trees turned into orange groves and lemon trees during the five-hour bus ride to Granada. Decorated with dramatic views of the original Sierra Nevada mountain range, the Spanish countryside appeared in full display. On one side of the bus, pink blossoms grew like flowers on trees—*almendros*, I was told. On the other side of the bus, mountains rose like whale jaws: rigid planks of rock with barnacled teeth. Carved into the side of the shale was a series of stained-white huts. Across the road from the almond trees, the cliff-cut huts were the only remnant in sight, but none of the Spaniards could say who had built them. "*Mira*," they said, pointing out the other window, toward the *almendros*. "Why look at old buildings when you can look at food?"

Earlier in the morning, my entire program of American exchange students had loaded onto a bus bound for Granada, the ancient capital of the Moorish world and the site of the last medieval Islamic palace, the Alhambra. Spring was in bloom, and with a group of Spanish guides, we were on our way to Moorish Spain.

∗ ∗ ∗

"You can't describe God," the main tour guide told us when we arrived at the Alhambra. "Not in physical form anyway. The Arabs, they use geometry to describe traits about God—His perfection, peace, and goodness."

I stood in a palace chamber surrounded by my fellow study abroaders and looked up. The ceiling air was still. Across the span and carved into the surface, a pattern of stars played out like the night sky. Inset into an octagonal star were sixteen windows, one on each influx, and inside the outer star were thousands of indentations that collided and formed a constellation. Some indentations were brighter or darker than others, but they all led the eye upward to the highest point, a dark ring that marked the inner circle and the top of the ceiling. "The Alhambra is an image of God, an act of worship in the entirety of its design."

The guide led us into the next room where we saw the Unending. Intricate geometric patterns of microscopic designs repeated in perfect unity around bends, archways, ceilings and all types of curves that tried to break the symmetry of a design that remained consistent through generations. A stalactite pattern inscribed with diamonds and script covered the ceiling of one room, then continued down the walls and through the cracks, enveloping the corners until they were lost in the unity of the pattern. Each room had its own pattern, and the beauty was that it was impossible to tell where one pattern began and one pattern ended.

I marveled at the geometry and symbols on the wall. How was it that something so intricate could continue forever, unbroken through all the trials of years and yearnings? Napoleon's assault on the Alhambra in the eighteenth century had destroyed much of the palace, and if all that we were seeing was the ruins, the palace had been even greater in its glory days. These patterns of lines and stars had endured through generations, and I marveled at the wonder of it. It was like the only other pattern I knew, family patterns. My family had frayed a lot with the passing of time, and while we hadn't yet come undone, perhaps we were on the verge of it. Dreams were hard to hold on to. "God is both the beginning and the end, the end and the beginning," the guide said. "At least that's what most people believed when this was built."

*   *   *

Growing up, Dad had two dreams. One, of course, was the farm, and the other was the family. He wanted to have his own farm someday, and he wanted to have a family. Most of all, he wanted a lot of life, and that meant a big farm and a big family. The two had always been connected, ever since they had frayed early on.

When he was little, Grandma and Grandpa used to send Dad and my uncle to stay with Great Grandpa and Great Grandma on their farm. "They knew how to make sure kids had fun," Dad said. "And they always knew how to keep us coming back. When Uncle Ken and I would run into their room each morning and jump into their bed, they would laugh and snuggle us between them. That was one of the happiest feelings. I wanted to have a farm ever since I was little."

That dream, of course, took a long time to pan out. I don't know what happened on that farm, but they received something there that perhaps they had missed at home. They'd spend the days picking cherries and chasing bullfrogs. It was a boy's paradise. They'd run through the fields and feel the wind rush across their faces on careless summer nights.

Summers at Great Grandpa's farm, however, quickly disappeared. Grandpa, of course, was run over and killed outside the supermarket when Dad was in his twenties, and shortly afterwards, Great Grandma sold the farm. She didn't want to, but she had to—she couldn't run that whole place by herself. Without the farm and both of them to hold it together, their dream of a farm and a home place fell into disrepair. Great Grandpa's old tractor was kept but retired to an old shed and forgotten for years. Most of the old equipment was sold as the rest of the family moved into town, but Dad always believed that he would return someday. He got along well enough with his parents, enough for a strained relationship and phone calls several times a year, but the farm was where the family had been the closest, closer still when there was a home place, somewhere to go back to. "I always thought I was going to return to Idaho, but life took other turns and it never ended up happening," Dad said. "What I wanted to build then, was the Home Place, so you boys would always have somewhere to come back to."

The Home Place, of course, was intimately connected to the other home place, Bohemia, and the ones who had sent us to America on that doomed night so many years ago. When the Bohemians had pledged their collective futures together in the Pact and sent my ancestor to freedom by sacrificing everything they owned, they had unknowingly bound us to them for eternity. The Home Place meant that there was always someplace to go back to. We were in this together, and we had to go back and find them. I called Dad about that earlier in the week to report my progress.

"What?" Dad said on the phone when I called to tell him I'd arrived back safely from Germany. I always thought parents were supposed to be glad when their kids made it home safe, but Dad skipped over that part. "You didn't even try to find the Germans?" He couldn't believe it.

I didn't really know what to say, so I told him that Aaron and I had been busy "seeing the country," but I left out the hooker part. He'd have been really mad if he'd known that was what I'd been up to.

"Do you know what you just did? Do you know what this means? No one has had the chance to go back. Ever. Now ... I don't even know what to tell you!"

I hadn't prepared a response for that. For years, the dream of our return to Europe had ticked away silently, held somewhere deep before getting lost somewhere along the line. I had grown up with the dream of the farm as the eventual Home Place, but never the home of the Bohemians. The Dream had been transmitted but never passed on. The pattern was broken.

The guide led us into an empty courtyard where a reflecting pool filled the space. At water's edge an arched fortress towered into view. Above the fortress, streaks of clouds slashed behind a Spanish flag that snapped and curled with the rhythm of the wind. At its base, a portico of arches ran the length of the building before steep walls became castle battlements; all of this was captured in the water's dark emptiness. In the glassy pool, I saw myself standing at the foot of the fortress, wearing Adán's sweater. The wind above fell to a lull, and I took a picture of my reflection in the pool with Adán's red *1968* embroidered on my arm. The guide motioned ahead and we continued through the palace to arrive at the royal gardens.

If the palace reflected Perfection, then the royal gardens reflected Beauty. "The Arabs believed that a good garden should appeal to all the senses," the guide said. "Including the spirit. Water and its reflection must always be kept in sight."

Water pulsed through inch-wide canals in the middle of stairways and walkways, diverting to fountains and winter springs. In the next courtyard, a chalice surrounded by three pine trees bubbled in silence as water spilled over the rim, creating a murmured drip. Hidden in the shadow of the trees, the fountain was only visible if you were looking for it.

The guide nudged us ahead. All around, the color of water changed from pink to orange to red to green with the surrounding colors. Straight ahead was the exit. Wind kissed my cheek as it hushed through a tunnel of roses that were waiting to bloom. Over the years, a tunnel had formed as roses fastened themselves to arch supports, eventually forming a frame that blocked out the sun, and I disappeared into it. The tour was over; it was time to head into the city. The wind brushed against Adán's sweater as I left, sealing off the garden behind and ushering me toward what was yet to come.

I returned home wearing Adan's sweater and telling stories about Granada. Dior ran to greet me as I entered the front door and knelt to pet him. He licked my face and peed on the floor as usual, jumping on my leg as I walked down the shadowy hallway toward Carmen and Asis, who approached from down the hall.

"*¡Mi amor!*" Carmen cried. "*No he oído nada. ¡Tu has sobrevivido!*"

"Carmen didn't sleep at all while you were gone," Asis said. "She prayed night and day that you would be safe from *los gitanos*—the gypsies. *¡Gracias a Dios!* Those are dangerous folk!"

Carmen ran over and kissed me on both cheeks before giving me a hug. "*M'ijo, ¿todo está bien?*"

"*Más de todo,*" I said.

I reached into my bag and pulled out a Moroccan magic lamp. "Give it a rub!" I told Carmen as I heard a sound in the living room. "What did you wish for?"

Another set of footsteps began shuffling across the floor in the living room while I waited for Carmen's response.

"The same thing I always wish for—*trabajo, dinero y salud*. Work, money, and health, if that's what God wants to give us."

Asis laughed. "Sometimes He gives it to us and sometimes He doesn't. How'd it go in Granada?"

I told them about how I'd bought the magic lamp from a swindler in a street shop and the rest of the stories came out in a rush: watching a flamenco show and going to the Arab tea houses. Carmen and Asis stood around me in the middle of the house listening intently when the footsteps I'd heard earlier moved into the hallway. Adán had been in the next room over and he'd heard about the whole trip. I always said Adán looked like a Spanish redneck with the look of a swooping hawk, and for once, my instinct held true. He'd seen the sweater.

"*Hola*," I said. "*¿Qué tal?*"

Adán pointed his index finger at me from across the hall. "*Te llevas mi suéter y le chingas a mi madre*," he said before storming into his room and slamming the door. "I have nothing more to say to you."

"*Un momento*," Asis said as he hustled down the hall. "Adán!"

Adán raised his voice behind his door. "So you think that little shit is your son, don't you?"

Carmen rushed down the hall in my defense. "*Adán, escúchame.*"

"No, you listen to me. *Me jodes*. I'm your son. And I'm the one who used to wear that sweater."

In little more than a moment, I had become Joseph, a favored son given a rainbow coat by his father, and I was the son who had taken the place of Adán, their actual son. Adán pounded the wall in his room. It didn't help that my middle name happened to be Joseph.

The walls began to shake and reverberate with their voices as they began rising and bouncing between narrow walls. *Te jode. Chinga tu madre. Perra*. Adán's girlfriend who had been quietly studying in his room suddenly opened the door and ran down the hallway to hide in the bathroom.

Asis seized the opportunity and stormed into Adán's room. *"Tonto. ¿No entiendes que Estif tiene nada sin nosotros?"*

Adán lashed back and their voices became more violent as they moved out of Adán's room and toward the hall and my direction. I ran into my room and shut the door. Through the uninsulated walls, I heard every word as I sat on the edge of my bed.

"You know his Spanish is shit," Adán said.

"We know," Asis replied.

"You know that he doesn't have any friends and that he leeches off you like a bitch on a leash?"

"We know," Asis replied.

"And you know that he doesn't understand anything about this country?

"Look, we know," Asis replied. "But he's our son too."

"Your son? Who's that—anyone born in America? You have more pictures of these foreigners around this house than you do of me and Asis."

"Por favor," Carmen said.

"Ever since he's been here, you've forgotten about us."

I heard the front door slam and suddenly the house went quiet. The wall in front of me turned to a blank shade of white. Light filtered in through the window, but it was a glaring affront. There were no footsteps in the hallway and neither Carmen nor Asis moved—nothing. In that empty apartment, we sat still, each of us in separate rooms. I don't think any of us knew what to do.

After several minutes, I heard Adán's girlfriend open the bathroom door to examine the scene. Adán was gone. Her footsteps muffled down the hallway and the front door opened and closed again. I didn't want to leave my room.

My real mother had divorced Dad when I was nearly two years old. While I had never witnessed any of the events that led up to it, I knew what it felt like to watch the world I'd tried to build come crashing down in front of me. Maybe I'd been a little presumptuous trying to talk to Carmen and Asis all the time, but I really had no one else. Without them, I was in a completely foreign world.

As I sat on Carmen's watermelon bedspread, it felt like I had just caused a divorce. I didn't understand how it had come to this. When the going got bad, I'd usually been able to imagine myself in other places or situations, but this time I couldn't. I could only imagine myself in this room on the first day when Adán shook my hand, flashed me a smile and said hello. I took off his sweater and laid it neatly on the bed.

WEEK 7
ALICANTE, SPAIN

THE NIGHT OF ADÁN'S SWEATER and the thought of divorce brought out a lot of things I would have preferred to forget. First of all, it brought out dreams, but these were always dreams unspoken. I'd tried not to hint at them before, and only vaguely reflected on them in moments when I saw them begin to disappear. Dreams were so fragile—they were like porcelain, you couldn't drop them like you would, say, a marble. *Oops, there it goes. Shucks.* No, you really couldn't do that. Dreams were something to be kept silent. They could be felt and acknowledged, but only in private, only in secret, only when you sat at the end of a watermelon bedspread all by yourself. Because for me, the Dream started with divorce and the idea of the Home Place teased like a knife. It meant that I would always have somewhere to go back to, even though I never really did.

"Well, I guess this is it," Dad said as we prepared to say goodbye at the airport. He tried to keep a straight face, but couldn't and his eyes dropped to the floor. "Till next month then?"

We stood with our backs pressed against the glass paneling of the airport rotunda. Beneath us, people in suits rolled black suitcases, but we had our backs turned to them, too. Above us, the height of the ceiling rose and swallowed the room like Jonah and the whale, except neither Dad nor I was Jonah. We were being swallowed by circumstance; that just seemed like the way life was going.

"I don't want to go back there," I said, in reference to Seattle and my mother's house.

"Someday you'll come home for good," Dad said, looking at me in his camouflage Cabela's hat. He looked so wonderful and confident in his answer, in blue jeans and a Marvin Woods Products t-shirt.

His eyes shone and I wanted to believe him. Ever since the divorce, I was supposed to come back home and be with Dad. That had been the plan all along, really, that I would return home, except it never quite worked out that way.

When Dad left Seattle for Baker and open pastures, I had decided to stay with my mother. I was eleven and I wanted to finish elementary school in Seattle, say goodbye to my friends, then move off to the farm that Dad and Mom would most likely have bought by then. But at the end of my sixth grade year, my return was derailed. My mother had an emotional breakdown and threatened the worst if I left her. That put a halt on things.

Maybe what she said that night has changed over the years and gotten lost in the recesses of memory or maybe it had been twisted in the process, but I remember the essence of what she said. *If you go live with your dad, you'll make me hurt so bad that you'll break my heart and I'll die.*

The night she said that, I believed her. I didn't want to be responsible for someone else's breakdown. And I won't describe the scene from that night any more than I have to because I don't really need to. Sometimes single sentences hang over you like an overcast cloud and cling to your worst regrets. Oh, I stayed with her, but I hated myself for it. The day after I told her I'd stay, she flew into a temper because I hadn't folded a towel just right, and I vowed that someday, maybe during high school, I would find a way to live with Dad. True, she might've had a breakdown if I went to live with Dad, but I would've had one too if I didn't get out.

The year I told her that I would stay with her, Dad moved to Baker and I was left walking on eggshells in Seattle with my mother. Once, when I was fifteen, she broke into my friend's house across the fence and searched it for my stuff. She monitored my phone calls too, so I had to borrow the neighbor's phone if I wanted to say anything private. Sometimes at night, probably when she suspected I was going to run away, she would sneak into my room and steal some of my things that I had saved money to buy. One day, I returned home to find that my six hundred dollar drumset had disappeared. I'd got it when I was twelve and saved all of my money for a year to buy it. When my mother divorced Dad, she took all of his stuff, too, except the dog, Fluffy, and his fishing boat. Usually when I said I wanted to live with Dad, I would lose some of my stuff.

I don't know how, exactly, she and Dad ever ended up together. All I know is that when I asked Dad about it, he would say that when you're young and when you go for a long time without being loved, sometimes you start to believe that maybe you don't deserve to be loved. Then you'd get desperate.

While I wanted to live with Dad since I was eight years old, I never imagined that he and Mom would one day leave for good and move to Baker. I understood why though. They had to get out of the city, the hospital and the traffic, the constant work was killing them.

"This was never the life we dreamed of," Dad said that day when I was twelve as we stood with our backs pressed against the airport railing, the rotunda bearing down above us. "We waited to leave until we knew that you would be strong enough to make it on your own."

Over the next several years the airport scene replayed countless times. Every month, Dad bought me a plane ticket to come visit them in Baker for a weekend. Dad and Paul would load up and drive two hours to the nearest airport to pick me up, then we'd all drive two hours back to Baker and get home long after the sun had set. On Saturday, we'd have one full day together and we'd usually do something as a family. Dad always suggested hunting or fishing, of course, but we were usually able to out-vote him and do something tamer—maybe get pizza or pick apples in the backyard. On Sunday we'd go to the little United Methodist Church in Baker, and afterwards we'd immediately grab McDonald's and rush off to the airport where I would fly out that evening and Dad and Paul would spend another two hours driving home, arriving late at night. Mom would have rode with us too, but she had to tend the home front and keep everything from falling apart. Adam had gotten into some heavy drinking and needed a close eye. "Those years were hard on all of us," Dad said. "But you boys got the chance to learn something very important: we were willing to do whatever it took to stay together, and we did."

For the forty-eight hours that we had together, those weekends meant the world to me. I dreamed of the day when I wouldn't have to go back and forth anymore. And every so often, usually on one of those Saturday nights when we were all gathered around the table after dinner, Mom and Dad would talk about buying a farm and building the Home Place. I knew right then that this was all I ever wanted. Somewhere to come home to.

As we stood on the edge of the railing at the airport, Dad gave me a massive hug. Neither one of us let go for a long time. He hadn't bought the farm yet, but gosh, he was getting close, and even closer to me. "It hurts me so much to see you go."

His blue eyes peered into mine from above the top of his Marvin Woods shirt and I could see his eyes begin to well up, and suddenly it all came out, all of the long car rides and the long hours at work, all so I could come visit for two days a month. I tried to hold back what I was feeling then, but I couldn't, it was too hard, and Dad grabbed me in another bear hug. I lived my whole life for that moment, the moment when Dad would take me in his arms once or twice a month, when he would wave at me and say goodbye at the airport because I never got to see him more than that.

When I got on the plane that day, the flight attendant said hello and asked me how I was doing. I didn't have an answer for her.

Time blurs, weaving cloudily in and out of time. The edges of memory are hazy, lost somewhere deep and surfacing only for a moment to breathe before they disappear again. This time we're in Mom and Dad's house in Woodinville, before they left Seattle, before the days of the farm, and before the Dream took hold of us. We're sitting in the living room. I have my feet crossed while sitting on the couch next to Adam, my older brother. Between us are four years of age and a bent NIV kids' study Bible. Neither one of us had read much of it.

"Let's all hold hands and pray," Dad said, "as a family."

We joined hands across the couch and bent our heads down. "Lord, you know how hard life can be," Dad began. He always spoke so honestly with God. There was an intimacy in confession, a closeness there, that Dad and God had developed during long talks at night, long before Dad's preacher days. Sometimes when the going got tough, he told us that he would argue with God, but this time he didn't. "Lord, we need You."

When we opened our eyes, Dad sat on a wooden chair in front of the couch. A worn, black leather Bible was on his lap. The gold letters on the front cover had mostly faded. Dad's eyes looked hollow, as if they'd been strained and lost some space from taking a constant beating. Mom sat across from him on the nearest part of the couch with Paul on her lap. Behind her glasses, her eyes looked strong and she put up a good front in spite of the circumstances.

"Mom and I were thinking that we should start having our own family church services," Dad said. "Like you boys all know, we don't really go to church anymore. The people there, they don't really like us, but that doesn't change the fact that we still need to come together as a family."

"Really, Dad?" Adam pleaded.

"Really."

The truth is that after all they'd been through, Mom and Dad had never been accepted into the church. "There's a lot of people who like to go there and shake hands and eat donuts," Dad said.

My brothers and I had learned that life wasn't always sweet like a donut. From what I knew, life was more like the donut with the cream-filled center. Most of it sucked, but the raspberry cream part, when you finally got to it, was pretty good. This was one of those moments.

Dad began preaching and I lost myself in between the walls and his words. The walls around us were covered with portraits of the things that mattered—ducks, geese, and hunting pictures, all hanging next to pictures of family. As the five of us sat on the long, brown-striped couch that curved around the walls and as Dad sat on the wooden chair in the middle of the room, the space stooped to meet us and his words hovered in between.

I don't remember anything Dad preached about that day, but I remember all of us sitting together in the living room because we didn't belong anywhere else, and how stories of a Father and a passionate Son made so much sense. Our family was designed to imitate that closeness, and while we failed at times, the stories, Dad said, always reminded us of the life we were called to. It was something more than this. Because this was a room with two people who never thought they would remarry; a father who had preached and felt called away from the ministry after his divorce, and a mother and a nurse who had left an abusive ex-husband. This was also a room with three hurting sons: an older son caught in the fold of a blended household, a middle son caught between two worlds and torn between two houses, and a younger son who would grow up and break his older brothers' toys because they were always gone. Here in this moment, we were bound together and all these stories converged, no matter what else was going to happen in the future. Maybe we didn't have it in us to shake hands and eat donuts at church, but maybe that wasn't even what mattered in the first place. The Dream began to take form.

In an hour, the moment would be gone, and in a day, I would go back to walking on eggshells all by myself with a mother who drew mind cords across my chest. When I got there, I knew that someday, things would change. They had to.

Time blurs again and brings us to one final moment. Eight years after our family church services, I'm crouched in weeds three feet deep, dressed in camouflage, trying to slow my breath. A dark hat is stitched across my forehead. My temples are drawn tight. Mom and Dad had disappeared to Baker years ago, and now, lost in a field behind a desolate church, I was running away from Seattle and on my way to join them. I reached into my pocket and grabbed an old Nokia phone and dialed one of the only numbers I knew. No one answered. I tried another number. The phone began to ring and the hollow tone reverberated through my ear and across the empty field. That morning, my mother had called the sher-iff to chase me down and get me—a wild ruthless son who had ran away and left her, because that morning, I decided to leave for good. The phone grew hot against my ear, until Dad's voice finally answered. *Steve, what are you doing? Are you safe?*

No. A car pulled up. I rose up slowly out of the weeds like a monster, covered in dirt, my hair long and tangled. Later that day, the cops would turn me in as a runaway and I would be taken to lock-up, that much was certain, but I was also on my way home; lock-up was just the first of many stops along the way. Through all of this, I knew one thing: what you never had was ultimately what you wanted the most.

The scene began to disappear. The field behind the church faded and slowly folded into the space of the past, and I was left sitting quietly at the edge of my bed in Spain with all these memories. I reached for my phone and dialed home.

"*¿Estif?*" Carmen knocked on my door several hours later. "*¿Puedo entrar?*"

I nodded to myself in the empty room. "*Sí.*"

Carmen opened the door and walked over to sit on the bed next to me. "Don't listen to Adán, he doesn't know what he's saying."

Carmen had her pajamas on and her hair had fallen behind her shoulders; her blue eye shadow was not as strong as it usually was. It had been a rough afternoon. I hadn't seen her since the fight started and since Adán had left the house several hours ago. Midday light danced and burned across the wall in front of us, a glaring, pale hiss that wove between the words that had been spoken that afternoon. I never doubted her, but I doubted what life would be like when Adán got home later that night. I'd had to walk on eggshells before and I never wanted to do that again. I definitely didn't want to do it for the next three months.

"I'm worried about you." Carmen reached over and put her hand on mine. "But I don't think Adán will be back until later. *¿Quieres comer?*"

"I could eat, maybe. But is it true—what he said?"

"No. None of it."

"So he won't be mad at me?"

"I don't know. But I know one thing." Carmen stood up and cupped her hand around her mouth like she was at a *fútbol* game. "*¡Papi!*" she called to Asis. "Let's eat!"

She began walking down the hallway and I followed her into the shadows.

In the fading light, Asis, Carmen, and I sat huddled around the kitchen table in our pajamas with a platter of wilting salad and a scatter of breadcrumbs between us. Our day-old chorizo spaghetti had been downed in a hurry, "*espaguetis*," Carmen called it. "*Los italianos no saben nada.*"

A silhouette of light flickered across the room, rhythmically, with the wind. Behind us and outside the kitchen window, a storm was brewing and the clothesline flapped in a coil that beat against the side of the apartment. With each flap, shadows danced across the kitchen in the dimming light. Of course we wouldn't turn on the overhead light. For a moment, then, dusk settled under Asis' eyes as he told his story. "Life was always hard growing up."

"*Estif, ¿sabes la historia de tu papá?*" Carmen asked.

"As I was saying," Asis continued, "*la vida es dura*. Life is hard. *Mucho trabajo*. But no one believes that in Spain, even though they know it's true."

As a Frenchman, Asis had free license to comment on the Spaniards, because until Carmen had come along, he'd never thought he'd live here. As such, he said things about the Spaniards all the time. Those lazies. "In France, you got up at six, worked all day, had a little fun, then went to bed and did it all over again. You were productive." In Spain, it was the other way around. Your life didn't revolve around work.

In Marseilles where he had grown up, life didn't revolve around work, either. It revolved around drugs. "*Muchas drogas*," Asis said. "*¡Dios mio!* Like Alicante."

Asis digressed into a lecture about *las drogas*. Of course, I already knew that they were *super peligroso*, but he told me again, just in case I'd forgotten. "You've really got to stay away from the smoke-smoke." He did a puffing motion. "That hooked a lot of my friends when I was growing up."

Lecture part two—what was worse than growing up in a drug town was growing up in a home without a father. When everyone else was doing drugs and chasing women, Asis studied and went to the gym. Well, he still chased women, but he was pretty good at chasing them away. "I just never clicked with any of them," he clarified. "Until I met Carmen."

Their meeting though, was preceded by one very important event— the loss of his father. When he was twelve, Asis had watched his father die. He saw it happen right before his eyes. This close. Asis leaned into the table for emphasis, but never said why his father had died.

In addition to his father's death, he had also grown up without any cousins or family close by. It was just he and his mother, and many years later, he watched her die, too, this time in an Alicante hospital bed with Carmen by his side. "The things you see, Estif, they shape you, even if you don't want them to. When my father died, I didn't want to be alone, but I ended up living many years alone."

Asis' voice trailed off and the room was silent.

"I started fencing while my dad was still alive, but I continued after he died. I got better and better. Then I started playing in tournaments and getting noticed, traveling all the time." When you have nowhere to come back to, he said, traveling in a way, becomes home. You were just on a plane or a train, all by yourself. He eventually became a champion, but no one was with him to claim the trophy.

"What it all comes down to is that we'd be pretty lonely without people like you to come live with us."

Carmen had fallen off a ladder and been beaten by her father. Asis had watched his father die and grown up without any cousins or family close by. And somehow, on a beach one day in Alicante they met, and over a series of subsequent and infrequent visits, they decided to build something together.

"We both had life hard when we were younger," Carmen said. "So when we got married, we thought life would be easy then. We knew exactly what we wanted, even if we never explicitly said it." Carmen's voice hung in the air as the wind rustled through the kitchen's open window. There was something mystical about it.

It was just like the old family gatherings we used to have back at home when old stories would be told and retold, the blending of the past and the present. Huddled around a table and hidden away at night, I heard many stories that were only meant for after hours, ones of promise and narrow purpose. The familiar themes were here, of dreams imagined but never fully realized, dreams of building a home and dreams of the Home Place. Between us, there was a safe place where dreams could echo and reverberate in the stillness. All of this, I knew, led us to tonight. Because from what I knew, dreams usually became more powerful when they went unspoken, when they gathered dust and communed in secret.

The room was now nearly dark, and Asis' muscular frame adjusted on his chair. He moved his hand across the table and brushed the crumbs into a pile in the middle, before sweeping them off the edge. "What we wanted was something we once thought would be simple. We wanted to create somewhere to come home to."

The wind whispered into his words as the last strand of light disappeared with the flap of the clothesline outside the window. It was a hard dream to build, because Adán didn't come home that night.

When I came home from school the next day, there was still no sign of Adán. I walked down the shadowy hallway and found Dior asleep on the toilet seat cover. In the room across from him, Carmen was asleep on her bed like a *momia*, wrapped in her blankets like a mummy as she lay straight on her back, her eyelids closed. I went into my room and set down my keychain backpack and turned to leave. It looked like a good time to get out of the house and head to the beach.

The streets were mostly vacant when I left the apartment. On either side of me, iron bars guarded store windows as *tiendas* closed up shop for the siesta. Spain was taking a three-hour break and business would resume, of course, after several beers and a few hours of sleep—sometime after five o'clock. I passed a government office that had closed for the afternoon, along with several other places of industry. The streets still swarmed with people making their way home, but their midday walks were lazy and indirect; it was a poor hour for beggars. Other than restaurants and the bus stop, Spain was silent at 2:00 p.m.

When I arrived at the beach, the sky was gray and I looked out across rolling waters. The waves on Playa Postiguet didn't usually rise much higher than three feet, but they rolled endlessly, crashing against each other below seagulls that streaked across the sky. Far to the left of me, the neighboring city of San Juan jutted out on a peninsula of skyscrapers, and I studied the high-rise through the misted haze. Spanish cities were always built so tall, but they were compact. You could fit everything inside them in one small area; like a footprint on the sand, they were self-contained. As I turned my gaze away from the distant city and back toward Alicante, I saw a swing set that faced the ocean. I made my way towards it. On the way, I found a heart drawn in the sand. Bright rose petals inset a hand-drawn frame scrawled in the middle with the initials of lovers. I looked up and spotted a couple holding hands and walking barefoot, kicking their feet into the surf and carelessly flinging bits of foam in front of them like white bubbles. By the time I made my way over to the swing set and looked out again, they were gone. There was no one on the beach for miles, and in the overcast sky, the sand looked like granite. I lost my gaze in the water, and when I finally looked up, I was transported by the waves to a place far away, somewhere I never thought I would go, somewhere three thousand miles away.

The Dream began here, one night ten years ago before Adam joined the Navy, on a night when all five of us sat huddled around the kitchen table. Most of the house lights were out and our empty plates sat in front of us, waiting to be removed, but no one motioned to take them away. Paul, as always, sat next to Mom and leaned against her shoulder. Adam sat across from her, a redhead just like Mom, but at six feet he was taller than the rest of us and determined to set himself apart with nipple piercings and tattoos. Who did he think he was? Naturally Mom and Dad didn't like that. I sat next to Dad at the end of the table, who as usual occupied the head, even though Mom was the one who powered all the decision making. Not that she was the sole decider, but she was the worker, the engine of the family who paved the way for Dad to dream dreams about boys and farms and tractors. Because tonight at our old wooden table, all of those things were about to finally come together. Dad was going to make an announcement. For the first time since Great Grandma and Grandpa Hanna had lost the farm and for the first time since Great Grandpa had been run over and killed, we were going to have a farm. What was once lost had been found, and of course Don Hanna was not going to miss the opportunity to call a family meeting and announce something special.

"Well, we've done a lot of searching and praying over the years," Dad began before taking a deep breath. "For two full years, we've been looking for a farm, and boys … we've finally found it. We just bought a farm!"

The farm was outside of Baker a little ways but not too far. Mom and Dad drove us out to see it. Overgrown, yes, but it wasn't too bad. The barn was a shack-barn, but it was still a barn. There was cow manure two feet deep right outside the back door, an abandoned shed suitable for a horror film one hundred feet from the house, and several odd bath tubs from the early nineteen hundreds rusting away in the riverbed behind the place, but it really wasn't too bad. When you dream big, you dream big.

"I want this farm to be the Home Place. Years from now, I want people to talk about our farm as the Old Hanna Place," Dad said. The Old Hanna Place was what he wanted to build: a place for us to come home to. For me, perhaps more than my brothers, the Dream took on a larger appeal. It was a dream of permanence and significance. While my brothers had always lived with Mom and Dad, I hadn't, and for me, the Dream meant having a place to come home to. Forever. "We're going to build something for eternity," Dad proclaimed.

Eternity started with the Year of Cleaning. For an entire summer, we cleared brush behind the house. In addition to two feet of cow manure the second you stepped out the back door, we fought against a yard that had never been properly planted, a wall of willow trees that had never been properly trimmed, and fences that had never been properly built. The place was a mess.

That first summer, Adam built fences and used old-fashioned eighteen year-old sweat to pound black posts every eight feet. Before he went into the Navy, Dad was going to make sure he built some character. Paul and I built a lot of character that summer too, hauling brush and sticks and building huge piles that we burned every week or so. We turned the shed into a chicken coop and painted it, and soon enough, the place was looking less abandoned, but still a little dilapidated. That was okay though, because we were making progress. When you're living the dream, it doesn't matter if it's derelict. When we finally cut down the trees behind the house so we could see the river, the Elkhorn Mountains rose to greet us and it was like the longhorned tall tales of Texas had merged with the Swiss Alps. I didn't know what either of those places looked like, but Dad told us that was what our place was like. Somewhere where the greatness wasn't quite so obvious, somewhere where instead it enveloped us.

"All this work—these things take time, and I'm going to get all the work I can out of you boys," Dad said.

The next summer marked Year Two of Cleaning. We hauled more brush, burnt more sticks, and hauled more bed frames and other pieces of rusted memorabilia from the riverbed. Bit by bit, the Old Hanna Place was coming together, and because it was the summer, I got to spend an entire month floating the river with Paul and building the Dream along-side Mom and Dad and my brothers. For thirty days, it was the best thing that ever happened. But at the end of thirty days, I would return to Seattle and the airport trips would resume, school would start back up, and summer would turn to fall and then winter. In between visits and far into the night, I'd dream of what we were building. Because in order to have something for people to come back to, you have to first build something worth coming back to.

"Mom and I had a plan in all of this," Dad said. "By working on this place, we knew that you boys would become attached to it. We knew that someday it would mean something to you."

In a little valley that most people drive by and forget, we were either being branded or we were doing some branding ourselves. I'm not sure which, exactly, it was.

After all, we weren't an ordinary family. Mom and Dad didn't go out for date nights and they didn't even like going bowling. We barely went to church. We didn't take vacations like most people. In fact, when the Dream finally took hold of us, we stopped taking family vacations, and Mom and Dad just took time off their hospital jobs in order to work more on the farm. Some people called us a blended family, too, but that really made Mom mad.

"We're not a blended family, and we never have been," she said. "You guys were always full brothers and we were always a family, even if the government didn't think so."

We knew right from the beginning that blood didn't amount to anything. Your family was what you made it, the rest of the world be damned.

When I walked back home from the ocean, Carmen was waiting.

"Estif," Carmen called down the hall when I walked in. "*Tengo algo mostrarte.*"

I found Carmen in the living room holding a brown photo album. Her hair was pulled back with a red stretch band from the Chinese store as she sat on the couch with her legs crossed and a photo album resting in her lap. Adán still hadn't returned, so she thought it was a safe time to show me pictures of her former students before he came home and yelled at her for doing so. "These are all of my sons," she said. "Look at all the places they've been!"

Page by page, Carmen flipped through two photo albums filled with pictures of former students in places ranging from Austria to Pamplona. "This is Mykel," she'd say when talking about Michael, an *hijo* from two years ago. "Or this is Estifen in Sweden with Asis junior." She pointed out pictures of Mitch when he was there and they were all gathered together for a big family dinner. Every student that had ever lived with them had travelled to other countries during their stay, but they always had somewhere to come back to—No. 9 Calle Alona. With each student went a story and Carmen had a story she wanted to tell me about Mykel.

She pointed to one of the shelves in the china cabinet. In a framed photo was a picture of a blond American family. "*Es la familia de Mykel,*" Carmen said. "Here he is. Ohhh, how I loved him! *Dios mío,* that boy broke my heart."

One day, Mykel's parents from the States came to visit and stay with Carmen and Asis. Carmen was sitting on the couch with Michael next to her and his parents were sitting on the other couch across from them.

Mykel's parents spoke a little Spanish, so both families were able to talk to each other and the conversation was light. They started off laughing and joking, but at one point Mykel's mom asked Carmen something.

"How is Mykel doing in Spain?"

Carmen and Asis immediately stopped talking. They looked over at each other. For a split second, the room was quiet. Mykel's eyes darted over to Carmen and pleaded. *Don't tell them anything.* Carmen's eyes flew over to Asis, then back to Mykel.

"Your son is doing really good here," Carmen complied. "Really good."

Mykel looked back at Carmen and let out a deep breath.

"Thank you for taking such good care of our son," his mother said to Carmen and Asis.

"*De nada,*" they replied. And that was the end of the story.

As we sat on the couch, there was a certain hollowness in the way Carmen told it. She couldn't forget the moment when the boy who was supposed to be her son had sat next to her on the couch and pleaded with her to speak low and say nothing.

"Right then, I lied to his mom," she said, "so that she wouldn't have to know what her son was doing. What else could I say? *No, your son's doing horrible—he's been doing ecstasy and marijuana and hasn't gone to class at all this week.* I couldn't break his mom's heart. I just couldn't, even though it would have been telling the truth. When someone else's son becomes your own, it's different. You want the best for them, even though they might hurt you. And even if they hurt you, you'd still cover for them, again, and again, and again, until you couldn't cover for them anymore. Because maybe that's what love is. Or maybe that's forgiveness."

She adjusted her red headband and got up. "You're just like Mykel. I really love you, and when you really love someone, you start to get afraid for them. *Nuestra casa es tu casa*—we want you to always have somewhere to come home to."

Later in the week, Carmen received a letter in the mail from Mykel. He wrote about his life in graduate school and how he was studying history and how well things were going for him. Carmen nearly cried. He probably had no idea that Carmen still thought about that conversation. All these years later, it was still with her. Years later, another moment would be with her.

Late that night, Adán quietly opened the front door and walked back into the house. I was sitting at the living room table doing homework, and when I glanced up to check the time, Adán was standing in the living room doorway, looking at me. His arms stretched across the frame, covering the space in rippled muscle, his shirt fastened tight. Our eyes met and quickly dispersed as he nodded. I nodded back in recognition. Carmen was on the couch between us and her eyes glanced back and forth. Neither Adán nor I said anything. Adán disappeared down the hallway and I heard his door shut. I went into my room and quietly closed the door.

Inside it was dark and I didn't bother to turn on the light. There was no need to, really. After a time my eyes adjusted to the lack of light and began to wander across the walls, moving and scanning as I sat on the bed in the middle, unable to focus. Sound and reggaeton filtered in, a little bit at first, then gradually more. Heavy bass and distant thud—Adán. It was strange to see him back.

As I looked around the walls of my room, my gaze settled on a postcard that Carmen had propped on my desk. *Estif, Marruecos.* She'd never told me what really happened there. Instead, I'd heard stories—the kids were so little back then. Hanging on the wall next to the postcard was Adán's class picture from the second grade. He was tall then, too.

My focus moved between the picture and the postcard, back and forth. The two were connected. With each thud of Adán's music, a suggestion began to arise. I needed to spend some time away from the house. And I wanted to learn what life in Morocco had been like; it must have been hard. Hidden between Carmen's secrets and Adán's picture was a country I would visit, a place ingrained in memory. Since they wouldn't tell me all of the details when I asked, I decided I would fill in my own.

Without knowing what was at stake, I would venture into Morocco.

WEEK 8
ALICANTE, SPAIN

I LEARNED REAL QUICK that a trip to Morocco was not going to be easy. Sitting at a winter barstool in the *barrio* of Alicante, I heard tales of the Southland and what Morocco was really like. "You have to look like you're already dead in order to go there," a man sitting across the table from me said. "Because Morocco will come and try to kill you."

That sounded like my kind of place.

Twisted orange lights murmured above us as I raised my Mau to my mouth and let the alcohol slowly drizzle down, burning with each droplet. At the end of my bottle, the last dregs clung hesitantly to the brown glass before dripping slowly into the space behind my lips. I set it down and brushed my hand against the front of my mouth. Sitting across the table from me, a friend of a friend told stories about Morocco in between NFL highlight videos. His eyes glazed over the large TV on the wall behind me and he was lost in something or other, I wasn't quite sure exactly what. *He knows about Morocco,* my friend had said. *Oh, he'll tell you about Morocco.* Jesse was his name.

"Nice catch," Jesse said to no one in particular. He took a quick swig from his bottle. "Helluva game."

I looked over my shoulder at the screen: 24-20 Vikings. "Yeah."

We sat silent for awhile as his eyes moved back and forth with the game.

"You want to talk about Morocco, right?"

"Yeah. Kate said you knew something?"

"She probably wants you to hear what happened in the alley."

"Sure. Let's hear it."

For the first time since I'd sat down next to him, he took his eyes off the game. "You're not going to believe this," he began before taking another swig and clanging his empty bottle onto the table. In the silhouette of passerby and orange bar lights, Jesse's bleached-blond hair looked exotic, like some sort of platinum dye that was exported from Japan. He was tall and lean, and though he wasn't the macho type, there was a toughness in his eyes that seemed unusual for a guy who dyed his hair.

Jesse leaned into the table and lowered his voice. His eyes squinted and finally the glaze over them rolled back, and his pupils bored into mine. "A man offered to guide me around Tangier. I didn't think much of it at first, of course, so I said yes. That," he pointed toward me, "was a mistake."

His eyes reverted once again to the game behind me and I watched them follow the ball in a straight line. The quarterback must have thrown a pass, but the ball was probably intercepted. "Dammit," he said.

His head dropped and then he looked back at me, windswept. Alicante was always a dusty, sandy town and it looked like a grain of sand had gotten stuck in his boot. The way he paused all the time, he should have been shuffling through six-shooters.

"The guide took me into this thing called the medina. I didn't know what it was, but believe me, I was wary. I tried to watch my back. And I tried to keep track of where we were, but the medina was surrounded by walls. There was only one way in and one way out. Anyways, the guide led my friend and me deeper and deeper into this maze until he turned a corner and we ended up in an abandoned alley. The second we stepped in there, I knew things had been rigged. All of the sudden, the guide's friends jumped out of nearby windows and sprung out from behind dark corners. I put my hands up and they surrounded us. They didn't point a gun at us, but they didn't need to, they had us right where they wanted, and besides, they probably had several knives on them. They skinned my wallet and if they could have made some money out of my dead ass, they'd have killed me in a second."

"*Una cerveza, por fav,*" he called to the waiter who made the rounds near us. "They're out for you, man. I'll leave you to chew on that."

Morocco wasn't going to be an ordinary trip, that much was certain. This was a big decision. A momentum shift, a game-changer. Because no matter what was about to happen, I heard stories like Jesse's without end. The Spaniards always pounced on an opportunity to get high-strung and talk about *Marruecos* because it was either the birthplace of honesty or the death pit of tall tales. *I was in Morocco and nearly got killed. Some guy led me down an alley and his friends jumped me. I was kidnapped for three months and barely escaped.* Or better yet, *I rode camels through the desert and lived to tell of it.* One guy told me about how the Moroccans came up to you and threw snakes on your shoulders so that you had to pay them to take the snakes off you. Whether this was actually true or not, I don't know, but I heard it and remembered it for a long time (like Indiana Jones, I've always been afraid of snakes). I even heard a story about a group of girls who walked into a rug shop, and as soon as they stepped on the entrance rug, the owner yanked it out from under them and they fell into a dirt pit beneath his shop. (I didn't hear what happened after that.)

Morocco was a dangerous place, that much was certain, but that was also why I wanted to go there in the first place. For being a small-town guy, I'd always considered myself a bull rider of sorts even though I'd never actually saddled up. It was more about your mindset, really—Bud or Budlite—about attacking life and going all in, or folding a hand too soon and moving out to the suburbs. There was nothing complacent about Morocco. You were either on that bull or you weren't; it required everything. I wanted a quest like that, a quest that would take me to the edge. Adán wanted me gone anyway, and while we hadn't said much to each other since he'd shown back up at the house, some additional distance between us might be a good thing. After all, I'd come to Europe because the horizon was burning. The only problem was that now the horizon burned like a signal fire, purposeful and directive, but a warning all the same.

It was just a normal Sunday night dinner. Carmen and Asis and I sat around the small table in the living room watching Cubans on TV. Adán and his girlfriend were in the kitchen talking, so we had the living room to ourselves. In my opinion, they were getting the short end of the stick because Carmen wanted all of us to watch a show where Cuban girls ran around the beach with their shirts off. *Jajajaja,* Carmen laughed, *¡Mira!* Look at her *tetas!"* she said, pointing at one girl's boobs. *¡Qué grandes son!"*

Asis laughed and tried to look over at Carmen every so often for approval because he didn't want her to know that he was getting a little absorbed in the show. I didn't mind though, the olive and ebony-skinned chestnut brunettes were stunning.

Our plates in front of us, however, weren't quite as interesting. Fried fish and *ensalada con* spinach, *"espinacas,"* Carmen called it—a typical Mediterranean meal. A full trout stared up at me from my plate, its eyes glazed over and frozen in a look of disbelief.

"What, you've never eaten one of these?" Carmen said. "Just grab it like this." She took hers with both hands and used one to steady the fish and the other to pry chunks of white meat from the bones. She raised a hunk of meat above her mouth. Light glittered off the scales before she dropped the piece on her tongue and swallowed. *"Es buenísima, ¿no?"*

I took mine carefully and nodded. When I looked up, Asis had changed the channel and topless Cuban girls had been replaced by a Spanish comedian. That was a bit of a letdown. For switching to comedy though, Asis took the conversation in a rather serious direction.

"Are you sure you want to go to Morocco?" he cautioned. "You remember what happened there?"

Several years ago, two of his friends went to visit Morocco and were kidnapped for three months. Tossed in an empty room and given survival rations of bread and water, they had been held for ransom in a room with only a window. ("In Morocco there's no money in death, only in drugs," Asis reiterated.) Night by night when the guard wasn't looking, his friends planned their escape. One day when the guard was taking a bathroom break, Asis' friends were able to pry open the door and run away. They made their way through the port city of Tangier, and with the help of the Spanish consulate, boarded a ship home and never went back. They had made it out alive, but as grown men in their fifties, they had never planned on being kidnapped in Tangier in the first place.

That was what Asis was worried about: I was going to Tangier next weekend. "*Ten cuidado,*" he said before I heard another story.

This time the sun cast an endless glare on the rise and fall of sandscapes as two more of Asis' friends were in the middle of a dune caravan in the Moroccan desert, riding camels. They'd found a guide who'd agreed to take them on a tour to an unknown oasis, but they hadn't reached it yet. Like the postcard image of Morocco where a white-robed caravan wandered into the uncharted heart of the desert, a romantic anticipation arose in their hearts. Just like Lawrence of Arabia, they were living the dream. But as they crested one of the sand dunes, they couldn't see what was on the other side, and as they reared their camels at the top, a group of black-robed men armed with rifles jumped over and ambushed them. The men were ransomed and their guide was paid quite handsomely.

There could have been a thousand more stories on the dangers of Morocco, but they all boiled down to the same thing: I couldn't wait to get there.

"What are you thinking?" Dad's voice was flush on the phone when I told him what I was about to do. "Do you have any idea what you're doing?" A *what-in-the-hell* should be thrown in there to really capture the extra emphasis.

Mom said the same thing. So did my program director, Luis. "I've never been to Morocco, but watch out," he said. "If you go, you need to travel in a group." Everyone from professors to the *gente* on the bus agreed on this point. Never go to Morocco alone. I told them that I'd be traveling in a group. It would be safe.

* * *

A blood-stained sky swirled to the edge of the night as the Mediterranean world looked on in disbelief. Myself even, I nearly missed it. Etched through palm trees and the forlorn roofs of white apartment buildings, the redness gathered and collected itself against the outline of the moon. All around, the sky was ablaze. Standing in front of the laundry room, I used the window to frame the sunset into a still moment. When I turned away and walked back into the kitchen, I found Asis looking over my shoulder. His black curls were ablaze with the color of the sun, and his strong face and brown skin became a yellow mesquite in the swirling red light.

"*Qué maravilloso,*" he whispered. *¡Madre mía!* Our sunsets in Alicante *me da fe.*"

As usual, we didn't have any light in the kitchen and streaks of sanguine shot into the room and wrapped themselves around Iowa State mugs, University of Nevada souvenirs, and the Barcelona mug I'd bought for Carmen and Asis on my third week. All the souvenirs on the shelves basked themselves in the red light that now enveloped the kitchen. On top of the refrigerator, bands of light wrapped themselves around yellow bananas and bursting oranges, creating a sudden collage of color. A little ways from the sink, Asis and I watched the end of one day and the beginning of the next. Never mind the fact that we were both wearing coats and clutching them rather tight, the warmth of the sunset was something to behold.

"What I've always wanted is the sun," Asis said, his eyes steady on the horizon. "For my whole life, I've wanted to live by the sun and the sea, sometimes in more ways than one."

Late on summer nights, he and Carmen would walk down to the beach at two o'clock in the morning and go swimming with the rest of Alicante. It got so hot in the summer that you couldn't sleep at all, you just had to go out and play. There were concerts and games and *música.* "*Oh, la música,*" Asis said. "We loved those endless summer nights."

The red sky began turning burgundy, then into a vapor of sangria that slowly evaporated from the kitchen. In a moment, the sun was down and we were left draped in our coats and the night. Asis turned back to the counter and began chopping peppers.

For the first time in two months, Asis and I had the house to ourselves for some *padre-hijo* time since Carmen was out with a friend for a Friday night social. Adán was at his girlfriend's house and so was Asis junior, who was, as usual, spending some quality time with his bikini-model girlfriend. She had big boobs.

That left Asis and me alone at the house drinking beer and doing something neither one of us had done before—cooking. And so began our father-son tradition—*La Noche de las Fajitas*.

"*Tu eres el jefe.*" You're the boss, Asis told me, as we flew around the kitchen with timers buzzing and meat to be sliced. "How do you cut this?" he asked.

After we had cut the meat and peppers, Asis walked over to the fridge and pulled out a white-wrapped package. "Don't tell Carmen about this," he whispered, "but I bought some cow intestine for us." As he looked down at the package in his hands, his body-builder face lit up. "*Ah, la libertad sin la mujer.* Estif, someday you're going to enjoy the freedom you get when your woman isn't around."

The meat sizzled on the skillet and an exotic aroma wafted over us, seasoned and *sabrosa*. Peppers, fajitas, cow intestine, and Mexican food weren't typical Spanish fare. In the whole of Alicante, there was only one Mexican restaurant and its tables were usually empty. Even though our fajita sauce was the Spain version (some sort of watered-down tomato paste without any kick), it was fajita sauce all the same. We doled out larger portions than Carmen would have allowed and ate standing up.

"Don't tell Carmen I'm going to use this," Asis said, and pulled out a small vial of Tabasco sauce. "She hates it when I use this stuff." He poured it loosely over his three fajitas and then sealed the bottle and slid it into his pocket where she wouldn't see it. "Give me another beer while you're at it."

I reached into the fridge and grabbed us two San Miguel 1516's from the six-pack I'd bought. He dug through a drawer for a bottle opener and cracked his top and I did the same. *¡Salud!* "Someday soon, I want to teach you how to fence." We clinked bottles and drank. I took a long, full swig and the taste lingered until Carmen got back.

When we were still eating and drinking, she walked in the front door and pinched my butt. "You little pig butt, you're getting fat."

"Carmen!" Asis said, with a beer in his hand. "That's quite the welcome."

"*¡Tú también!*" Carmen said, her face still flush from the wind outside the house.

Asis glanced down at his belly. "I don't think I'm fat."

"Well, that's debatable."

I left them arguing in the kitchen and went into the bathroom to check myself out. A basket of old toothbrushes sat on top of the toilet and one of Carmen's Piglet stickers from her Winnie the Pooh sticker collection stared back at me from the mirror.

Naturally, then, when I pulled off my shirt and scrunched my abs together in an attempt to make a six-pack, Piglet appeared right in the middle of my ripples. A ring of runny olive oil fat hung over the edge of my jeans and I vowed to start going to the gym. I had been fit and trim when I arrived, but now that wasn't quite so obvious. After taking a quick look at my butt (which I was now painfully self-conscious of), I ran back into the kitchen to find one of Carmen's favorite packages of chorizo lunchmeat. A quick scan at *los datos de nutrición* revealed that just the meat in my lunch sandwiches supplied more than one hundred percent of my daily fat intake. I promised myself that I would start eating turkey instead. If I was going to slug it out in Morocco, I needed to get fighter-ready. That probably wouldn't happen in a week, but at least I'd feel better about myself.

The following day, sweat tinged my face as I made my first foray into the Spanish gym at the University of Alicante. For being a school of thirty thousand students, you wouldn't know it by going to the gym. Locked away in the basement, the gym was about four times the size of the average American living room with three times the level of sweat saturation. Fifty bodies crammed into an eight-foot high space and I saw nothing but tight black pants and dark brown hair. For thirty-five euros and a semester-long pass that was "*muy barato,*" according to the gym manager, I gained access to ten exercise bikes (two of which were broken), two treadmills, a set of mismatched kilogram weights, and several old lifting machines from the nineties. At eight o'clock in the morning, the Spanish gym types were out in full force—slightly more muscled versions of the typically lithe Spanish body. In several months, however, they were going to look like my host brother, a 2006 runner-up for Mr. Spain, or his bikini model girlfriend, Leticia. Hot puffs of air and the sound of *¡Qué fuerte, tío!* filled the room as I waited in line to grunt and bench a couple of kilos, before wiping myself off with a towel that someone else had already used and taking my clothes off in the changing room.

When I got home later that night, Asis and I shared a beer after he finished *haciendo gimnasio* (literally, "making gym"). With the beer, it marked a true Spanish gym experience—*tan fuerte*. Adán was in the kitchen with us too, and even ventured a joke. "Eating, drinking, and … you've almost run the Spanish triathlon," he said. "Now you just need a girl."

That was first on my agenda. Not a girl, per se, but a companion, a traveling partner or several. I needed to assemble a strike team that was willing to venture into Morocco with me. This posed several challenges. One, I wasn't on good terms with most of the Americans, and two, I was looking for people who would watch my back as close as I would be watching theirs. The search for travel partners began in cooking class.

"What are you doing this weekend?" Rachel asked me as she skewered a hunk of marinated beef and slid it onto a shish kabob. She placed the end of her metal skewer on the long stainless steel countertop and looked at me through strands of straight blonde hair. For all of the things I'd heard about her, I liked Rachel. She was one of the crazy study abroaders known more for her drinking, smoking, and anorexia than anything else, but she was a tough little *guapa* and she spoke good Spanish. I'd heard that the Moroccans liked to smoke a lot, so she could be a real asset in helping us acculturate. The Moroccans also liked blondes, but I didn't learn that until later.

"I'm going to Morocco this weekend," I said. "You want to come?"

Without hesitating, she gave me an answer.

* * *

My next recruit was my friend Eder from Brazil. He was a Ph.D. student in International Politics, and although he was actually forty years old, he looked and acted twenty-eight; you never would have known that he had a kid and an ex-wife five thousand miles away. In fact, his olive-skinned baby face was so endearing that he had acquired a hot Spanish optometrist girlfriend who paid all of his bills and did all of his laundry. He planned on dumping her when he graduated.

Eder and I sat at the bar in Lizarrán that looked over La Rambla de Méndez Núñez while sampling tapas we couldn't afford. Between our flurry of Spanish and Portuguese and the constant rotation of tapas that the waiters brought to us on large black trays, Eder's eyes followed palm trees in the street that swayed with the wind. Below the palm trees, Eder also kept a close eye on *las alicantinas*, reserving a special tongue-twisted smile for the long legs of pretty girls that ventured their eyes in our direction. "*Tío*," he said, "*tenemos que viajar.*" He wanted to travel somewhere, pronto.

"Just tell me where," I said.

"*Dondequiera.* Wherever."

"Well, I'm going to Morocco next week."

"*Aí, ¡sí! ¡Quiero venir!*"

Eder's baby face lit up as his voice rose to inflect. He was in. "Let me check with my research professor, but I'm pretty sure I'll be able to come. My girlfriend will probably complain, of course, but I'll tell her that she has no choice if she wants me to keep making love to her."

Our third adventurer was a girl from Chicago named Madilyn. "How's her Spanish?" Eder asked when I dropped by his study room on campus to tell him we had another traveler.

"It's OK."

"I suppose that's good enough. But is she hot? Is she a *guapa*?" He bumped his arm into me and winked. Underneath his green-skinned baseball cap, I saw the beaches of Brazil in his eyes, filled with taut girls in thongs and I suddenly found myself wanting to go there quite badly, the lust was so alive in him.

"I think she has a boyfriend."

"Come on, *hombre*, that doesn't mean a thing!"

My final recruit was a guy named Alec from Maryland. He was from my study abroad program, and although I didn't get along with most of the other study abroaders, I liked Alec. He had a sprawling lot of golden hair that covered blue eyes and gym-boy arms, and like Eder, he was a bit of a womanizer. While he liked to get a little crazy at times, he had worked his way through school and he knew how to buckle down and bear a load; he got good grades and was debt-free. Since our study abroad program had only ten guys total (compared to fifty girls), all of us *hombres* stuck together in an odd sort of brotherhood. Even if we didn't necessarily get along all the time, we had to hold up the testosterone quotient together.

I told Alec about Morocco and immediately he said yes.

It was settled, then. After the group was assembled, I double-checked with everyone to make sure they still wanted to go and they all said yes. We scheduled a time to meet at the bus station and buy tickets. We exchanged emails about the trip and talked about the things we wanted to do. We chatted about the trip in between classes. With five of us, no one was going to jump us in the alley and steal our money.

In between now and our meeting at the bus station, I had several loose ends to tie up. First things first, I had to find a book about Morocco and figure out what, exactly, we'd just gotten ourselves into. My friend Devin told me that the school library had free guidebooks for checkout, so I made my way over to the *biblioteca*. A large dark-hued building, it occupied the iconic center of campus, and unlike American universities where everything was online and students hardly ever went to the library, the place delighted with the scent of paper and perfume. I wandered the building and discovered a first floor devoted to American celebrity magazines and a second floor devoted to computers from the nineties. On the third floor, tall glass windows overlooked a canopy of fountains, orange groves and red flowers that sprawled across the campus below. Next to the windows, students sat curled over notes and the personal laptop was a rarity.

I returned to the first floor to find the guidebook section. In between tan metal racks of books on African culture, I found a book about Morocco.

Late at night, I lay on my bed reading about sand dunes and Moroccan medinas. The medina, I learned, was the old bazaar found in most Arab towns. In the port city of Tangier it sounded particularly bad. On most maps, the medina looked about one-fourth the size of the city (population: half million), and it was big and entirely walled off from the rest of town. There appeared to be one way in and one way out. Cops patrolled the entrance, but generally didn't venture in. What awaited was a labyrinth of tiny alleys and streets crowded with people, bikes, dogs, goats, and snake pits. At least that was my interpretation anyway. The medina was almost entirely lawless and without help, it sounded like it would be hard to find your way around. Even if you were from Tangier, the guidebook said, it was easy to get lost. That was why there were guides, and that was how they scammed you: because you needed them.

Be careful who you ask to lead you around the medina, the guide said. *There are many false guides.* In order to find an honest tour guide in Tangier, the book said to look for someone wearing a laminated name badge. If your tour guide wore a name badge, it meant that they were a government-sponsored tour guide, and thus only half as corrupt. *Don't trust anyone else*, the guidebook said. The sentence was underlined.

On a page that had been folded over, I found a map of the medina. *Bring a copy of this*, the guide said, *because you won't be able to buy a map once you're inside.* Once you were inside the medina, you were at their mercy. That was my interpretation anyways, but not a far cry from the guidebook's call to *avoid being robbed.* That sentence didn't get my hopes up. The next one wasn't any more encouraging, either. *Look as poor as you possibly can.*

I realized, then, that if I was going to look poor, I was going to need different equipment. While my keychain backpack already looked frazzled and impoverished after weeks of use, I would need a backpack that couldn't get sliced off my shoulder by a street thief. What I needed was something Chinese-grade, a little tougher but not much. Hanging on the wall one day outside a Chinese trinket store, I found a brown-sandbagger, a real bargain. *Shenzhou* it said across the front. Four buttons had been placed in random places across the front flap as if the backpack had been sprayed in gunfire and haphazardly patched up in Beijing. Both of the pocket zippers didn't work, and the water bottle compartment was already torn across the top, preventing access to the main zipper. It was exactly what I wanted. If I couldn't open the compartments on my own backpack, someone else wouldn't be able to either. "I'll take it," I told the sales clerk, and handed her five euros.

Theft, after all, was a serious concern. Last week, a girl from my program was robbed outside her front door and lost her keys and her credit card. The week before that, a man in the street had pulled a knife on Carmen and cut her purse off her shoulder while she was shopping. After she got robbed, Carmen bought a Dolce & Gabbana knock-off that had reinforced metal straps so it couldn't be cut from her shoulder. Theft, Carmen said, was something you should just prepare for. "But that still shouldn't stop us from cutting off the hands of thieves and beating them like we used to."

In the waiting time before Morocco, I caught a glimpse of the old days when some friends and I went to the Plaza del Toro for a Spanish bullfight. In the stadium, scarlet drapes covered white sunlit arches as a strange pageantry unfolded in the wooden arena. A pep band was assembled on the third tier, *todo vestido,* wearing top hats and marching band uniforms that sparkled in the sun while grandmothers in bonnets ate hot dogs with their grandchildren on the tier below. It was like the Spanish version of a baseball game, except with Disney music. Loud music and boisterous conversations continued until a man in green velvet and gold-plated armor strode into the arena and waved at the crowd while the band began playing the Spanish national anthem. The stands rose to attention, then sat down when the last note hung in the air—silent, almost haunting.

Seconds later, the moment would be lost in a flurry of pink sheets, colonial triangle hats, and charging, drugged bulls. When the bull was worn out, the music died down again and the green velvet matador appeared once more, this time with sword in hand.

A white outer circle had already been drawn in the sand, and two combatants—man and beast—stared at each other, eye to eye. There was nothing else. The bull let out a snort and suddenly thrashed toward the matador, but with a cool sidestep the bull thundered past him. Again, the bull charged, and again nothing. He charged and charged again, until he had nothing left to give and blood began dripping from the end of his mouth in a curd of sweat. The matador raised his sword. Light glinted off the blade and flashed across the crowd as his green and gold suit sparkled in the sun and he raised his sword for the plunge. The bull stood still. Right before the kill, time slowed and sound murmured to a dull hush.

Days before this, I had stood alone in the middle of the arena and marveled at the silence and size of it when no one was present. Sun had shone down on the sand floor, creating a deadening effect. I remembered how it had beat against my forehead and how I had stood there in the absence of sound. It was the sort of moment when you knew that cars were honking in the street thirty feet behind you, that busses were stopping and unloading, that people were yelling and shouting, doors opening and closing, but in the middle of the arena, all of the noise disappeared. In that moment right then, right when time slowed down, the matador plunged his sword into the bull. The crowd twirled their shirts above their heads in circles and began shouting. The stands began to shake and a thunderous roar rattled the arena's wooden frame as hundreds of people stamped their feet in unison. The sword plunged into the bull's spinal cord and blood spurted out its mouth as it collapsed onto the ground and began thrashing in the sand. As if on cue, a judge on the scarlet balcony above the arena rose to stand and put his hand on the railing like Caesar once did, nodding his approval.

The matador took a bow and saluted the crowd, the drums and carnival music continued, popcorn eating resumed, cars honked on the street behind us, and the TV crew worked their way through the crowd with live, up-close footage of the kill that would be shown in slow motion on televisions across Alicante while families ate dinner together. Lines formed at concession stands as the band prepared for another romp through circus pageantry. A carriage of six white horses dressed in gold armor and head feathers entered the ring to escort the dead body out of the arena. Sweepers mobilized and swept the blood from the sand and re-drew the white boundary circle while a new matador prepared for battle. Six slain bulls and three hours later, the rest of the show was over.

"I know this seems rather barbaric to us," my friend Devin said afterwards, "but think of what they probably imagine when they see American TV. They probably think the same thing when they see some of our entertainment—UFC fights with tons of blood and people attacking each other."

Although bullfights weren't popular anymore, they said a lot about the role of tradition in Spain that Carmen had alluded to when she mentioned cutting off the hands of street thieves. Until seeing the bullfight, I had never understood the pull of tradition in Europe. An older man on the bus had once told me that the bull, the *toro*, was the symbol of Spain. For Spain to be reborn, the toro had to be killed.

For forty-five years, General Franco's dictatorship had cemented Spanish traditionalism in the psyche. The nuclear family was encouraged and women were closely watched if they left home without their husband. Birth control was forbidden, and bullfights became the national pastime and the only government-sanctioned entertainment. Other traditions were also cemented. The Catholic Church became the church of the state, and to get a good job, a priest had to recommend someone for a position, but he could, of course, be bought off. Flamenco became the national music and *la roja*, the Spanish flag, a symbol of national unity enforced by the military.

With Franco's death in 1975 and the ensuing democracy in the eighties, Spain tried to put its traditions in the attic, but refused to fully part with them. While the Spaniards now have bullet trains, Internet cafes, McDonald's, and the eighth largest economy in the world, they still clung to the siesta and bullfights, odd eating times and midnight strolls, because to lose them might mean the loss of Spain itself. Spanish economists for years have argued for the abolishment of the siesta in order to

boost national productivity and GDP, but the Spaniards remain staunch-
ly opposed. Meal times remain as irregular as ever, even if they force the
Spaniards to work on a schedule that is uniquely their own. Women are
still expected to clean the house, cook dinner, and do the dishes afterwards, and most men never learn how to cook. If you even suggest eating at a different time or helping a woman with "women's work," expect
opposition. They may change a national pastime, but never, ever suggest
eating lunch at noon.

I did just that.

"*Estif, por favor,*" Carmen said. "Now what kind of idea is that?"

The day before the Morocco trip, I was greeted by an even more unwelcome idea.

"I don't think I'm going to be able to make the trip," Rachel told me in
between classes. "There's going to be a big party this weekend."

"But didn't you say you wanted to go?" I countered. "You said you
were in. You planned on going, right?"

"I say a lot of things I don't mean," Rachel said.

After my next class, Alec swung over to talk to me. Something had
come up and he couldn't go. I nodded.

"Look, I really want to go," he said. "I was planning on going until
some of the other guys asked me to go with them instead during Spring
Break. Sorry."

Right after Alec, Madilyn approached me. "I should have told you this
earlier," she said, "but I made other plans for the weekend."

One by one, they came in succession, and it was finally down to Eder
and me. Right before we were supposed to meet up and buy our tickets, I
called Eder. "Eder, are you still in?"

"*Hombre*, of course. I just have to ask my professor. I'll meet you down
at the station."

In a matter of hours, the plan was beginning to come undone and was
in serious danger of falling apart altogether. By now though, I had invest-
ed too much and I was all in. Whether it was just the two of us or myself,
it didn't matter to me. I would go to Morocco and I would live to tell of it.

* * *

It was cloudy when I arrived at the bus station. A chill breeze drafted through the open doors of the bus platform and the wind carried the cheap scent of wadded up fast-food wrappers and sticky soda pop. No matter where you'd been, the bus station was someplace you could always go to find someone worse off than yourself. When the cops weren't looking, drugs and money changed hands behind the dumpster out back. Inside the waiting area, beggars sat on soiled plastic bags and held up yellow cups bristling with dirt. Teenage mothers clutched babies to their breasts with one hand while fiddling with lighters in the other. Life was hard— you saw that at the bus station. Hidden under my beanie and jet-black coat, I dropped my eyes and tried to look worn down like everyone else.

Around the edges of the ticket area, bus representatives sat behind bulletproof glass and sold tickets to faraway places. Because Morocco was only fourteen hours from Alicante, it made sense to take the bus.

I scanned the crowd again for Eder, but still no sign. I stepped outside into the clouded February day and looked up as raindrops fell and smacked me in the face. I turned my head back to the ground, leaned against a wall, and put my hands in my pockets and waited. About fifteen minutes later, my phone began to ring.

"*Dime*," I answered.

"*Estif, soy Eder.*" He wasn't at the station.

"Are you coming?"

"*No, tío. No puedo*. I can't, even though I want to."

"So that means you're not coming?"

"Yes, but *hombre*, you know what they say in Spanish. Five minutes is an hour and yes usually means no unless outside forces intervene."

"Unless outside forces intervene?"

"*Lo siento, tío*. I'm sorry. But I can't go if my professor says I can't go."

"Well," I said. "Next week?"

"Next week."

I tucked my phone in my pocket. All around, I watched people walk up to ticket counters in groups and order tickets. They smiled and nodded and said *gracias*. I wouldn't do that.

I approached one of the ticket counters with a red sign that said Tangier. Behind the glass, a middle-aged man was sitting on a stool. His flax, graying hair looked like the day had taken a long draft of him and puffed him out; he needed a cigarette.

"You want to go to Tangier?" he said, dropping his chin and raising his eyebrows.

"Yes."

"By yourself?"

"Yes, that's correct."

"Do you have any idea what you're about to do?"

"Not really."

He nodded and reached under the scratched bulletproof glass to hand me my ticket. "Your bus boards at midnight."

When the Morocco plan fell apart it was like dominos. Plans never fall alone. Always in sequence and always in order, one fall always leads to another.

Over the years in Baker, we'd made a lot of plans for the future. We planned ahead for the hay harvest, and we bought cows and began planning each spring for when new calves would be born. We planned around school events and PTA meetings, and when I was sixteen and finally living in Baker, we began to plan as a family, believing that the Dream would come full circle and that, for once, things would finally work themselves out.

The summer when I was sixteen, the Dream was finally realized. At long last, we had the farm and we were together as a family. During my sophomore year in high school, I ran away from Seattle and my mother twice and endured ten days of juvenile lock-up in the process. After a long series of custody trials, the court eventually turned me over to Dad's custody, and after the legal battle was over, the rest of the dreams we'd harbored over the years managed to fall back into place. My older brother Adam cast off his nipple piercings and got married and had two kids. Paul started playing the saxophone and began falling in love with music. Together, Paul and I spent our afternoons running around the farm, chasing cows, floating down the Powder River on inner tubes and building forts. Mom continued to expand her influence and became vice president at the hospital in Baker. After quitting his job to work for the government, Dad finally had enough time to devote to fixing up the farm, and he began developing a multi-year plan where we would begin tackling various summer-long, fixer-upper projects until the farm was finally complete and the Home Place had been rebuilt.

Home Place reconstruction, then, started with the Year of the Fence. Every winter, Dad began planning ahead to the type of work he wanted us to do the following summer. "I think next year is going to be the Year of the Barn," he would say as he sat at the kitchen table in the middle of winter, hunched over an engineer's grid sheet, doing some drawings. He wasn't an engineer by trade, but he was pretty good at engineering a lot of things. "I have to get all the work out of you kids while we still have you around."

Mom never objected to the Year of the Fence, and she constantly brainstormed other ways to keep us busy. "You know I'd really like to have the house painted," she said one day. Sure enough, the next week Paul and I would be out painting the house. Adam was off in the Navy sailing around the South Pacific by this point, but he'd put in his time. Mom and Dad helped with the work, of course, but more as a means of instruction. We were being trained.

For the Year of the Fence, we built two miles of electric fence that Dad had specially designed. During the day, Dad was kept busy working his other job for "the government," so Paul and I were left on our own driving four wheelers and swimming in the river when he wasn't able to keep an eye on us. Dad had several jobs, so we always had plenty of time to play and work while he was gone. In between running a bioterrorism outfit for the government and starting his own consulting business, he had the farm and us boys (although secretly, I think he really wanted to be full-time Dad).

One section of the fence he'd designed was set to run two hundred feet in a straight line, then we'd set the corner post before building the next section. It was a simple design that would prominently feature rusted wire and bent steel t-posts every eight feet.

"You're still putting the damn posts in a crooked line," Dad hollered at us, as he adjusted the angle of one of our fence posts by bending it back and forth inside the earth. Paul and I had tried using a rope and marking it every eight feet, tying the end of the rope to the corner post to form a straightedge, but that wasn't precise enough.

"A good fence has to be straight." Dad shook his head and jumped in the truck and took off. Before we knew it, he was back with the deer hunting rifle and a tripod. "Now we'll get it straight."

Dad sighted the fence line with the scope and told us how far to move each post. We probably got some odd looks from the neighboring ranchers, but so did all of our farming methods. We still farmed with Great Grandpa Hanna's 1948 International tractor, even when our neighbors had new air-conditioned John Deeres. For us, it wasn't really about what we had, but whose we had. An old tractor owned by one of the Bohemians was going to win out every time. "You boys have to learn how to work like they did, because someday, you'll have to learn how to sacrifice like they did."

The year after we built the fence, we learned how to sacrifice like the Bohemians. Mom came home one day and was strangely quiet. *What's wrong, Mom?* She wouldn't tell us what it was until later, after dinner. We mostly sat in silence while we ate, picking at our plates until we learned the truth. She had lost her job. In a patient care dispute at the hospital, Mom argued on behalf of a patient, but in doing so, she ended up losing her job and we ultimately lost the farm.

Baker was an awfully lonely town when you were on the edge. Without Mom's work money as vice president, we couldn't afford to live in Baker and keep the farm. It was time to sacrifice, then. Mom and Dad decided it was more important to keep the Old Hanna Place, so they rented out the farm and moved one hundred and sixty-four miles away for new hospital jobs. Every few weeks, they would return to work on the farm, but it wasn't the same. The Dream had been deferred.

When they moved to their new house in West Richland, Washington, I was in my second year of college and I hated coming home for Thanksgiving. We had neighbors that were younger than eighty. We had sprinklers in the yard, green grass, and a suburban fence. We had a green trash bin where you were supposed to put your yard trimmings, and we even had a mailbox in front of the house. Something had gone horribly wrong. Dad called it the Tame House.

"Someday, hopefully within five years, we'll move back to the farm," he said, but usually after saying this he would fall asleep in his armchair, resigned to doing Sudoku puzzles to bide the time. He started making wine in the backyard to keep himself busy, but work was taking a lot out of him, and being away from the farm had already knocked the wind from his lungs. He started to eat a lot and get fat, at which point he began eating less and less. Just like I used to live every month looking forward to the one weekend I got to spend in Baker with Dad, Dad began living for the one weekend a month that he got to spend on the farm. Weekends were fleeting though, and his job as a neuroscience administrator at the hospital got harder and harder, and soon it became tough to cut away for a weekend here or a weekend there. Slowly one year turned into two, two into three, and soon enough, the Dream was further away than it had ever been before.

The death of a dream is much harder than the maddening, squealing birth that dreams are born into. When the Dream failed us, it didn't die, it just began to wither, and we would be finished the moment it shriveled up small enough to be forgotten. But one part, the secret part, still boiled in Dad's heart of a dream long unspoken. The farm hadn't been called the Home Place for nothing. Even though we might have temporarily lost the one in Baker, there was another Home Place, the original one, and he wasn't going to count it out just yet.

Before I left for Morocco, the whole family gathered together for a midday lunch. As was our tradition for special dinners, Carmen made *paella* in a big black pan and shrimp curled their whiskers over grains of yellow rice. Adán's girlfriend made a massive salad drenched in olive oil, vinegar, and hard-boiled eggs, and Asis opened the living room cupboard and pulled out two bottles of hard Spanish cider. All seven of us—two parents, two girlfriends, and three boys—gathered in the living room that wasn't quite large enough for all of us. We sat down regardless and ate, some of us on couches, others of us at the table. We weren't celebrating the fact that I was going to Morocco, in fact, I didn't even know what we were celebrating, it was just a fiesta for *cualquier razón*—who knew?—it didn't really matter, anyway. In Spain, you never needed a reason to eat and drink. When Asis popped the corks on the cider (some of the good stuff from the Galicía region), the dinner party became New Year's Eve for no apparent reason.

"Everyone in your travel group is ready for Morocco tomorrow?" Asis asked.

"Yep," I lied. "Everyone including myself."

"Just remember what I told you before," he said. "Stay in your group and don't leave the city. The center is always safe."

Growing up, Dad always sang the old hymn, *Abide with Me*, before my brothers and I went to sleep. He'd stand inside the door of our room and the light and chirpy sopranos of our young voices would find steadiness in the sweet tenor of his voice. That song and our dad were something we could count on, and the last sound I remember falling asleep to was the sound of Dad's voice. Every night we sang our song, and in the midst of a broken and blended family, we knew that we could abide in Him and our family. It was something that always drew us together. On nights when we were younger and when Adam and I slept in bunk beds and looked up at our ceiling of glow-in-the-dark sticker stars, Dad would come in and teach us about the strings of love.

"When you boys were small, I often tried to explain the invisible ties that bind our hearts forever across space and time. They're little strings that are designed to tie our lives together. When we move away from each other, when we have to leave for a long time and go somewhere, even for just a moment, the strings tug at our heart and pull at us until it hurts and until we cry. Love is like those little strings that tug us closer, pulling our hearts in and out of time, weaving inward in rhythm, towards each other and away. No matter where we are or what happens, they are always with us because we will always be together."

At church today in Spain we sang *Abide with Me* in Spanish, and although the lyrics were a bit different, I immediately recognized the song and it brought me back to that moment when I was a little boy looking forward to Dad coming to kiss me goodnight and sing to us. Like the ties that bound our hearts together across space and time, that song made the sun beat inside my heart. I couldn't help but remember singing that song when we were all safe and small in the house, singing it with Dad. I remembered when the light from the hall would filter in. When he'd lean over and whisper in our ears and say goodnight, his whole frame outlined in gold from the door's light, and when he'd finally shut the door and Adam and I would talk into the night. Under the faint green light of our glow-in-the-dark stars, we would dream, our eyelids would shut, and we'd slowly fall asleep. Those nights had been filled with so much tenderness and safety.

As the clock ticked toward midnight, I gathered my things and shouldered my bag. I turned off the light in my room and quietly said goodbye to Carmen and Asis in the living room. I walked the length of the shadowy hallway one last time and turned my key in the lock to shut the door. From now to the end, there would be no safety.

II

The Pact

WEEK 9

TANGIER, MOROCCO

AT MIDNIGHT, the outline of a ghost stood outside the Alicante bus station. In the drape of a shadowed silhouette and the glare of phosphorescent lights, a man with dark-greased hair hovered over two large suitcases. The suitcases had been taped and re-taped shut, the contents of which nearly spilled out through the few loose strands of gray that held the package together. Over the bags, the man stood with his arms crossed, waiting. Smoke pulsed out of his mouth like a whispered gun as he stood watch and shadows covered the rest of his form.

In the darkness the rest of the scene unfolded. Other than an old woman sitting on a bench wearing rusted glasses and a burka, the platform was silent. In front of the watchman sat a large bus that had turned vacant hours ago. The people inside it had filtered out and wandered into the streets, never to return again; the bus driver had abandoned it too and fallen asleep inside the station. Everywhere, there was the sound of faintly buzzing streetlights, eerily noticeable, but providing a murky din all the same; the place had a way of capturing the cold in open space. Other than the empty bus parked in *Plataforma Uno*, the other three raised cement landings were empty. If something went wrong, no one would be there to help.

I approached the station wearing a dark gray beanie that I'd borrowed from Asis junior and my jet-black coat. I wore pants that didn't fit and a shirt that sagged in places, trying my best to look like the man on the platform. Underneath my beanie, my hair was slicked and jumbled from bed-grease, and underneath my armpits was the last bit of deodorant that I would slather on. Slung across my shoulders, the Chinese backpack I'd bought hung limp and inside of it were just enough supplies to make it through the three-day weekend: a roll of toilet paper, a disposable toothbrush, a map of the Medina, and a change of clothes. I kept one hand on my Shenzhou backpack and the other in my pocket fingering my knife. As I approached the platform, the man standing in front of the bus remained motionless, his back turned to me like a monolith, and when the old woman sneezed and blew her nose, he didn't turn or flinch or look at her. Vapor peeled from his mouth and evaporated in the glare of the orange lights. I moved closer to the cement landing.

I stepped onto the platform and stood next to him, keeping my eyes trained forward before looking over. He had a cut above his eye, a scar of some sort, and the station lights caught his face at an odd angle and drew shadows across chiseled marks. He was missing both of his front teeth and the air from his words slithered through the gap. "You going to Morocco?" he hissed.

I paused and my breath began smoking in front of me, but there was no wind to hide the consonance. "Yes, if this is the bus."

"Well, it isn't."

As if on cue, a man swung out from behind the back of the bus. Disguised in shadow, I saw the outline of his movement before I saw him. When he stepped into the overhead light at the far end of the platform, he was holding two bags of gas-station snacks in his left hand, and I couldn't tell what was in his right. He had a ballcap on, a braided goatee, and two matching pigtails. He began walking toward us.

"Morocco, huh?" the man next to me said, as he turned and nodded to the man with the snacks.

"Morocco," I said. I moved my finger onto the blade release latch on my knife. "You from there?"

"Used to be. Before I moved here to be a dishwashing Moroccan. Now I can't even get a job doing that. What I need though," he began before glancing over at his friend and then back at me, "is some money." A husked voice grated through the gap in his teeth. "I'm looking for some work."

As the braided man began edging closer, the man next to me began talking faster. He was in Alicante without papers and without a job. If I knew of anything—any job—I should tell him. He had lived a hard life in Morocco and he deserved something for once, something other than trouble. He stopped and checked his watch. "You American?"

"Spanish."

"Your accent's French," he said.

When the words left his mouth, the man with the snacks reached us on the platform and now stood facing me. His braids were rough and course like rope, scented like fleas and tipped like a dripping candle. He looked like he should have been in a Middle Eastern metal band twenty years ago, except for the fact that he had brown hair and rough-cream skin. He handed a pack of snacks to his friend before pointing at me.

"You should meet my friend," said the man with the missing teeth. "Because you're going to need some help in Morocco. Don't worry, though, Aban can help you."

The braided man reached out his hand for a handshake and I took it. *Encantado.* His shirt stretched above his wrist when we shook hands. There were needle marks on his arms.

Aban reminded me of a man who'd tried to sell me cocaine on a Greyhound bus when I was sixteen. I'd taken the bus to visit my older brother and I ended up sitting next to a guy with needle marks up and down his arms. Clutched tight in his hand was a ten-dollar CD player that you could buy at the gas station, and over his head he wore the old Walkman-style headphones with the wire frame. Metal poured through the speakers as I tried to quietly read next to him, and he would stop and turn every so often and ask, "What you readin?" I would tell him and then he'd forget and ask again. "What you readin?"

Whenever the bus would pull into a new gas station every hundred miles or so, he would sit motionless in his seat and pull out a pack of hash and look at it longingly. Then when the bus would pull away from the pit stop, he'd stand up and sit back down. "Missed my chance to smoke," he'd tell me. "Can you believe that?" Then we'd go through the same routine at the next stop. "Dammit, missed my chance to smoke!"

That's what I was trying to get away from when the bus to Morocco pulled up at a quarter past midnight. I looked up and saw faces pressing themselves against rows of windows. Hot circles of breath clouded the glass, but dark eyes lit up like fireflies through the windows, watching us and watching our luggage even closer. The elderly woman got up from the bench and adjusted her burka on her head before moving to board the bus. As she neared the steps, the toothless man slid behind me and grabbed his suitcases and lifted them into the underbelly.

When he had finished loading the suitcases, he slapped his braided friend on the shoulder and whispered something in his ear.

"Where you going?" he asked me.

"Tangier." I turned to board the bus.

"If we don't meet again," the toothless guy called after me, "welcome to Morocco."

I released my grip on the knife in my pocket and moved to stand in line behind the old woman. The bus driver checked her ticket, nodded, then waved her on board. When he waved me into the bus, I stepped out of Spain and into the Middle East; the bus was full of dark haired, light-skinned Arabs. I found a window seat at the back and laid my head to rest. When I opened my eyes, Aban and his marked arms leaned over the seat next to me. "Hello there, amigo. It looks like we meet again."

For the next fourteen hours I tied the straps of my backpack to my feet so that Aban couldn't steal it from under me while I tried to sleep. I kept my fingers on the edge of my knife, even though I was barely awake. Every hour or so, I would wake to occasional headlights that seeped through stale curtains and the smell of congealed sweat that permeated the cloth seats of the bus. At 3:00 a.m. we stopped in Granada. Several weeks ago at the Alhambra I'd learned that Granada was a Moorish town, but I really hadn't seen much evidence other than a few Arabic teashops where you sat on cushions and smoked. When I walked behind the gas station to look for a restroom, I stumbled upon a tent with a TV in the corner that was transmitting the Moroccan news in Arabic. A group of four Moroccans huddled around the shopkeeper, speaking a language I didn't understand. I left the store and walked back outside. Trash littered against a chain link fence and wild cats sipped the last dregs from overturned beer cans, while people from the bus huddled under low trees and ate sandwiches from plastic bags. I went back into the bus and slept.

We arrived at the Spanish port of Algeciras sometime in the early morning. When I'd bought my bus ticket in Alicante, the ticket man had told me that roundtrip ferry tickets were included in the fare, but they were nowhere to be found. I asked Aban about it in Spanish and he said this was normal. "Just follow the people in front of you and they'll let you on the boat." Aban stepped in front of me and I followed him around the port security gates, up the stairs and onto a concrete lookout area similar to the waiting station in airports with sleek black seats and sterile overhead lights. The morning was quiet, although no one knew what was going on. That was normal for Moroccans, Aban told me. "No one ever knows what's going on."

The ferry was supposed to leave every half hour or so, but we hadn't seen a sign that said anything. I wandered downstairs in hopes of finding somewhere to buy a ticket. At the ticket kiosk, I was told to be patient; someone would come and show me how to get on the ferry.

By the time I returned, everyone in the waiting area was gone except for a line of five people holding tickets. One by one, they stood in line at the far end of the terminal as a security officer looked them up and down before letting them proceed through a narrow passageway. The line grew shorter and shorter and I began to frantically search the room. As I scanned the perimeter, I saw a Moroccan walk up to a counter and grab a white paper stub from a stack that was barely noticeable. He approached the security guard and handed it to him before disappearing. In like fashion, I stole a ticket from the stack, handed it to the guard, and was let onto the ferry. I didn't know how tickets would work on the return trip, but I boarded the boat and kept a firm grip on the deck railing. As bits of morning light began to fill the sky and light up the red Moroccan flag mounted to the back of the boat, I watched Spain move further and further away. Across the Strait of Gibraltar, we began drifting into the sunrise. I went into the compartment below to buy some cigarettes before tightening my grip on the railing.

"The first thing you'll learn is that the Moroccans are really friendly," Aban said. He had seen me leaning over the deck railing with my hands clasped over the edge and had walked over to say hello. "You're going to a great country."

As we talked on the railing and as the waves curled beneath us, Aban told me several important things about Morocco. The first thing I learned was that for his braided hair, braided goatee, and the five rings that jostled on his left hand, he didn't look like the typical Moroccan. The typical Moroccan was a harlot, a drug dealer, or worse. As we leaned over the side of the boat with the Moroccan flag beating into the wind behind us, I heard stories of villages in the mountains and cities in the basin. "I wish you could come to my mountain village with me," Aban said, "because then you could see something no one gets to see."

In his village, foreigners were loved and embraced as locals. You did pottery with the elders and ran barefoot with children in the street. You rode camels through the village and ate stew at night while watching the stars—at least that's what Aban liked to do. He hated the city. And that was also a subtle warning.

"Several things are going to happen to you all at once when you get off this boat," he said. "When you step into Tangier and they see that you're not a local, they will begin coming for you."

"Who's they?"

"The guides."

I thought I understood what the guides did. "Don't they just try to lead you around town and then rob you in an alley?"

"Not necessarily. They do all sorts of things and you never know when they're watching you. They're always watching you. You could be in the port or the meat market or the fish market and they'll be watching you.

All you have to do though, is say no when they offer to lead you around."

The guides were going to be forceful, he said. I told him about the prostitutes I'd run into in Germany and asked if they'd be like that.

"Well, they're not girls. Morocco is a country for men."

Over the railing, azure water glittered in the distance as Africa approached. Behind us and in front of us, the shoreline was visible, and a low, brown horizon appeared ever more steadily. I was expecting (perhaps wrongly) to see sand dunes, but instead low grassy hills offset by mountains bordered the water and low waves splashed and lapped against the boat. It was a wonderful, glorious morning, perhaps best captured by two Moroccans sitting on a white table laughing, pointing at mountains and other places further in the distance. Underneath black hair and black coats, I saw two friends pressing their hands against their foreheads and shielding their eyes from the sun while they stared directly into it. It was a moment of friendship and defiance. They sat alone at the back of the boat, surrounded by empty space and surrounded by the weight of the future. It was either going to be wonderful or it was going to be horrible.

I pulled my beanie down tighter over my head. We talked about many things on the ride over—the craftsman economy in the mountain villages, the trials of youth and the lack of jobs, how fathers often sold their daughters for forty camels if they were pretty or ten if they weren't, how the Moroccan king filled six private jets each year with guests for a government vacation on the country's dime, and how in the bartering market of the Medina you had to trust everyone even though no one was worth trusting—in all of it, it boiled down to one thing: this was a man's country. If you were a woman, you shut up, wore the burka, and made crafts or got sold for camels. But if you were a man, then you had to be one. Little boys didn't grow up in Morocco—there were no children. Maybe there were a few kids in Aban's mountain village, but life was still hard. You either took life or life took you.

When Aban and I snapped a picture together at the back of the ferry with the water boiling around us, his face was resolute and mine was framed into a smile. There was a hardness in his face while we talked, and I got the sense that if he could take back everything that had happened to him, he'd like to forget most of his life.

As it was, Aban was leaving Spain for good. He'd worked as a cook for six hundred euros a month for long enough, well below the poverty line, and he was going to go back to his mountain village, maybe this time he could make something out of nothing. He had to believe so anyways, he said, because Morocco was a country of big and broken dreams. He'd gone to Spain to try and change his fortunes, but without skills or schooling, he'd been unable to do so. He loved music and hated money. That was a bit of a problem in Spain.

The ferry began slowing down as we neared the harbor. From the top of the boat, we could see the whole city as it unfolded from the top of a rolled hill. Tangier was a white city, but it was a shade of white that had faded and stained with time. Over the passage of years, the original purity of the square-stoned buildings had been lost to a city where everything was always up for bargain, where anything could be bought or sold. I asked Aban one final question before we parted ways.

"What's going to happen when I get off this boat?"

"I don't know. But you need to go find a hotel room with bars in the window and a good lock on the door," Aban said. "That's the first thing you should do."

As we got off the ferry he reached out his hand and we shook hands like we had done fourteen hours earlier at the bus station. "My friend," he said, "I wish you the best of luck."

Instead of being swarmed by rough-necked guides like I had imagined, I was left off at the top of a ramp overlooking a massive parking lot filled with junkyard cars. From my view at the top, I saw a low rise of money exchange kiosks lining the far edge. Beyond that, the sun ripped across the sky, illuminating a walled hill in the distance filled with old houses. Before the hill, there was a massive white archway, and before the arch, the parking lot. I began weaving my way through the Fords and Fiats of twenty years ago. About halfway through the parking lot, a turquoise taxicab with a yellow stripe drove by and offered me a free tour of the city in English. I responded in Spanish. *Never talk in English*, Aban had told me on the boat. *They'll spot your American accent three kilometers away.*

Not only would the lowest price for anything increase by three hundred percent, but my life would also be in serious danger. "Besides the fact that I want to see you survive," he said, "I want to see you experience Morocco unfiltered by English."

When most people visited Morocco, Aban said, they went to Marrakesh and never saw the real Morocco. As far as I was concerned, the parking lot I crossed and the city I entered represented the Real Morocco. The parking lot ended at the white-stained archway that I'd seen earlier, marking the entrance to the city. I walked next to a line of dusty cars waiting to enter, and looked over and saw drivers hunched over the wheel. From their stereos came the sound of Arabic guitars in minor chords; the feeling was of turbans and Kasbahs, exotically familiar but tinged with a sense of danger and intrigue. I walked past the line of cars and handed my passport to the guard under the arch. He greeted me in French, *merci*, and I proceeded in.

The country opened up to a broken main avenue. Split in the middle by a strip of wild grass, a cracked pathway, and a thrush of wild palm trees, the Avenue d'Espagne was divided in two, very much like the country itself. On one side stood the red-bannered money exchange kiosks, cheap restaurants and souvenir shops with their sliding yellow signs. On the other side of the divide, the scent and glimmer of the Straight showed itself between buildings that were in use but that should have been abandoned long ago. Beyond and further in the distance, resort hotels looked fit for the king's visit. In between the money exchange kiosks and the worn-down houses, a rough strip of pavement and chunky grass divided the road and held the country together. Festering heat and people were everywhere. Burkas marked space in the crowd while men in black coats bartered and exchanged information. Old men in beige robes looked over their shoulders once or twice before diving into dumpsters to search for food scraps while gaunt dogs wandered the streets between white walls that bristled from years of misuse. The sun beat down upon gaping holes in the road, women and children sat in mud puddles behind broken-down vans, weeds shot up through cracks in the cement, stores were splattered with spilled sodas and broken bottles, flies hovered over rusted dumpsters, and produce rotted in restaurant windows. Ticket men selling ferry tickets to Spain were everywhere. With a passport and three hundred dirhams, a Moroccan could take the one-hour ferry to Europe and forget the dregs of their previous life. For the Moroccans that couldn't afford three hundred dirhams, a stock of paddleboats were hidden along the harbor. Come nighttime, they would be loaded with passengers trying to cross the Strait in search of a better life in Spain (where there was over twenty percent unemployment).

Spanish, then, became a very important language to know, and it gave me what little power I had. If I could do nothing else in Morocco, I would at least be able to talk to people, and I did so entirely in Spanish. I invented a persona, and I became Josef de España. There were some blondes in the Basque Country, maybe they would believe me.

I moved to the kiosk side of the road divide and people began following me with their eyes. "Hello friend!" someone called out in English. "I can show you around." Other voices lingered, and kids stared as I walked by their game of soccer in the middle of the street. A man in a robe waved at me. "*Amigo, ven conmigo.*" Come with me. I ignored him.

My first order of business was finding a place to stay that night. Aban had mentioned a street where all of the cheap hotels were located and I began making my way toward it. On the way I took several wrong turns and ended up in back-alleys where the concrete was crumbling and inaccessible to cars. Men working in metal shops stared at me and began to move toward me and I retraced my steps back to the main street. Wandering in the shadows of whitewashed buildings, I found the street of *pensiones* that Aban had pointed out. It curved up around a hill where each three-story building was a budget motel marked by a sign that draped over the road, a *pensión* designed for budget travelers. I toured several different pensions to get a sense of what to expect. One innkeeper showed me a room that was "very safe" and prominently featured an eye-level window and a door that didn't lock. Another innkeeper showed me a room that had mold spreading across the walls but that could be mine for a wink and forty dirhams (less than four dollars). The room I ultimately settled on had an innkeeper who spoke Spanish, a second story view with iron bars in the window, a porcelain hole in the ground for a toilet, a bed free of bedbugs, and a door that locked—all for eight dollars.

The innkeeper tried to get me to pay ten, but I told him that was too much. He had a thick head of coarse black hair and his defining features were a mustache, a blue polo shirt, and a long gold chain that he kept tucked underneath. It was obvious that he was a man of intent—he meant what he said, but that of course meant that he avoided saying a whole lot in the first place. The danger was always in the details. "Be back by nightfall," he said.

What he really meant became immediately apparent when I stepped outside the pension and began walking toward my Mecca, the medina. As I curved up a hill and passed a store selling knock-off flip-flops, the shopkeeper walked out of his store and tried to entice me inside. He had many things I needed, he informed me. I shook my head. *No, no gracias, estoy bien.* I passed a shoe store, a cheap belt shop and a vegetable stand, and at each one, watchful eyes followed my every move. On either side of me, blond tourists walked intermixed with dark-haired Moroccans, but there was one difference between them and myself. They traveled in groups.

I felt a bubble of space slowly collapse around me as robed men and young men with chains wrapped around their necks began to close ranks beside me. Dark eyes scanned me up and down, looking for bulges in my pockets. "*Amigo*," they said. "What are you looking for?" I kept walking and the air closed in with the smell of molded oranges and camel hair, the throb of tribal drums and oasis guitars. The closer I got to the medina, the more intense the crowd around me became. I was hailed by shopkeepers and men in long robes who I assumed were guides. "*Amigo, ven conmigo,*" they said, but I kept my thoughts in front of me and pulled my beanie further over my eyes, slitting them into a glare. A nearby man in a black coat probed my eyes and pockets for money. This obviously wasn't Aban's mountain village where kids walked barefoot through dusted streets. This was a land of big dreams and broken dreams, but where dreams were always suspect. If you had money, it could be easily taken. Because to get something, you had to be willing to use anything and anyone, including your own family. I watched a father send his five year old son after a group of tourists to lead them into his shop, and like any Moroccan, the boy would get his share of the commission, especially since he was already fluent in five languages other than his own. I made my way closer to the medina.

As I rounded a corner, the street opened up to a wide plaza that was heavily patrolled. Police whistled and hollered at foreigners while protecting the entrance to the medina, although they rarely entered. It wasn't their territory. All over the plaza, locals and foreigners looked on either side of them twice or three times and walked with narrowed eyes. We were being watched and the weight of an unspoken contract hung in the air. The cops would do their job outside the medina, and inside, someone else would take care of business.

In the center of the plaza, sunlight beat upon a cracked stone fountain. Water flowed through the broken granite and spilled onto the stone below, before seeping into the sand where it was swallowed whole. Across the expanse of people and palm trees, a keyhole was cut into the wall. Next to the keyhole, a map from long ago had been drawn onto white stone. Etched in black, it marked the beginning and end of the medina. Walls four feet thick kept police out and thieves in, and although I couldn't see much through the keyhole, it beckoned me to enter. As I made my way toward it, something began to happen behind the scenes that I wouldn't realize until much later in the afternoon.

Sitting under a red tea tent near the entrance to the medina and shielded from the sun and public eye, a group of old men with hats and turbans studied passersby and whispered to one another in hushed tones. Their eyes followed the arms of Spaniards carrying shopping bags, the wrists of a Brit taking a picture of the arch, and the breasts of two Japanese women who wandered carelessly through the crowd. As each tourist passed in front of the tent and entered the medina, a puff of smoke would seep out from under the shadows as they whispered to each other without turning their necks. The police never entered the red tea tent. When a tourist would pass by the front of the tent to enter the medina, one of the men from the table would quietly get up and disappear into the crowd behind them and follow them into the medina. Several more minutes would go by, then another whisper, and another man would disappear just as another reappeared. As I moved closer to the entrance of the medina, the men in the tent began to whisper without craning their necks, and from within the shadows of the tent, an old man in a red sweater was dispatched. I proceeded into the medina.

Color dazzled and burst as I entered. Bright colors met my eyes from every angle—scarlet cloth on winter garments, yellow-painted hand signs, purple tents, and green produce on vegetable carts. Aromas spiced the market's murmur as incense and jasmine for sale juxtaposed with the odor of a man leading his goat through the crowd. On every side, voices rose around me, engaged in haggling and bartering under canopies pitched on the side of the road. You could buy anything in the medina, anything from a woman to an embroidered rug, and one was often traded for the other. In a city where everything was suspect and everything was up for purchase, the only question was price.

I became the price. At once I was beset by the guides I'd heard so much about. A white robed man approached me from the right, his face buried in his hood. "Friend, you can trust me." On my left, a man in a brown robe gargled a hello before grabbing my shoulder and trying to lead me off the street. As soon as I said no to them, two more men appeared in front of me, one in a striped robe, another in a black hat. Our short conversation went like this.

"Do you need us to show you around?"

"No."

"Of course you do."

"No, I don't."

"Then you want some trouble?"

Usually at that point in the conversation I would reach into my coat pocket for my buried knife and turn away. They would swear and yell at me and tell me that I'd be sorry. Maybe I would, I didn't really know. All I knew was that as soon as I said no to one guide, two more appeared and by the time I had made it one hundred feet into the medina I was beset on all sides and scared for my life. "You'll be sorry, amigo," one guide said. "*Te jodes.*"

As I turned around and retraced my steps back to the entrance with guides threatening me on all sides, I realized one thing. They were right.

*   *   *

I escaped to the fish market. The smell of stale blood and the faces of gutted fish looked up at me, but offered little solace. I struck up a conversation with a bearded vendor in a blood-flaked apron, but after a few questions, he figured out that I wasn't going to buy anything so he began talking to someone else.

The smell of dead fish swirled and froze in the air as I stood in the corner of the market looking down at a marlin engulfed in a tub of ice. Somewhere in the tub, I lost my gaze and found consul in the sight of congealed water. It was so beautiful, so frozen. The heat and the medina—at once it was too much and I was scared for my life. What if the guides were right and they really did come to hunt you down? Alone in Morocco, I didn't stand a chance, and the trip was starting to feel worse by the minute.

As I stared long and hard into the marlin ice, an old man in a red sweatshirt began working his way through the fish market.

"Aí, me odio a los españoles," Carmen ranted. "I hate our neighbors and I'd do anything to have the people in Morocco back!" A week ago, we had stepped out of the elevator in our apartment building and she was fuming. That afternoon, one of the neighbors had ridden the elevator with us and had barely given Carmen an *hola*. That did it. We stood in awkward silence as the culprit, a neighbor with an ugly perm, glazed her eyes across the elevator floor as we slowly climbed one, two, three floors before the doors opened and the neighbor turned heel without saying *ciao*. Carmen had been a member of the apartment's social committee for years and she hated people like this. "The people in Alicante aren't nice like they are in Morocco," Carmen said as we entered the apartment carrying shopping bags. "When you get to Morocco, Estif, you'll realize one thing. The people there are really friendly and anyone will come up to you and invite you to tea. When they do, make sure you say yes."

The door to the house closed behind us as we passed into the shadowy hallway. Further still and somewhere far away, it would be teatime.

* * *

When I turned around in the fish market, an old man in a red sweatshirt began walking down the aisle next to me. "The fish are sure fresh, aren't they?"

In the low light of the fish market, the dampness barely illuminated his face and I saw a dimly lit figure begin working his way toward me, slowly, perhaps deliberately. I saw him lean an arm against the wall as he helped himself down a hobbled stairway. Shots of white hair pecked a rim around his head that was decorated by a red beanie that matched his sweater. He carried nothing in his hands.

There was something about the man, the way he carried himself and walked straight and deliberately, even at old age. He was the only elderly man in the fish market and he moved quicker than everyone else, almost like an acrobat, even as his body clung to the walls and stone shadows for support. There was a sense of deception about him, as if he was trying to hide something, but as soon as he stepped into the light it was gone.

In the main light, the old man became a larger version of himself. There was a bright whiteness to his face, and the stubbed outline of his beard wrapped itself neatly around his smile. I saw him joke and banter with vendors as he made his way down the aisle. He was clearly headed my direction and he looked like he could have been a thinner version of my grandpa. "You looking for some fish?"

I was glad to hear his voice.

When he reached the bottom of the stairs, the rest of his bearing entered the room. He was old, that much was certain, perhaps sixty-five, but there was an odd warmth to his face. He moved to stand next to a trout display and motioned his arm over it. "In Morocco, we have almost as many beautiful fish as we do women." He winked.

I agreed.

He put his hand into the display and rifled it through the ice before holding it up in front of him and wringing it out. "It's cold in here."

I nodded and put my hands in my pockets. "So what do you do?" I asked in Spanish.

"I run a pharmacy," he said. "But my friends, they run a tea shop." For a moment his words hung in the air, almost foreboding, but he brushed them aside. "What about you, amigo? Is this your first time in Morocco?"

"No," I lied. "My parents used to live here."

"Really," he said. "Where?"

"Rabat," I said. "You know the place?"

"I know many places." He reached out to shake my hand. "But let's talk about that over tea."

Without thinking, I said yes and shook his hand. "*Soy Josef*," I said, using my new persona. "Good to meet you."

"*Encantado*," the old man said. We shook hands, but he never told me his name. "Follow me."

A red flag went off in my head, but I ignored it. I had nothing else to do and no one else to talk to. I may have been following a complete stranger, but he hadn't offered to lead me astray, and after all, Carmen had said this would happen. Someone would ask me to tea and I would say yes. We left the fish market.

"Morocco you'll learn, is a wonderful country," said the old man. "There are so many nice people. In Morocco, we go to tea with anyone. It's not like that your country—Spain."

"No, it's not," I said. "But I heard from my parents that Morocco was like that—really friendly."

"Then they told you that we love tea?"

"They did."

"Good," he said. "Because I'm interested in talking more."

The old man led me back into the plaza outside the medina and gestured toward the red tea tent. "I would like to introduce you to my friends and their tea shop. They have a wonderful tea shop." From the sunlit plaza, the tent appeared heavily shaded and I could see a group of old men huddled around a table taking long drags from pipes. He gestured toward the entrance stakes and I followed him in.

Smoke brushed my eyes and faded into the air as a group of older men held pipes between yellowed teeth and sat around wooden tables on folding chairs. "My friends," the older man said, "I want you to meet our new friend, Josef, from Spain." Immediately conversations halted in Arabic and resumed in Spanish as the group of men rose one by one to shake my hand, before sitting back down to watch the plaza. As we made small talk, their eyes moved in lines behind me, watching people move in the plaza. Every so often as someone passed underneath the arch they would stop talking in Spanish and whisper to each other in Arabic. They never took their eyes off the plaza and never craned their necks, but sat almost entirely motionless, blowing smoke. "Let me get you something to drink," the old man said, before disappearing further into the tent and leaving me in the midst of his bearded friends.

A probing series of questions followed in his absence. What was I doing in Morocco? Why Tangier? Was I alone? I created a response for every question they asked, but my sense of suspicion increased. Of course I wasn't alone, I told them. My friend Eder and I were visiting Morocco and we would be meeting up soon in the plaza. We loved Morocco, I said, but we really would have to get going soon. "But you'll join us for tea, of course," they said, and motioned to stand as if they were insulted.

"Of course," I said. They relaxed back into their seats and resumed smoking.

When the old man returned with our tea, it looked like a combination of spinach and marijuana shoved into a steaming glass. I was a little worried. Here was an uncommonly nice stranger. I didn't know his name, and he was giving me a free drink from his friends' shop. Should I turn down the drink? And if I turned down the drink, what then? In Arabic culture, I obviously couldn't refuse it—that would be a slap in the face to my host and all of his friends, and perhaps that would be more dangerous than actually drinking the tea. Which is why, I think, he gave me the tea. I had to drink it. *Bébelo* they said. I drank it.

"It's good, isn't it?" the old man asked.

"It's good."

From under the shaded promenade of the tent and a cloth chair, the keyhole arch of the medina beckoned from across the plaza as the old man sat down next to me. His skin wasn't too dark, but it was dark enough to be weathered by the sand, dark enough so that when he squinted, his eyes seemed to get lost in his brow, folding into the total effect. He squinted a lot and when he looked at you, it was as if he was staring straight into the sun; you couldn't tell what he saw in you. I turned away from his gaze and continued watching the plaza.

Palm trees shaded the cracked fountain of water, and although grass grew unhindered across sections of the plaza, the whole effect was of a dusty, metallic day, almost as if you were in a mechanic's shop looking out through the dust and grease that had accumulated in the heat of the summer. It was a country where the postcards show pictures of white-robed people riding camels through sand dunes in the desert. While there weren't any sand dunes in Tangier, it felt like there were. The Moroccans guarded their skin from sun and sand.

The plaza was filled with people, and the ones that stood out were the women in burkas, the priests in beige robes, an American in a Steelers sweatshirt, and a group of Spaniards wearing aviators. My faithful observer didn't notice the women or the priests, but he saw the Brits, the Frenchmen, the girls from Tokyo, and the same group of Spaniards.

"Look at all those Spaniards from your country, buying all that stuff," he said, pointing to the Spaniards leaving the medina with plastic shopping bags. "They must have come from Market." Or he would point to another group of people, "Those Brits are so easy to spot, look at the way he walks and how he takes pictures of everything. My friends and I, we know all sorts of stuff. We just wait for someone like you to ask about it." So I did.

"When I'm not running my pharmacy shop, I sit here with my friends and we watch the city move. And we talk. We like meeting new people and showing them our country. We're Moroccans, of course, so we want to be friendly. That's important."

Every Friday, he told me, was Market Day when people from the mountain villages rode camels into town to buy goods that would last them through the coming week. It was a most interesting day for sightseeing, he said. "Do you want to go to Market?"

As I leaned back in my seat, his suggestion increased my suspicion. Was he a guide? I'd already run into several of them, but he seemed different. In Morocco, however, motive often masked intent, and he could be anyone. I'd heard about the infamous *guías* of Tangier that would show people around the medina and then rob them at the end of the "tour" that usually included stops at stores their friends owned (he'd already mentioned how he had a friend who owned an herbal shop). If the old man sitting next to me was one of those guides, I didn't want to go to Market with him, or whatever that was.

I told him that I had to meet my friend Eder soon, so he let the matter drop. I began to trust him a little bit more.

We resumed talking about regular stuff and mountain villages, international travel and North African customs, and he told me again how nice the people in Morocco were. They were so nice, *gente muy simpática*. He asked me if I wanted another glass of tea. We continued drinking.

We resumed talking about everything and nothing and he explained the history of Tangier and the history of the medina. Tangier was a wonderful city, he assured me, and the Medina was a wonderful place, even as the mouths of his friends whispered to each other in Arabic, their eyes swinging back and forth across the plaza, hunting for something.

After more conversation and a pause, we finished our tea and relaxed again to the view of the plaza. Half an hour after he'd first suggested we go to Market, he made the suggestion again. "Do you want to go to Market?"

Again I told him I had to leave soon and he switched topics to the history of the craftsman in Morocco. A craftsman was both a welder and a wielder, I was told. A master of both, he answered to none. "The spirit of the craftsman is still alive in Morocco, but you'll have to go to Market to see it for yourself."

Red flags went off in my head when he mentioned going to the medina again, but after an hour or so of talking, I thought he was just a friendly old man. To be safe, I again lied about having to meet Eder in fifteen minutes.

"We can be back here in fifteen minutes if you want to go," he suggested. "What do you say?"

What was there to lose? I said yes.

When I gave him my answer, his face brightened and he looked at me as if he was squinting into the sun, studying my whole being. "We'll go and see my friend at his herbal shop. He loves talking Spanish and meeting Spaniards."

"I only have fifteen minutes," I reminded him.

"Of course."

He got up from his chair and began walking toward the white keyhole entrance. As I walked next to him through the arch, something was noticeably different this time around. Instead of looking like they wanted to rob me, the Moroccans began to smile in passing and they bowed their heads at the old man. This time around, no one hassled us and none of the guides approached me. We stopped to talk to several of the old man's friends and all of them asked about me. "This is my friend, Josef," the old man would say, as we stopped and talked to random people every fifty feet or so. They would nod and smile and say hello. "Josef is such a nice man."

The streets became less crowded as we began moving deeper into the medina. Wide avenues became claustrophobic as alleys clung to each other, twisting and turning. Shops began to give way to houses and broken windows as we moved deeper into the labyrinth. The noise from the bazaar began to die down and the sound of our footsteps echoed across flaking walls. As we moved farther and farther towards the Kasbah at medina's end, I became the only non-Moroccan. The old man began walking faster and making more turns. One street began to look like the next and soon enough I had no sense of where we were anymore. "I have to meet Eder in five minutes," I said. "We need to leave now."

"But I want to introduce you to my friend," the old man said. "It will only take a moment. He has a wonderful herbal shop."

Halfway down a deserted alley in the heart of the medina, we stood in front of an open door. From the street, the opening appeared ready to swallow me; it was dark inside. I checked my watch. Twenty minutes had passed beyond our fifteen minute agreement. He suggested that I go into the store, but I told him that I wasn't interested in herbs.

"Of course you're interested in herbs," he said, and moved to block the way in front of me. "Come on, let's go." A scimitar crossed his lips and he waved me into the dimly lit store. Musked in shadows and cloaked in the scent of sandalwood, the room had a tough, masculine floor that quarried over dirt. Other than the light from two small windows above the entrance, it was nearly dark.

The old man nudged me into the store and brought me to the center of the room where an old wooden table stood at chest level. The table that had been cut in places, and above it, a light bulb hung suspended from a rusty chain, but remained unlit. The chain hung still over the table, ready to shrivel its rust and strike. Dust rose from the floor with our footsteps, and I noticed that along the walls of the room, glass jars had been capped and stacked like specimens, covering most of the boarded space. When we reached the table, the old man turned around and retraced his steps to stand in front of the entrance. He crossed his arms to block my escape. The scimitar I'd seen earlier danced across his face, and on the other side of me, the rusty chain hung suspended over the table. It was a trap.

The light from the small windows above the door blasted onto the floor in front of me, splicing into my eyes. When I reached up to shield them, I saw the outlines of two figures begin to move. Behind a bare countertop that sat beneath the windows, two thugs looked at me from across the room. One was tall and rippled with muscle; the other was shorter and thicker across the chest. The larger of the two Moroccans, probably six foot four, moved into the light that broke across his face to reveal a bone-set jaw and rattlesnake eyes. Dressed in a plain white shirt that was stained in places, he began to advance towards the circular table and the rusty chain as if to beckon me. There were herbs and soaps on the table and he took one in his hands and examined it.

"Do you know what this is?" he asked.

I didn't know, so I remained silent.

"It's jasmine." His eyes locked mine in place as he turned the block of white jasmine deliberately in his hands. "Do you know what we use this for?"

The other thug stepped out from behind the counter and moved towards where we were standing at the table. Dust rose with his footsteps and smoked into the light as the old man held guard at the door.

"Stop," the taller thug commanded the other, as he looked over his shoulder and set down the piece of jasmine he was turning. "I'll handle this." He turned back to me and again held up the block of jasmine. "Do you know what we use this for?"

I couldn't answer right away, because I began thinking frantically. How had I fallen for this? I couldn't escape until they got what they wanted—my money or my life. I wasn't going to give up easily, and I had one advantage. I knew this was a game, and maybe if I play-acted, I would be able to find a way out. My life was worth the gamble. "That jasmine looks interesting," I replied and surprised him by reaching to take it from his hand. "Tell me about it."

The thug let me take it from him and I rolled it in my hand as he had done, fascinated by what I saw. "Do you use this like perfume?"

"No. We use sandalwood." He stepped around the table and led me to the wall of jars. We spent the next ten minutes going around the walls of the store opening and closing jars, examining different herbal soaps and I began to feign interest. *Lily—fascinating. How do you use it?* I didn't even wait for him to start the bargaining process, I beat him to it and placed two things that looked the cheapest in the center of the table under the rusty chain. "Five dirhams."

He clenched his jaw tight. "Those are worth a lot more than that. One hundred and twenty."

I didn't have anything close to one hundred and twenty dirhams to give away. "Sixty."

"One hundred, no less." He paced around his side of the circular table and ran his hands through the cuts in the table. Between us, the chain and the unlit light hung ominously, as if he would use them against me.

"Sixty and two packs of cigarettes."

He immediately stopped running his hand across the table and paused at my suggestion. I had touched a nerve: foreigners weren't supposed to know the secret about cigarettes and bargaining. He could have strangled me if he wanted to, but by suggesting cigarettes, I had gained the upper hand. I knew the secret.

"If you have four packs of cigarettes, it's a deal," he said, and pushed my items together, wrapping the tiny piece of broken jasmine in a plastic bag.

I reached into my coat pocket and pulled out four packs of cigarettes that I'd bought on the ferry ride over and handed them to him. After examining the Marlboros, he turned and nodded to the guide at the door, who stepped aside and waved his hand. I was free to go; they weren't going to ransom me.

Three months ago, Asis' friends had been in the exact same situation and ended up being held hostage for three months. A guide led them into a store to buy something and that was the last the world heard of them. That was what should have happened to me. Other people had died standing in front of the table with the chain, but somehow, I had survived.

It's hard to pinpoint a single reason why I survived and they didn't. I believe I made it out of the hornet's nest because of one man's offhand comment in the Alicante bus station. When the ticket master saw that I was about to buy a bus ticket to Morocco all by myself, he told me to buy cigarettes and use them like money. He told me that when the standard of money changed from coins to necessity, a new currency emerged in the form of Marlboros, and whoever knew this secret would increase their bargaining power. I had learned the secret to Moroccan bargaining, but I wouldn't stop using it just yet.

When we left the shop, the old man in the red sweater wanted to lead me further into the medina. "My friends in the herbal shop really liked you. I want to introduce you to another friend in my pharmacy shop."

I didn't want to meet any more of his friends, so I pointed to my watch and began walking back down the alley the way we had come. "We're late," I said. "I have to meet Eder. Now."

"Wait, amigo," he called after me. "Let me lead you back."

For some reason or another, he offered no more deception and led me back to the red tea tent. "Now a tip for your wonderful guide."

"I never asked you to lead me around town."

"Come on." He held out a hand in front of him as his friends in the tea tent studied my every move. I coughed up ten dirhams, but he threw it back at me in disgust and said I needed to give him more money. When I gave him twenty, he said it still wasn't enough, so I gave him a pack of cigarettes and left him standing in the middle of the plaza. He yelled over my shoulder as I walked away, but didn't give chase. He didn't need to, because later that night, someone else would follow.

The second extortion happened Friday night after dark on a walk back to my pension. I was wearing my beanie and signature Moroccan murder look when a guy walking next to me gave me a random compliment. I turned to him and said something in Spanish and he swung in closer to me.

The first thing I thought was that he talked and looked like he was an eighteen year-old guy from Columbia. His Spanish was as spotless as his white hoodie and as slick as his gelled hair, which seemed out of place in the plain, rougher styles of Morocco. Since he had spotless sneakers, he must have been a foreigner. He told me that he was visiting from Brazil, so we began a conversation about travel and life in South America.

On a boulevard by the sea that streamed with waves and people, we stopped to sit at a bench and continue talking. In the dark, that was a mistake.

Twenty feet away from us, Moroccan families took evening strolls as the guy from Brazil suddenly told me that he was dying of hunger and hadn't eaten in three days.

"I'm hungry," he said as he reached his arm over the back of the bench and over my shoulder. "I just need a little bit of money."

I leaned forward on the bench to escape his grasp. After seeing three people in the span of half an hour dig through garbage cans looking for food, I was slightly inclined to believe him. *Can you give me some money?* didn't look like a question, it looked like a dagger.

My eyes studied the road in front of us. Parents were walking their kids home and old people were out for late walks on the beach. From all I knew, it was just another night in Tangier. "Look, I don't have any money."

"Then you don't get it!" He threw his arms down on his lap and bored his eyes into mine, trying to coerce me. "You don't know what it's like to starve of hunger, to have your stomach devour you from within. If you knew what it was like to live like I have to … you would help me. Now."

Twenty feet away from us, Moroccan eyes wandered over our bench and toward the ocean.

"You don't need food," I said. "You need cigarettes."

"That's not worth anything," he said. "What else you got?"

"Nothing." I pulled out another pack of cigarettes and threw them at him. "Sell these and get your money."

As he ran his fingers along the plastic wrapping, I stood up from the bench and put my hands in my pockets. Without looking back, I walked off into the night and joined the people walking on the street. Behind me, all I could see were his spotless white sneakers weaving through the crowd and appearing and disappearing into the night.

When I got back to my pension, I fell to my knees in prayer. *Father, if tomorrow is like this, I don't know how I can make it through.*

As always, He would send an answer.

When I walked into the downstairs lobby of my pension the following morning, I found a group of ten New Zealanders. Dressed in Quicksilver hats and aviators, their long hair curled around the brims of their caps. "Have you been here before?" they asked. "We need someone to show us around."

When they invited me to join their group, something immediately changed in Morocco. Morocco changed. Almost immediately, we were welcomed into shops. Waiters treated us nicely. Only a few guides approached, but with ten of us, we had the power to tell them no.

When I told the group what had happened yesterday in the medina, they immediately wanted to see it for themselves. Since things had been different traveling with them, I agreed to lead them in. We passed the red tea tent and entered the medina with one goal. We were going to go further than I'd gone yesterday. We were going to find the Kasbah, an old military fortress that sat at medina's end. Boldly we set forth, and I was reminded of the words of my guide from yesterday.

"Look at all those tourists," he had said while we were drinking tea in the red tea tent. "They're so stupid. They have no idea where they're going."

After he had led me astray yesterday, I had gone back to my room and studied the map of Tangier. I was not going to be misled again.

As the group of New Zealanders and I neared the Kasbah, one of the guides pulled us aside and said that our destination was in the opposite direction. "I'll take you to the Kasbah," he told us as he tried to lead us in the opposite direction. "Come on."

Since I had studied the map beforehand, I knew that he was trying to deceive us—the walls of the Kasbah were two blocks in front of us. "He's lying," I told the group, and we strode straight into the Kasbah in full view of the false guide. He wasn't the only one we caught trying to deceive us.

During our journey to the Kasbah, the New Zealanders and I encountered an old friend—my guide with the red sweater from yesterday. In a crowd of mostly beige robes, I spotted his red sweater in the middle of the street as he held up a box filled with fake sunglasses, trying to sell them to tourists. When we made eye contact, his expression dropped back a bit. Yesterday he'd claimed to own a pharmacy, but today he was out selling counterfeit sunglasses in the middle of the street. His yellow teeth turned ugly in the light. *"Hola amigo,"* he called out. *¿Cómo estás?"*

When the New Zealanders walked by, he asked them if they wanted to buy any sunglasses. They said no, of course, but right behind us my old guide found a willing buyer. A Swedish girl was wandering through the medina by herself. As soon as she said hello, he began leading her off the street.

"I wish our neighbors were more like people in Morocco," Carmen said before I left. *"Uff, los alicantinos."* She swept the floor as she said this, her eyes trained on dirt specks that vanished into the dustpan with each stroke. "Our neighbors never ask us to do anything." She kept sweeping and remained silent. It was a sober thing to say, really. Even though Carmen had stared down the barrel of a police officer's gun while living in Morocco, she still loved the people there. "Sometimes they don't know any better. They either love you or hate you, but at least they express something. There's always life in that."

When Carmen and Asis had lived in Morocco, they had seen the vibrant, lovely side of people. *"Los marruecos* are open and friendly and anyone will invite you to tea," Carmen had famously boasted. She was right about that. The criminals sure would. How had I missed all of the wonderful people she had encountered in Morocco, people who came up to you for random conversations without ulterior motives? It turned out that I just hadn't met them yet.

When I finally met them later in the trip, they were not who I expected them to be. They were a taxi driver who spoke only Arabic, for whom I had to draw a picture of a camel for him to understand that I wanted to ride camels. They were the three camel owners who sat on shards of broken pots while tending a dying fire within view of the ocean and smoking hash. After they let me ride their camels, they invited me to spend part of the afternoon talking with them, nothing more. When you're lonely and being taken advantage of across the world, that's something that stays with you. There was no backdoor deal with these folks, no game of deception, no market place haggling, no squinted eyes-in-the-sun looks, no sunglasses to hide intent. When the camel owners invited me to come sit with them and "just talk," that was what I'd been waiting for, and strangely, that was what Morocco was known for.

At the end of my last full day at just around sunset, an old man approached me at the end of a broken pier "just to say hello." We talked for an hour and he didn't invite me to tea. As time marked the end of the day, the light was just right and his voice was just soft enough. In between the interplay of our words in French and Spanish, what I'd been looking for began to appear.

At the end of the last pier on the harbor, the horizon was burning. Standing in front of the Strait of Gibraltar that faded into mid-light flames, my Moroccan friend looked out across open waters as his kofi tilted across his forehead. The sun glinted off his face and in one glimpse he held both Europe and Africa in his eyes and the connection was close but distant. In the mellowing light, Spain appeared through the mid-February sun-haze that dusted across a sanded sky in the middle of winter.

Light filled the air at the end of the broken pier. There was nothing left here, nothing more to see. White clouds drew shadows across tumbled rocks inlaid like tiles. It was a raised and leveled form of disorder that calmed with the unbroken seashore, decorated with the footprints of kids playing soccer. In between all of it, I stood next to a man I'd known for five minutes. Above us, the descending sun transmitted the essential part and its dying fade looked like Apollo had just landed. I couldn't speak French and he couldn't speak Spanish, but here we were, underneath airplanes and in front of white-sanded beaches, here at the end of the pier, talking like this was normal. On that pier, my journey through Morocco and Europe began to take on a life of its own.

In the previous weeks, something strange had begun to happen. I had come to Spain to watch the horizon burn. I had come to stand under a table with a rusty chain and nearly get killed. I had come to sit at the edge of a pier and hang my legs over the edge and laugh at death, but I had also come for something deeper. I had come for a quest. And now that I had been brought to the edge, now that I had lived to tell of it, I began to feel that maybe it wasn't quite enough. If I ever made it back, I would return with stories worth telling, but those stories would never be dreams. Straddled between two continents, I began to dream.

The old man and I walked side-by-side down the pier as the horizon rolled behind us in wandering flames. Next to the old man, I kept my hands quietly clasped behind my back, almost in meditation. The wind whispered into my ear and sand drove into my face, hard. Spain loomed behind in the now-darkening sky, and in the echoes of our parting words, the old man smiled at me until his face burst in sadness under his kofi. That afternoon, he had needed someone to talk to. "Thank you," he said. "It's been a pleasure."

Somewhere indiscernible, somewhere off in the fading light, somewhere where it didn't quite make sense, there was a purpose for all of these hard lessons and all these hard times.

It wasn't over yet.

Six hours before I was supposed to leave, I reached into my pocket for my ticket home and it was gone. I didn't know if it had been lost or stolen, but I had my suspicions in Morocco.

In light of the circumstances, I figured it made sense to go to the bus company's local office where they would be able to look up my purchase in their database. Then they would print me a new ticket and I would go back to Spain. When I went to the bus company's office, however, a dose of reality struck. There were no computers in Morocco, at least not at this company. I wandered back into the street.

My next stop was the Moroccan Port Authority, but they didn't have any Spanish or English-speaking workers. I tried visiting the police to report a theft, but they didn't speak any of the tourist languages. Even the tourist companies were no help since they only spoke French and Arabic. This was surprising because in the medina, even little kids could speak four or five languages. But since languages were the key to tourist money, it made sense that the guides were fluent.

In true Moroccan spirit, an old man overheard me trying to talk to one of the ticket salesmen in Spanish and came over to help translate. The man turned out to be a broker at the port, and announced that he was going to make me a special offer. He couldn't believe that someone had stolen my ticket. "Now what kind of Moroccan would do that?"

With his help I was able to get a ticket for sixty euros, "a really good price," he assured me (twice what I had paid in Spain). He claimed that it was refundable upon arrival, but I never received a refund. He sent me off at once to catch the ferry.

I began walking towards the port to catch my ride back, but this was Morocco, it couldn't be that easy. Although I had my bus ticket home, I now had to track down my ferry ticket from an unknown man at the port. "Sa'id has your ferry ticket," the broker said. "Just show him your receipt and he'll give it to you."

"How do I find Sa'id?"

"Don't worry about that. He'll take care of finding you."

If someone would have said, *this is right out of a thriller movie*, I would have believed them. Sa'id was supposedly waiting for me outside a coffee shop. As I made my way through a half-empty parking lot, a man I'd never seen before had already received intelligence about me from a runner. From across the parking lot, he began to make his way toward me in all-black biker's leather and slicked-back hair. With every movement, the silver zippers on his jacket dangled and clanged against each other. When we met in the middle of the lot next to a broken Cadillac, he reached into one of his zippered pockets and took out a folded magazine. Instead of giving me a ticket, he tore off a one-inch strip of what was once an advertisement and handed it to me. "This shows that I took your receipt," he said as he pulled my ferry receipt out of my hand, taking the only evidence that I had bought a ticket. The piece of magazine he gave me in return was unmarked.

"How is this a ticket?" I said.

"Don't worry about that," he said. "I'm looking out for you." He motioned for a runner. "Take him to the waiting area."

Sa'id's man took me to the waiting area for the ferry, which turned out to be his friend's coffee shop. "You're encouraged to buy something," the runner told me. It looked like Sa'id would be getting a cut of the profits. "Wait here for two hours, then Sa'id will bring you your real ticket," the middleman said in Spanish before leaving. Whenever they spoke your language, there was cause for concern.

I sat down at a table with a Muslim couple from Barcelona who were also headed back to Spain. "Are these tickets normal?" I asked and showed them my piece of torn magazine.

"Relax," they told me. "This is normal. We just have to wait."

I asked to see their ferry tickets and they showed me similar one-inch magazine strips. If what the runner said was correct, then Sa'id would be back in two hours. The ferry was supposed to leave in an hour and a half.

Sa'id returned in an hour and a half without tickets. "Just be patient," he said before disappearing again. Moments later, I watched the ferry I was supposed to board sail away. The couple sitting next to me was also supposed to be on the ferry, but they reminded me that this was normal. "*Tranquilo.*"

An hour later Sa'id returned with actual tickets, but he gave them to other people who had been waiting longer than us. "*Tranquilo,*" he told us. "Your turn will come soon."

After waiting three hours, the couple from Barcelona was furious and decided to take matters into their own hands. "Come with us," they said and motioned for me to follow. "Otherwise, you're on your own." Announcements blasted through the loudspeakers in Arabic and French and I couldn't understand a thing. We approached the security counter.

The husband spoke with several of the port officials, who told us that we would be able to ride the next ferry without real tickets. I wasn't sure if money had changed hands during their conversation or not, but half an hour later, we were on our way to Spain.

*   *   *

Of course, it couldn't be that easy to get home. Once we arrived in Spain, the seven o'clock bus wasn't there, but we were told that it would arrive on the next ferry "within the hour." In all, sixty of us waited for the next ferry—fifty-nine Moroccans and myself. The other Spaniards had learned that it was smarter to fly to Morocco and avoid this whole mess, but since I hadn't learned that yet, I sat on a bench outside the one-story building in front of a chain link fence. In the space cut by darkness and illuminated by hazy streetlights, I looked between the holes in the fence and across restless water. There was no sign of the ferry.

At eight o'clock the Spanish port received a call from the Port of Tangier—the bus was on the next ferry. Several minutes later the ferry arrived but the bus was nowhere to be found. *They made a mistake*, we were told over the intercom. *The bus will be on the next ferry.*

The rhythm of the power-glass door marked time, as every minute or so someone would wander out and look for signs of the ferry crossing the Strait. We didn't have to ask them if they saw anything. Seconds dripped like oil out of a leaking pan and minutes became droplets that clung to worn patches on the floor—dirty. Hours were marked by the number of times we called the company and by the number of times they told us *don't worry, the bus is on the next ferry.* Every two hours we'd huddle in front of the chain link fence outside the customs building to watch a new ferry arrive, unload, and return to Morocco void of its promise. We watched the rich Moroccans arrive and get off the boat and get in their cars and drive away, their red taillights disappearing into the night. We watched ferries leave three times, and we knew that the fourth would likely be the last.

By midnight I'd become desperate enough to try my hand at some forlorn poetry on a scrap of napkin like I was Yeats or something, but by one o'clock I'd tired of poetry and had fallen asleep on the floor of the customs building. It was just me and the Moroccans and we sprawled out across the floor like it was a homeless shelter, except we didn't have blankets or pillows, just hard concrete.

"*Tranquilo, tranquilo,*" the Moroccans tried to tell me when I started to get mad. Calm down.

"How can you calm down when this is happening?" I told them. If this ever happened in the United States of America, well, we had a thing called justice. You could file a lawsuit. You could yell at the company and get a refund. Maybe we could even get some sort of human rights money for having to sleep on concrete. I would have pounded my fist against a government cubicle for a handout, and I don't even believe in handouts. This wasn't fair—it was just how life was in Morocco.

My heart began to sink. You can only look across dark, empty water for so long until you lose hope and resignation begins to set in. Hope is what had kept us going for five hours in a place where there were no waiting rooms, vending machines or magazines to read. There was nothing and no one but us, and we had been lied to, again. For the Moroccans, this was nothing new, but for me it was a cultural experience I never wanted to go through in the first place. What would I tell Carmen when I went missing and didn't arrive home when I said I would? She'd think that I'd been kidnapped for good. With each empty-promise ferry, I watched our chances retreat as it disappeared back to Morocco across uneven waters, slipping further and further away.

After waiting six hours at the Spanish port, it was about time for the final ferry to arrive and all sixty of us gathered in front of the chain link fence. Talking came to a standstill and we felt the crisp air press against us as we pulled our bodies tight under moonlight. No one moved until we saw a faint light in the distance break across the water. The last ferry was here. When it docked, we watched cars and people disembark, but saw no sign of the bus. Five minutes went by, then ten. Alone in front of the fence, we waited and no one moved. The bus had to be here. When it looked like we were out of luck, we heard a sudden throb as a diesel engine sounded in the belly of the ferry. It was here.

As the bus crawled its way out of the ferry, we learned that there was a catch. Over the loudspeaker, the Spanish port informed us that there weren't enough seats for all of us. The Moroccan company had sent the wrong bus—the short bus—and someone was going to get left behind.

Panic struck and violence took over. We'd had enough of patience; it wasn't a virtue anymore. I'd seen something similar this past Christmas when I worked Black Friday at Old Navy. I'd seen the animal within that was willing to trample toddlers and shove babies aside to get a twenty-dollar gift card for being the first person in the door, and that was just to buy cheap clothes. When your life depended on being the first person in line for the bus ride home, it became much worse.

I fought right alongside everyone else. While we'd all spent the last six hours together talking and becoming friends, we all knew that we'd only done that to pass the time. Now we went for the throat. Old and young men clawed each other; women and children were bulldozed out of sheer desperation. After the fights, the source of our fear was quickly dispelled when everyone realized that there were, in fact, enough seats. Then we went back to being friends. We were all in this together, really—for ourselves.

We were forced to work together once again when our certified bus driver got lost on the way back and we had to help him navigate southern Spain. As we approached each destination, a new passenger from the bus would walk to the front of the bus and tell the driver where to turn, before shouting at the rest of us to announce the next stop. *¡Ésta parada es para Granada!* The driver, however, remained clueless so two twenty-something Moroccans sat next to him in the aisle and attempted to guide us toward home and the *autopista*. A seven-hour bus ride became nine, and tempers heated the already congested space. There was no deodorant, no trash cans, and none of us had seen an ounce of hygiene in over twenty-four hours; there wasn't any sleeping on the way home. If you were asleep when the Moroccans called the name of your town, then you weren't going home. When we neared Alicante, I helped one of the Moroccans from Barcelona navigate us up the Costa Blanca and finally, after thirty-five hours in Morocco, I was home.

When I opened the front door to the shadowy hallway, Dior came bounding down the hall to lick me and pee on the floor in his usual fashion. Carmen and Asis sprung out of the living room and rushed to throw their arms around me. Carmen gave me kisses on the cheek and said that she had stayed up all night, every night praying for me. Somehow, she had gotten a strange feeling that I had been in danger. Even Adán came over to say hello, and when they asked about the trip, I didn't quite know what to say. Part of me was proud of what I'd survived, but part of me also wanted to bury what had happened because I had lied to them about going alone.

As we sat in the living room at day's end and I told them the story, I revealed the important events, but kept one part secret, the part about the horizon burning. As I lay in bed that night before falling asleep, I stared up at the ceiling and at the outlines of the pictures on the wall. All these lives and all these people had learned something. This weekend I had learned a lot of hard lessons, and from somewhere deep within, I prayed that somehow, maybe in some distant place, there was a reason for it.

The room disappeared before me, and refocused itself on a small five by seven photograph of a family standing on a farm by a snowy river. If dreams were only as good as their dreamer, then maybe I had become a little stronger. Dreams come and go, and like the picture on my dresser of a family clutching their coats in the cold, they would have a hard time letting go.

Week 10
Valencia, Spain

I didn't know it at the time, but Morocco would prove to be the turning point of my journey. There's a certain amount of confidence that comes when you walk to the brink of death and live to tell of it. When you stare dark shops with chains and tables straight in the face and spit on them. Yeah, I did that. Maybe that's an exaggeration, but it captures the essential part. Surviving Morocco gave me guts. And it made me a believer in miracles, if I wasn't already. Those were the two ingredients necessary to set off on a larger, more dangerous quest. I had begun to formulate several ideas as to what, exactly, that quest would entail, but I was keeping my options open. While I thought my Moroccan survival expedition made for a great story, Dad had some other things to say about it.

"How stupid can you get? That was D-U-M-B *dumb*," he said when I told him the story over the phone. "You could have gotten killed! Then what would Mom and I have done? I'd have had to hop on a plane to Morocco and drag your carcass back to the Dead Pile at the farm. Did you at least learn *anything* from it?"

The only lesson that would count in his book as a "lesson learned" was never to go off on my own again. Of course, that wouldn't be happening—I would be running off on my own again this week to an explosives camp. While I didn't want to hear Dad yell at me, there was a part of what he said that took me out of Morocco and back to when I was three years old.

"Jump to me," he would say. We were in the swimming pool, getting used to the deep end—three feet. I climbed out of the pool in my blond hair and tiny swimsuit and stood on the edge of the chlorine water. Dad smiled up at me, his dark hair wet from the water, his arms open, ready to catch me. "Jump!" he said, and I laughed and jumped into his arms. "Wherever you are, I will always be there to catch you."

We knew that he would be there for us. From when he held my older brother in his arms and Adam's heart nearly stopped beating from alcohol poisoning when he was sixteen to when Dad took my younger brother to the ER when I had speared him with a stick, we knew what he meant when he said, "You boys will always grow up knowing you have a dad who will do whatever it takes to find you." We were learning to jump into deep water, but perhaps something more.

When I was fifteen I ran away from my mother's home for the first time. My parents divorced when I was one or two, I can't remember, but what I can remember is that I was always being trained to jump. I ran away from a chaotic home with my mother and put myself in juvenile lock-up for five days. When I was in lock-up, Dad drove four hundred miles to come visit me for the fifteen minutes that the staff allowed. I saw him burst into the waiting room as I sat there in my solid blue detention pants and shirt. I saw tears in his eyes as he ran to hug me, and I went right back to being three years old and jumping into the swimming pool. He was still there to catch me.

Two months later, I was in lock-up again, this time as an at-risk youth. The first person the caretakers called was Dad to let him know that I was safe. He drove another four hundred miles to see me for fifteen minutes. By the time he arrived, the lock-up facility had transferred me to a low-risk safe house outside of Seattle, where another girl was staying with me in captivity. Esther was sixteen and had gotten AIDS from her foster dad when he raped her. As her body was ravaged by the disease that her foster father had given her, she watched me sit silently at the windowsill of the safe house, watching and waiting for my real father. The only thing she'd ever known about fathers was that they did bad things to you; they never loved you. She listened to me talk about my father and yearn for him, and when the big diesel truck sounded on the sidewalk next to the safe house, and when she saw us run to hug each other, she ran into the bathroom and started to cry. She told me later that seeing Dad come to visit me was the hardest thing she ever had to watch.

I think what Esther felt that day was similar to what I put Dad through when I went to Morocco and lied about going alone. It wasn't exactly the same, of course, but it hurt all the same. One of the hardest things to watch is when someone you love takes their own leap, even if it's foolish, even if it could kill them. Can you jump far enough, so far that you can't be caught? I might have just landed there. But to this day, I am convinced that if I had turned up missing in Morocco, somehow, against all odds and possibilities, he would have been the first one to come find me, even if I was somewhere I could never be found. There are no odds or chances with love. It wins against the greatest odds, and I had certainly put them to the test.

From Morocco on, there was a falling out, a loss of trust. There's no one waiting to catch you when you swim out in the middle of the ocean against all advice and sound wisdom, there's only someone who has to watch you drown from the shore, unable to break the waves and come help. Sometimes you need to swim out there though, in order to get stronger, in order to do bigger things. At least that's what I tried to tell myself. Dad had tried to dissuade me from going to Morocco in the first place, but I hadn't listened or been particularly honest. And now here we were, talking on the phone, tension pulsing from the mouthpiece as it grew hotter against my ear.

"Do you realize you had Mom and I scared to death?"

Maybe now I did. It wasn't unforgivable, but something had come between us, perhaps a realization. I would have to learn how to jump all over again.

The search for new lifeguards began.

The search started in the kitchen. Over and over, Carmen and Asis had raved about how friendly the Moroccans were, and it was about time that we got to the bottom of this. I had trusted their advice to go to tea with anyone and it had nearly gotten me killed.

"*Los alicantinos*," Carmen began on one of her usual rants about the people from Alicante. "If you even put a mattress on the street, they'll steal it in five minutes!"

Coincidentally, as I walked down the street later that day, I saw a bed mattress sitting next to a garbage can. As I passed by the same street again an hour later, it was still there.

On Friday night, my friend Scott from Maryland came over to test the waters and meet Carmen and Asis for himself. Over the past two months he'd heard a lot about them and wanted to meet them. "They sound larger than life," he said, even though he was himself, quite larger than life. Scott was an international business major who had traveled all over the place. Before Spain, he was in Thailand and China learning business strategies, and before that, he had grown up with the Cubans in Miami, where he was the proud owner of a swampland *¡Florida Gators fútbol!* impression. Naturally then, we became great friends. Scott and I went out to grab kebabs for everyone, then brought dinner home to talk with Carmen and Asis, who were, of course, watching comedy shows on TV. Dior peed on the floor for Scott when we arrived, and when Scott held him up in front of us like Simba in the Lion King, Dior's tangled white fur formed a sharp contrast to Scott's thinning black hair and smooth white skin.

When Scott put Dior on the floor, we sat down for dinner. The food was great, the wine was flowing, and we heard some interesting stuff.

"Did you know that 9/11 was a plot by the US government?" Carmen calmly asked us as she sat on the couch in her pajamas, her hair pinned atop her head like she was in a Chinese hair salon. Asis sat next to her, his hands folded neatly in his lap, his eyes glazed over as he watched TV, almost in a coma. He looked like he had fallen asleep, but his mouth moved when he talked. Not one to jump into a confrontation, he never said whether he agreed with Carmen or not. His mouth hung open, dry and devoid of moisture from being motionless for so long. He didn't blink, either.

"No, 9/11 *did* actually happen," Scott tried to tell Carmen. They have evidence: the voice recordings from the flight, testimony, hell, didn't you see it on TV? Why would our government destroy our own country?

"That's just what I read in the magazines," she said. "Did you know that the Spanish president and his wife are both gay?"

At one a.m. when we finished eating dinner, Scott and I stood outside the apartment building in the slickness of newly fallen rain. "I don't know what magazines Carmen reads, but she sure seems to believe them," he began. "They're great people to talk to, but Carmen's crazy—she's a motormouth—and Asis is a little kooky himself. They're perfect for each other."

"You're right," I said.

Scott reached his hands into his pockets. "Do you believe everything they say?"

"Well …" I began and paused to look down the street. "I don't know. Before Morocco, maybe I used to."

We said goodbye and *chiao* and *adios* and *hasta luego*—all three of the goodbye expressions that you had to say in order to bid a true Spanish goodbye—then Scott disappeared around the apartment building and the mist took his place. I would see him again tomorrow, but I would hammer out some truth beforehand. I would say *lo siento* for lying to Carmen and Asis about going to Morocco alone, but they had some explaining to do.

The following morning I tried to apologize to Carmen and Asis about going to Morocco alone. Actually, I fudged a little bit here and told them that my friends had ditched me (which was mostly true), but they wouldn't buy any of it. *Lo siento, lo siento.* I tried to apologize extra hard, but they didn't seem to understand why I was apologizing.

"In Spain, we're never sorry for anything," Asis said. "Just *viva la vida*—live some life." He stood up from the couch and wandered back into the kitchen to get the telephone that was as thick and old as a brick. He carried it into the living room and ran his fingers across yellow buttons.

"We're going to have some fun," he said. He dialed the number of his best friend and handed the phone to me, his face beaming like a middle schooler about to make a prank call. "Talk to them in English," he said. "And tell them they owe the bank a lot of money."

On the phone, Asis' friend bought the whole gimmick, hook line and sinker. He would write a check to the bank tomorrow for one thousand euros, but *hombre*, he wasn't happy about it. *¡Aí aí aí tío!* Asis snagged the phone from me before I could get his friend to pay the bill and rout his funds to my account. "*Hombre*, you just got scammed," Asis told him.

"Really?"

"Yeah, now how do you feel about yourself?"

"I feel like your son sounds like a banker. He speaks good English," the friend said.

"Of course he does," Asis responded. "He's American."

"Oh."

Asis went into the other room to talk, and since Carmen was out buying oranges at the street market, I had the house mostly to myself. Since I would be leaving for another trip tomorrow, I decided to immerse myself in Spanish culture and sleep the afternoon away.

That day I came to the conclusion that Carmen and Asis were one quirky, fun, and lovable couple. On one hand, they said they were poor and that everything from toothpaste to oranges was *muy caro*, really expensive, but on the other hand, they had two cars and a motorcycle, when most Spanish families only had one car, if that. Even though Asis drove a new Mercedes, they ate at cheap restaurants (and complained if their meal cost more than five euros), bought their clothes at the Chinese store for ten euros, and drank quarter beers at home because Asis hated going to the bar. When I asked him about the Mercedes, he said that he had gotten it for free from work, before changing the topic to Asis and Adán. *Muy trabajadores.* Both of their sons earned their own money, in contrast to most Spaniards who thought that it was normal to depend on your parents until you were either thirty or married. Both Adán and Asis junior had also attended private schools all the way through high school. But even as expensive diplomas hung on the walls of their rooms, the house was covered in dollar-store trinkets that Carmen had collected over the years, and the whole family preferred pajamas to normal clothes; they didn't like to frequent street cafes like the rest of the Spaniards. To top things off, both Adán and Asis junior didn't smoke or drink, even though Asis junior was the pinnacle of Spanish fashion and womanizing as Mister Spain. (Not only did he have a bikini model girlfriend, he told me once, he had other girlfriends, too.)

In all, they were a family of contradictions, which of course meant that whenever they said one thing, it would contrast with something else they believed. "*Las naranjas son muy caras,*" Carmen would say about how expensive oranges were, then she'd walk home with a potato sack full of them. Or "you can only take one shower per day," and she would take two, then wink at me if I needed another one.

They believed in telling the truth and in believing, mostly, what they heard. Carmen may have read a lot of tabloids and thought that President Zapatero was gay, but she also happened to be right about a lot of other things. Asis' warning had proved correct my first night in Alicante when he told me to watch out at the port. Several weeks ago, Carmen had given me her suitcase and Adán's sweater, and while she'd given me the sweater without knowing all the problems it would cause, there was something very significant behind the gesture. Both Carmen and Asis knew a lot about the world, but I was learning that there were a lot of things that they made up, too. One conversation was particularly telling.

"What's wrong with this sentence?" I asked my writing professor, Paloma, one day after class. It was always intimidating to approach her because she was a gym-toned forty year-old in tight jeans, but I had gotten an F on a paper and couldn't understand what I'd done wrong. Carmen had helped me edit the paper and had even corrected my grammar and verb tenses. It must have been right.

"From now on, don't ask your host mom for help," Paloma said, looking me straight in the eyes even as her shirt drooped in front of me. "By this point in the semester, you already know more correct Spanish than she does."

For the rest of the semester, I followed Paloma's advice and shied away from Carmen's help when she pestered and looked over my shoulder. "You're writing this wrong," she would say, even as I eventually went on to earn straight A's. In the important things, however, in the life talks, I trusted her with my whole heart, but I began to take in new information outside of what they told me at home. I began talking to new people on the bus ride to school or the store clerks I met in the afternoons while wandering through Alicante. Sure enough, I was learning new things. The president wasn't gay (actually I already knew this, but I sought some extra verification, just to be sure), and the Spanish economy was much worse than I'd understood before. Maybe there was a place for tall tales and truth that was larger than life and maybe that was what growing up was all about, but there were some stories that I didn't want to decompose. Stories that whether they were true or not, I had to believe.

NEBRASKA, 1922

I remember big stories from growing up.

"How much longer till we get there?" Adam and I asked from the backseat of another road trip. Outside the windows of our Aerostar van, open wheat fields and the scent of mountains rushed by as we drove off to visit family that conveniently lived in the middle of nowhere.

"About five," Dad would always say. We learned that it was "about five" till we got to the next bathroom, gas station, or motel swimming pool. There was almost a holy reverence about the number, where everything seemed to align alongside the stories we'd hear.

In between our asking Dad how much longer the trip would take and in between Dad's about five's, we heard stories, big stories, about our great ancestors. "Those Bohemians were really something," Dad would say and launch into another story about our very own Manifest Destiny. "The Bohemians were running from something!"

Indians! Cowboys! Farms out west … they were only the beginning of what we heard. Our great grandma had been a real pioneer, a woman tough as an oak, who at age nineteen had somehow decided to hop on a train bound for the Middle of Nowhere, Nebraska to teach kids how to read. Well, she actually thought she was going to teach Bohemian and German kids, but when she got off the train, she was surrounded by Indians. Dad repeated that line again, just for emphasis. *She was surrounded by Indians.* Now why would she do that, go live amongst all those Indians by her lonesome self? ("My theory, he whispered to us, "was that they wanted to buy her because she was so pretty!") She was the first person in the family to graduate from college, the Northern Nebraska Teacher's College, and her diploma still hung above the washer in Grandma and Grandpa's house. Wasn't that something?

When she arrived in Nebraska, she decided to stay and teach some school, Dad explained. The kids she taught didn't know any English, so she had to start all the way at the beginning, even with the older ones. She'd grab a book and hold it up to the class and say, 'book. This is a book.' And they'd repeat after her, 'book.' She had to do this with everything from books to chalk boards, but with old Frances, if that German woman was going to teach you something, why, you'd learn it. Another thing you'd learn was that she was quite pretty. Joe Hanna sure thought so. While she was teaching, she fell hopelessly in love with your Great Grandpa, a Bohemian, and they moved out west after their son broke his leg and the insurance money paid for the trip to Idaho.

"You boys got some family to be proud of," I heard the relatives often say. "Not every kid gets to inherit the story of a family and a woman who would move all alone into the middle of Indian Country. Those're some brave folks." Yep.

In my imagination I saw Joe Hanna working on "the Old Hanna Place," as Dad put it, the original farm, wearing a white cotton shirt and sweating as it clung to his body, but this wasn't ordinary man's sweat. No sir, I'm seeing a man who traded with the Indians and lived to tell of it, a dust on the boots look without horse manure—movie star sweat. This was my family, and I never envisioned them seated in chairs like the boxed-up, boring versions of people found in black and white photos, that would be too easy.

In later years, I learned that sod houses and Indian country weren't typically first choice destinations for new arrivals to America. Our Bohemian ancestors bypassed the New York and Boston factories in favor of someplace largely uninhabited; they were being hunted. "You didn't go to the middle of Indian Country unless you were running from something," Dad said. "I don't know what it was, but I think someone was after them."

There was other evidence that they were being hunted. One of the first things they did when they got to America in 1870 was change the family name. Haná dropped the accent and became Hanna "because it sounded more American," and they settled down to forget what life was like in Bohemia, even as they continued speaking Czech. Other than that, we didn't really know much more about our Hanna ancestors. We didn't know what they did, who they were, or why they went to live and trade with the Indians on the Great Plains and live in a house made of muddy grass, but the legends endured. They were larger than life.

"*Jak se máte, jak se máte!*" Dad would say as if it was some great Czech phrase. How are you doing! How are you doing! "I used to hear my uncles say that to each other when I was a kid. *Jak se máte! Jak se máte!*"

In the far corner of Dad's bookshelf sat an old copy of *Teach Yourself Czech.* "My dream ever since I was a little kid was to have my own farm," Dad told us. "And now, even though we've lost it, we still sort of have a farm." But there was another dream sitting on his bookshelf waiting to be read. Someday and somehow, we would find them.

While the stories about the Hannas were great for road trips, they were not suited for the night. We had other stories that were reserved for the quiet reverence of the fire or the lonely glow of an off-kilter lamp after midnight. Through Dad, all the Bohemian stories converged, bound together in him through his parents who had somehow found a way to merge two halves of Bohemian poverty together—the Hannas and the Belohlavys. Under the cover of darkness, we'd hear the Other story, the haunting story. On cold winter nights, the Pact would be reborn.

One night one hundred and twenty-five years ago when the moon was probably full, our ancestors gathered in an old building under the cover of darkness. One by one they filed into the shed. Inside the walls were bare; there was nothing except a round wooden table that had been cut in places and worn over time. A rusty chain should have hung ominously over the table, but was absent. In its place, a candle sat on the table, and its lonely flame pulsed in and out of time as wax grew hot and began to drip down below the wick. In the shadows of the flame, faces became visible as they slowly entered the shed and gathered around the table. From one side of the table to the other, faces were covered in dirt, bodies dressed in rags, feet shoveled in dirt and already prepared for the grave. An eight year-old boy looked up into the flame, his blond hair twisted behind his face as a smear marred his cheek. He didn't go to school; he had been herding geese all day. Next to him, an old man drizzled his long beard across the table, his head bent down in silence. Next to him, a middle-age woman leaned over and resolutely looked into the tiny flame, cradling a newborn baby. As each of them arrived one by one, the last of the Belohlavys stood together, until the table was lined shoulder to shoulder in silence. Aunts stood next to nieces and grandfathers next to grandsons as the entire family gathered together to bind themselves forever to a pact. Tonight, they would pool all of their money to send one man to America and give him the chance to have a better life, but a heavy price would be required. To set one person free, they must all become poor. From now to forever, whomever they set free would never be seen again. Once the money was pooled, one member of the family would disappear forever.

The family stood around the table, their heads bent in silence. The toll would be heavy. They would never see the fruits of their sacrifice and they would never be able to join the one they sent or see what the family would become in America when their fates would finally have the chance to change.

The flame in the center of the table flickered, buffeted by shifts of air and heavy breaths on all sides. Whatever the Pact would cost, it was desperately worth it. The Belohlavys knew what it meant to come to the table. It meant that you would give everything you owned to someone you would never see again and trust that somehow, they would make good use of it. You would never see them arrive on the boat and get welcomed to America with a handshake. You would never see the open skies of Nebraska on a starry night and get to stand beside them and whisper in their ear. You would never see the births and weddings of their children. All the Pact meant was that you would watch the people next to you starve and shrivel in pursuit of a fleeting dream that had disappeared across the Atlantic, a dream that someday, maybe sometime far from now, the ones you had freed would return and together the family would rejoice. In that moment of return and remembrance, the cost of the Pact could finally be justified. Whoever was sent must instill in their children a desire for the Home Place. No matter how long it took, the Return was necessary. It meant that the Pact had not been in vain.

The little boy reached his hand into the middle of the table and placed all the money he had earned herding geese that day. He would continue herding animals for the rest of his life and would never learn to read. Having given all that he had, this night would be the highlight of his life. The old man next to him stretched his hand over the center of the table and dropped a pouch of coins. He also herded animals. The mother of the young baby stretched out her hand and dropped coins that clanged and jangled until the sound deadened. She kept the family's shack clean. In the stillness of the cold air, their breath became visible and clouded the table like smoke, hazing the low light from the candle. The baby began to whimper. In eight years he would be herding geese like the rest of them.

One by one, hands dipped into the center of the table as the family gave everything they owned. When it was all counted, it was just enough to send one person to America. Through one randomly chosen person, the Belohlavys were going to change the course of family history. They would not be poor anymore. They would be miserably poor.

On the shoulders of one fated man, they would place their hope. They drew lots and a young man won the drawing. He didn't want to win. The day the train arrived that would send him away from the family and Bohemia forever, he couldn't get on the train. It was too heavy a burden to bear. One man from the family offered to go in his stead. A stoic figure pushed through the crowd and took the ticket and boarded the train. Hard faced and resolute, he would face their future. Leaving his pregnant wife and future child behind, Vaclav Belohlavy boarded the train and sailed to America. He didn't cry or smile as he left. My great ancestor would bear the burden and would carry the weight of the charge because the Pact required another price. Whoever was sent would most likely die alone.

In my memory the scene fades slowly into the night, wrapped in the grim light of the candle. Whether that was exactly as the events happened, I don't know, but my imagination fills in the details. What's certain is that one day one hundred and twenty-five years ago, they had paid a price to set one person free, but the hope of what they had done followed them for six generations. They had set him free to pursue a dream.

Tomorrow I would be walking through explosives in Spain headed for the brink once again. I called it survival training, but maybe, it was something more.

In the early morning I got off the bus to the sound of rockets and Valencia. As I stepped off the bus and onto the curb, fireworks screeched across a clouded sky that was partially obscured by eight-story apartment buildings, crowded storefronts, and a plaza filled shoulder to shoulder with people streaming in one direction as the shadows of buildings hung over the walkway; it was just enough to feel confining. Coupled with a bourgeoning population of three million people in a city designed for 800,000, the air began to coagulate and tighten with each breath. Wearing my signature beanie from Morocco and my black coat, I stood with my face to the crowd, ready to once again face off against the world. When I looked over, Scott stood beside me and nodded. Several other students gathered around us and together we headed into the crowd. "You guys need to experience this firsthand in order to understand Spain," our study abroad director, Luis, told us. "But watch your step. In Spain we don't believe in liability waivers, so you might end up losing a leg."

We saw what he meant. Packed shoulder to shoulder, the streets pulsed with people shoving and fighting, moving and weaving between each other as they stood on tippy toes to peer over the crowd before disappearing inside. A father placed his daughter on his shoulders, and when she pointed at movement in the distance, he began walking in the opposite direction. Wives kept their arms wrapped tightly around their husbands, who craned their necks over the mass of people. Not only was it difficult to know where you were going, but every now and then, partial sticks of dynamite would be thrown into the crowd and sudden blasts would tear groups apart as people scattered and reconvened in the vacuum of the explosion.

As Scott and I turned sideways to squeeze through a narrow passageway, an eight year-old boy threw a string of firecrackers on the street in front of us. Scott grabbed my arm and pulled. Right where I was about to step, firecrackers ripped across the ground. I looked down at my foot in disbelief. A step later, my foot crunched on the remains of red packaging that had just been shredded. Smoke circled over the pavement as similar blasts echoed nearby. Moments later, I saw another Spanish kid grin wickedly as the crowd suddenly evacuated in front of me and a shot cracked in front of my right foot. That little devil. The kid laughed, and I watched his dark hair bounce before it folded into the crowd. We had arrived at Las Fallas.

Other than Spain's famous running of the bulls in Pamplona, Las Fallas in Valencia was one of the country's biggest fiestas. For an entire week, I'd heard endlessly about how excited the Spaniards were to "burn shit" at Las Fallas. Carmen and Asis hated it because the festival meant what it implied. You destroyed old stuff. As Scott and I led our group into the main plaza, the crowd opened up and we saw a group of teenagers drinking boxed wine and hurling firecrackers and M-80's in front of an old couple as they slowly made their way across the plaza. A boy set down his wine and crumpled a hamburger wrapper on the ground before throwing an M-80 several feet in front of the old couple. Immediately the husband reached over and touched his wife's arm to stop her and they waited for the explosion to sound before they continued walking. Several seconds later, another kid threw something in front of them, and again the old couple looked down and paused. The wife reached over and placed her arm inside her husband's. In the background, city flowers decorated balconies, while the young jeered at the old. The man bowed down his head and lowered his eyes to the street in front of them and his glasses slid to the front of his nose. He never should have done this.

"Looks like another Fallas," someone next to me said. "We're burning everything to the ground again—including ourselves."

For an entire year leading up to Las Fallas, neighborhood associations and the Valencian government hired special craftsmen to build giant caricatures, known as *fallas*, that were designed to burn in fifteen minutes or less. Often eight stories high and wildly elaborate, crews were authorized to spend anywhere from 6,000 to 600,000 euros per falla, and there were usually over fifty of them scattered throughout the city at every major plaza and intersection. When the clock struck midnight, the burning would begin and all of the fallas would be destroyed. "The fallas are like spring cleaning," an event flyer said. "Sometimes you just need to burn the old stuff!"

After the old people had crossed the plaza and disappeared, we got our first glimpse of one of the fallas that would be burned. Covering half of Valencia's largest plaza and nearly the size of a city block was an elaborate caricature of Philadelphia's red LOVE sign, an old cartoon painter who was pointing at something, a cupid angel with a Pinocchio nose in the shape of a trumpet, a restaurant waiter, and Barack Obama, all fused into one giant wooden sculpture. The Spaniards said there was a meaning behind the mishmash, but all I could determine was that it was just as tall as the eight-story buildings that surrounded it and three times as colorful. "It's pretty, isn't it?" a woman standing next to me said. "Tonight, we get to burn it!"

For the rest of the afternoon, Scott and I walked around town looking at fallas to the soundtrack of explosions in the distance, while homemade bombs blew up on the street in front of us. It was like a bigger version of the Fourth of July, except instead of seeing American flags everywhere, I saw green Moby Dick statues and pink mermaids with purple nipples.

As we saw more and more fallas and more and more old people getting fireworks thrown at them, I began to wonder: wasn't there *la crisis* going on? Where were the signs of the recession? Other than crumpled hamburger wrappers and cheap wine boxes littering the sidewalks, there was no limit to the lavish. A twenty-foot statue of *La Virgen María* that was made entirely of roses towered above us in one plaza, and right next to it, *La Plaza de las Flores* featured a massive wall of flowers that had been woven together. The feeling was of colors and scents and confetti, but lurking deeper was something somber, the sense that this was all just something to burn. Hidden behind the dollar-store coats and ripped jeans of young Spaniards were the real signs of *la crisis*. In side glances down alleys, I watched kids jump into dumpsters and forage for food even as they carried hundreds of dollars of explosives in their hands.

"Fallas is so much squandering and so little sacrifice," Asis had said before I left. "It's fun, but it's entirely built on something we never had in the first place."

Scott and I wandered for most of the afternoon until we found ourselves sitting on a silver sidewalk rail, waiting for the next big thing to begin. To the sound of gunshots and a wall of smoke, a massive red dragon led the Parade of Fire, swinging its claws back and forth in front of us. Behind the dragon, rows of trumpeters in red capes marched in unison, followed by lines of dancers dressed as skeletons. Scott breathed out some pent-up air and dropped his hands onto the rail.

"What I hate about Spain is there's no aspiration. There's no motivation. There's no incentive to do anything other than party and have protests and parades. 'You want to become something?' they say. 'You want to do something with your life? You want to have an idea for a business other than a *restaurante* or sock shop?' Forget about it. But if you want to build a tax-payer funded *falla*, go for it!' I don't understand these people—they're so happy when they're not working."

"Believe me," I said, "it makes sense."

For the past few weeks I'd been teaching English to local middle school students, and I'd noticed an unusual phenomenon. In America when you asked a kid what he wanted to do someday, he would usually tell you that he wanted to be an astronaut, a doctor or the president, or all three. At least that's what kids in my classes growing up always said. No one wanted to be just a middle manager. But when I asked my Spanish students what they wanted to do someday, they told me they wanted government jobs so they would never get fired. Everyone wanted to work for the government. "In a government job," my students told me, "you don't have to do anything. Once you pass the test to work for the government, they can never fire you."

Government paper pushers—that was what young Spaniards dreamed of becoming. In all of my wildest dreams, I never dreamt of doing data entry for the government. There had to be more to life than spreadsheets and spending reports, and that was where Spain differed from America.

"Long ago our ancestors left Europe to leave mediocrity," Scott said. "Sometimes I forget about that, until we have to watch it every day in person."

As Scott and I sat on the rail with our backs to a plaza, a boy snuck up behind us and tossed an M-80 that exploded under our feet. The kid laughed as Scott and I jumped off the railing in shock. I looked at Scott and he looked over at me. We were through with this.

We wandered into one of the city parks, assuming it would be safe, but quickly learned that it was harder to see smoking fuses in the dirt than on black concrete. We passed kids smoking dope and lighting firecrackers in oranges, sending pulp spattering across the air where it stuck to palm trees in little bits of yellow. For me, the show was nauseating. Here in all this sudden wealth and all these fallas and all these fireworks was a city clinging to a dream. It wanted to be known, but the price was extravagant.

The burning began with the arrival of darkness. Huge sculptures of everything from The Lady and the Tramp to Moby Dick suddenly were draped in cords strapped with pieces of dynamite and drenched in gasoline. A match was lit, a spark was struck, and a flame slowly crawled along the cord, igniting a chain of engineered explosives that burst the falla into a column of fire. As I stood near the front of a million-strong crowd, my face began to scald from the heat as the people around me started to step back. I followed their lead as ash began to swirl overhead and rain down on the fleeing crowd while firefighters frantically hosed flames that began crawling up the sides of neighboring apartment buildings. As the falla and the buildings around it burned, the crowd began to cheer. Once the falla had burned through its outer layer, its wooden frame appeared as a black skeleton covered in flames. The wood began to splinter and creak as the Spaniards toasted the falla by clinking their flasks. ¡Salud! Minutes later, the frame tumbled to the ground where I had been standing, splintering the charred wood as it collapsed eight stories below. In fifteen minutes, a year's worth of work had come to an end.

On our walk back to the bus after the burning of the fallas, a familiar smoke swirl began to rise in the area where I was about to step.

"Watch out!" I jumped back and shoved my friends aside so they wouldn't get caught in the blast. Like a fuse, a slight wisp twisted and rose, then nothing. *Joder*. It turned out to be nothing more than a cigarette that someone had thrown on the ground, but I was still scared; it was indicative of the whole fallas experience.

Maybe that was why kids threw fireworks in front of old couples. One generation had sacrificed so that another might have enough to squander. There was value in squandering. It meant that you had made it. I didn't want to ever squander, but maybe I already had.

At night's end, we boarded the bus and left Valencia. As the city lights whisked by my window at one hundred and twenty kilometers per hour, the scene of the burning falla replayed in my mind and juxtaposed with the scene of the table and the Pact. Long ago, Vaclav Belohlavy had known what it meant to come to the table. With every penny they had, the family had set him free. Bought at a price, he had been given one chance to turn the family around—there would be no squandering.

I returned home just in time for Father's Day. Dior ran over to pee on the floor and Carmen hugged me and whispered into my ear. *Asis papí va a llegar en un momento*. I nodded. Asis would be here soon and I needed to help get things ready.

I walked down the shadowy hallway and placed my backpack in my room before going to join Adán and Asis junior in the living room. Together, we assembled a dining table that Carmen had borrowed from the neighbors. Then we sat on the couch to wait. Carmen disappeared into her room and returned dressed like a rose, wearing a red sweater and a thick shade of red lipstick as her soft brown hair fluttered across her back. Her face beamed. *Ojalá que esté bien*.

When the front door opened and Asis arrived back at the house from an errand, we all waited silently in the living room. "*¿Hola?*" he called down the hallway. "*¿Alguien está aquí?*" When he walked into the living room, we jumped and rushed to greet him.

"*¡Madre mía!*" he said. "*¡Qué sorpresa!*" All of us gave him hugs and we sat down to eat a giant pan of paella that Carmen had prepared. Loud conversation rocked back and forth across the room as we ate. We were a rather boisterous bunch. We ate too much and drank too much.

As the afternoon sun filtered into the room, we leaned back in our seats and loosened our belts. Adán said he needed to run the third leg of the Spanish Traitholon with his girlfriend that night and we all laughed. Asis suggested that he do that outside the house and we all laughed again. As the afternoon wore on, we remained at the table, even as we were falling asleep in our chairs. For us, *El Día de los Padres* was an opportunity to come to the table. Unlike Las Fallas, we were building something that could never be destroyed.

Earlier in the week, Adán, Asis junior and I had gathered to give Asis our Father's Day gifts. Adán gave him a belt that actually worked, I gave him a plate that I'd hauled back from Morocco for use at our next fajitas night, and Asis junior gave him a new cologne that Carmen liked. Asis junior sprayed him with a quick shot of it and Carmen buried her face in his chest hair.

Asis and Carmen went into their room and closed the door. I heard them giggle. Adán disappeared to run the third leg of the Spanish Triathlon with his girlfriend, and Asis junior and I lay down on the couch in the living room to watch *fútbol* and take naps.

A quiet peace fell over the house as we drifted off to sleep. The light outside the window dimmed. The air chilled and settled. Lulled to sleep, there would be plenty of time for pacts and whispered dreams.

WEEK 11
BENIDORM, SPAIN

THE LIGHTS WERE OFF in the hallway when I came home to the sound of the juice-making machine. Under a dull light and a beige cupboard from the eighties, Asis was making carrot juice. His back was turned to me as he grabbed a raw carrot and began beating it against the countertop like a baseball bat, raising it over his shoulder before bringing it down hard with a *thwap*.

After he'd hit the carrot against the counter several times, he tossed it in the blender next to him. When the blender started whirring, Asis began humming to himself. "*Mi amor, ¡cántame, cántame!*" My love, sing to me, sing to me! From the kitchen doorway, he didn't realize that I had been watching him for quite some time.

As he sang, chunks the size of vomit swirled inside the blender that spat them out occasionally, and soon enough, Asis had become decorated by his work. Dressed in his baby blue pajamas, his chest was sprinkled with orange specks.

"*¡Oh, mi amor!*" he sang again, before turning around and jumping back when he saw me. "*Estif, ¡qué sorpresa!*" A hint of embarrassment crossed his face.

"Carrot juice." I laughed. "Is this what you do when no one's looking?"

"Looks like you caught me in the act," he said as Dior ran into the kitchen and peed in the corner. Asis shrugged and didn't scold him. "This is my deep dark secret, my worst regret." He walked over to whisper in my ear. *Just don't tell Carmen, ok?*

I smiled. *Ok, I'll keep it a secret.*

"Here," he said, handing me a glass of water mixed with carrot chunks, ground up bananas, and yogurt. It looked like a shake, but worse. *"Pruébalo."*

I tilted my head back and took it like a shot. The carrot chunks stuck to my tongue as I swallowed, making juice pulp look tame. "It's good," I lied.

"Let's try another mix," he said. "Let's do the same thing with apples. Let's make apple juice!"

"No, I really think I'm good," I said.

"No, you're not." He handed me another glass. *"Está bien,"* he said. "But it needs a little sugar."

I nodded before trying his apple juice; a tiny sip. It would need more than just sugar. As I walked over to the blender to examine his concoction, we heard the front door open.

"Mi amor," Carmen said as she walked into the kitchen. "Asis, what is this? I want some."

As Carmen and Asis took shots of carrot juice, Adán walked in carrying Carmen's grocery bags. He looked at me and shook his head. *"Joder, tío."* He'd never seen his dad make carrot juice before, but he hadn't ruled it out, either. "You guys are ridiculous."

We all laughed. Carmen and Asis continued taking shots of juice and Adán and I worked together to put away the groceries. Since Morocco and Las Fallas, Adán had developed a new respect for me. Since he mainly doled out respect based on what you'd done or how far you pushed yourself, I naturally received it quite well because I'd pushed myself once again this week. Adán was impressed, but it hadn't come easily.

That morning, two friends and I had set out to *barranco aquático* and go waterfall jumping and repelling. For only twenty-five euros, a guide led us and a group of Spaniards deep into the Sierra Nevadas where we hiked several kilometers in *neoprenos* ("wetsuits") to an alpine stream that was famous for its waterfalls and narrow cliff jumps. We would then work our way down the stream, using whatever means necessary to get to the bottom. It sounded fun, of course, but it began with a warning. "*No me importa si mueres*," our guide said. Our lives were our own to lose.

That morning, I had stood at the edge of a waterfall. Water rushed beneath me, surging like a boiling pot ready to foam over. Above me, clouds dotted the sky and sunlight beamed down between mountains and the scent of pine. In the distance, hills rolled in blue-green succession until they met the horizon and further still, the sea. Next to me, my guide stood ready in a red wetsuit and whispered into my ear. This would be the first of many waterfalls, he said, just a fifteen footer. *You can do this.*

I grabbed my harness, checked the rope to make sure it was anchored, and lowered myself over the edge. My feet swung out in limbo until the rope tightened and I hung suspended in front of the waterfall, dangling in midair. Water pummeled my helmet as hundreds of gallons per minute rushed over my face. Hand by hand, I lowered myself down the face of the waterfall, twisting and swinging as I went. A rock jutted out beneath me—"watch your head!" said the guide. Just below the rock, my hands became slick and I lost my grip and fell into the pool below. After surfacing, I wiped the water out of my face and looked up at the fifteen-foot *cascada* that had just been conquered. I gave a thumbs up to my friend Meg as she stood at the edge, ready to descend.

With each splash, water shot between us and hung in the air like sun crystals that rose and fell as we waded our way to the next waterfall. At the edge, the guide reached into his pack and pulled out a long cord of rope and began tying it to the rocks for our next *cascada*. A low-hanging tree partially obscured the descent, casting a shadow over the pool below and shrouding it in darkness.

The guide called the first person to the edge. Behind the first climber, I saw shoulder bones sit firmly between mountains in the distance. We had a long ways to descend. My eyes followed the red rope over the waterfall as I watched the first climber fight against the face of the rock as he moved his feet across a fissure to better position himself for the drop. He let go and plunged into the black pool below. When he resurfaced moments later, I heard a *tío, tu turno*. It was my turn.

Water surged beneath me, urging me forward. This descent, it would be hard. I breathed in and tightened my rope. "Are you ready," the guide said. "Because your training is about to be over and the real thing is about to begin."

I clasped the rope and hung suspended over the rocks.

Training comes easier when you're younger, when you're on the edge. In our family, at least, it had always worked that way. You just worked—that was training. At least Dad thought so anyways. Don Hanna was training his sons so that one day, we might be able to complete what God had for us. Hopefully, that would be the Return, but if not, it would be whatever we were put on this earth to do. "And whatever that is, you will need to know that you have a father, two Fathers, who are crazy about you."

To show us how crazy he was about us, Dad put us through Poverty Camp. Actually, that was a term my younger brother Paul had coined, but the feeling was the same. It was a joke really, we weren't really poor, but we made ourselves feel that way; our poverty, it was self-inflicted. The summer after we lost the barn, Dad made us live in murderous poverty, which meant that we lived in front of the farm in an RV camper that we didn't own, microwaving store-bought corn dogs on shreds of old Cheez-It boxes. Oh, we built lots of character that summer.

How Poverty Camp went was that each day we would work on the south side addition to the barn. Dad had drawn up the plans for it and we would build it, even though we wouldn't be able to use it in the foreseeable future. Since Mom had lost her job, they had rented out the farm to new ranchers, so Poverty Camp meant that we lived in front of a house that used to be ours but wasn't anymore, building something we might never have, "something made for eternity," in Dad's precise words. The farm, it wasn't really ours anymore, but Dad couldn't let go of the Dream. He had to build the barn; it was now or never. Someday when he retired, he and Mom would move back and they would reclaim the Home Place, and that was that. The Dream wasn't lost forever, he reassured us. You boys are going to be a part of something great. We were going to take our hundred year-old barn and make it last for another hundred years. What was once lost, we were going to restore.

The plans had to be just right. The boards just square. If our template was an 1896 shack-barn where half the roof sagged, where half the boards were grayed and garishly worn in places, where the inside dirt floor was constantly covered in starling poop, then we had a lot of work to do; the original barn had no foundation. We mixed and re-poured concrete. We had a contractor tie chains around the original barn posts and pull it up-right so it wouldn't sag anymore. We set the now-upright barn posts in a mix of cement and steel, solidifying them in the new foundation. When the chains were finally released around the posts, the building stood straight on its own accord. We were making progress.

When the old barn had been partially fixed, we shifted our work over to a 1,700-square-foot addition that Dad had envisioned on grid paper. From June to August, Paul, Dad and I framed new walls, hauled pieces of plywood from a massive pile next to the barn, and tacked them into place. We drew lines and calculated measurements. Each night we would sleep next to each other in the camper in sleeping bags, eat rotting sand-wiches on torn pieces of cardboard, and take showers where dirt would cake off our bodies and drain in a run-off valve beneath the camper. Dad would talk to Mom each night and miss her, but he understood that she had to work her new job in order to finance Poverty Camp. Late at night we'd watch movies together or play dice games before falling asleep. We'd talk about dreams, big dreams, like the barn and the farm and of some-day being able to return for good. In between the sweltering heat and the sweat that lined the brims of our cowboy hats, something was growing between us. We were being trained to build a barn that we'd never really own, but that would eventually own us. We began to long for it.

As that summer drew to a close, several events marked our progress. The ribs of the frame went up first, and we celebrated accordingly with drive-thru ice cream. About a week later, the strandboard went up, cover-ing the previously ribbed frame. Several weeks after that, the trusses and roof went up, and Paul and I hauled the trampoline over to the edge of the barn to jump off into the sunset. But even as we jumped into the sunset and even as we went out to a real restaurant to celebrate the end of our work, an unspoken feeling hung in the air. Poverty Camp was over. When we finally drove away in August, a dust cloud began to rise behind the blue diesel as Dad slowed to a stop at the end of our driveway. When we turned to admire the reconstructed barn at the end of old Taggert Lane, the barn became more than a barn. It became our Pact, and it became our Dream. Through the barn, the Pact was reborn.

We sat in silence and no one spoke for a while. Dad was at the wheel wearing his cowboy hat and his bug-eye sunglasses that had gone out of style years ago. His beard was graying and his usually lively expression began to droop. As we turned off our gravel road and onto the frontage road that would take us back to the Tame House, Dad glanced to the left again, then over at the road in front of him, then back to the left toward the Home Place. Standing in front of the Elkhorn Mountains, a row of willow trees, and the Powder River was a plot of fresh-cut hay fields, a white house, and a beautiful new barn. Once again, we would have to leave it.

Dad cleared his throat. He wanted to lecture, but his voice stopped in his throat. "No matter where you boys are, you will always know that you have a father who's crazy about you."

I looked over and saw something wet and dark begin to form in the back of Dad's blue eyes. He blinked several times as he clenched the wheel tighter. "Someday God is going to show you guys miracles," Dad told us. "The problem with miracles, though, is they're never the way we want them to be." The Pact was a miracle, but its timing was never ours to own.

"Just keep your eyes open," he said as his words faded. "One day, we will return."

After rappelling down several larger waterfalls, the neoprene group and I advanced to a new challenge. Knee-deep, we sloshed through pools of water that reflected an exotic version of the Sierra Nevadas that I had known from boyhood visits to my grandparents in the Californian mountains. White-rocked cliffs loomed on either side of us, and wet vegetation and thorny bushes prickled over the water, slithering across our

foreheads and wetsuits as we moved further into the canyon to arrive at
a simple four-foot drop. "Jump," our guide said, as he jumped off a small
boulder and splashed into the three-foot pool below. We formed a line
at the edge of the overhang to follow his example. After belaying down
twenty-foot waterfalls, it shouldn't have been a big deal, but the last girl in
line didn't want to take the jump. Married and twenty-four with her hair
neatly styled in a ponytail, she approached the edge cautiously, and after
peering over, she sat down and began to scoot her way across the rock.

"*Guapa*," the guide yelled. "*¡Párate!*"

She continued to inch her way forward until she was about to drop
into the pool. Standing twenty feet in front of her, the guide picked up a
rock and threw it at the boulder next to her. A deadening sound echoed
across the canyon. "Stop!"

The girl scuttled back onto the rock.

"You have to jump," the guide said. "There's no other way back."

The girl slowly tip-toed to the edge, then looked down at her ankles.
"I can't do it."

"You have to. If you can't jump when it's easy, you'll never jump when
your life depends on it."

She looked down again at the three-foot pool and closed her eyes. The
rest of us stood still and watched the guide coax her. "Come on now. You
can do it."

Nothing. She stood with her arms crossed and her eyes closed. I
looked away and up at the shoulder of a mountain next to us. Bristled in
pines, it was hard to see much. I looked back at the rock where the girl
had been standing but she was gone. A moment later, I spotted her wading
across the shallow pool toward the guide. We continued on.

As we worked our way down the mountain riverbed, the stakes began
to rise. Instead of sunlight and an open view of the horizon, bone-
white cliffs towered thirty feet above, enveloping us in a sort of water
cave. In the isolated light, the water became a crystalline *azul*, and we began swimming through the caves. Inside, a dead snake lay upside down,
twisted on one of the rocks, and a dead rat floated in the water.

"Now a warning," the guide said. "The jumps are about to get harder.
From now on, cross your arms and feet before you jump." He did a brief

demonstration, crossing both sets of limbs as he jumped over a ten-foot fall and into a tiny crevice. "Hopefully you make it."

The final waterfall was an eighteen-foot thriller that started on a ledge the size of a plate. There was no opportunity to run and gather speed. Everything depended on your ability to stand on the plate and hurl yourself into an adjacent cave shielded from sunlight. The canyon opening for the jump was barely more than Spaniard shoulder-width, and the Spaniards have small shoulders. One by one, we took turns standing on the plate and looking over the edge before backing away. After each of us had taken a look, the guide stood at the edge of the plate and jumped. "Who's next?" he said.

Everyone backed away, leaving me closest to the plate. I stepped onto it.

"¡Americano!" the guide yelled from below, his head smaller than a nickel. "Jump!"

I didn't.

"Amigo, what just happened?" The group laughed. "Okay, I'm going to count for you like a *niñita. Uno.*"

"*Dos.*"

"*Tres.*"

He barely made it to three before I flung myself off the edge.

"Catch me!" I had told Dad so long ago when I had first jumped into his arms. Now in the thin air of the mountains, the scene was the same as before, a washed background of colors and emotions, chlorinated blue and dark water and one man standing in the water to catch me. Only this time he wasn't there and this time the water was darker and murkier. It was the same scene, really, just a different time and a different place, a deeper swimming pool. This time I had stood on my own two feet at the top of waterfalls and I had jumped.

There is a parable of a man who when given the choice, must choose between three roads. On the first road, he is guaranteed to return to where he came from. On the second road there is a chance that he will be able to return, but if he takes the third road, he will never be able to return. If I had been given the choice then, I would have taken the third road. I wasn't the first one to make that decision.

* * *

The year was 1885 and Vaclav Belohlavy had arrived in America. I imagined him making his way out west with some fellow Bohemians to Nebraska so they could do things "the Bohemian way." But the open expanse of Nebraska can be a lot of space to take in when you have to stand alone in the middle of it and look up to the sky with your arms pressed against you. In all of the newness, Vaclav had no one to share Nebraska with—he'd left his wife behind.

"The Bohemians, Vaclav particularly, were very lonely during those early years," Dad had said. "They didn't have anything. They lived in sod houses made of muddy grass and probably did farm work on someone else's place, working for next to nothing." Vaclav worked for one of the area farmers, and I imagined that he dreamt of his wife while he worked, so much that he never wanted to send her a letter. Maybe when you dream of something for so long, it loses its impact if you ruin the ideal and send a letter that might never get returned. If you never send it, at least your lover has always been faithful to what you haven't told them.

"We never knew why he didn't send a letter to her," Dad said. Vaclav's wife was pregnant with his child, maybe that was enough of a burden to bear.

While the Pact might have sent Vaclav to America alone, he didn't want to die alone. Bit by bit, he began to save his money. One day—he didn't know quite when—he would send for her.

THE LETTER

By the time I arrived back from waterfall jumping, Carmen and Asis had received a letter in the mail. "*Estif, ¿qué es esta?*" Carmen asked, and showed me a *carta* written in a language she couldn't understand. I immediately recognized the Hanna brand on ranch letterhead.

"It's a letter to you from my parents."

Later that night we sat in the living room and I translated the three-page letter, just like the oral historians used to do. Asis had his feet on the sofa table and Carmen sat on the other end of the couch with her feet on Asis' lap.

"*Jefe, un masaje, por fav,*" Carmen asked. "Boss, a massage please."

"Girls always want you to do something for them," Asis said.

While he massaged Carmen's feet, I read the letter and we covered Hanna history in America. I told them about the Oregon Trail and Indian attacks, and we might have hit a little Manifest Destiny somewhere in there. The three weren't necessarily intertwined, but for storytelling purposes they made us Americans seem larger than life. Did they know that there was a California gold rush in 1848? Sure enough, there was! Personal histories were dissected. Paul was in high school and played the saxophone. Adam was in the military and married with two kids.

"*Qué joven,*" Carmen said. "I didn't think anyone else but us was dumb enough to get married that early!"

When I told them about my parents and how they had met while working at Steven's Hospital, Carmen asked if Mom had ever dreamed of owning a ranch. No, I didn't think Mom had ever dreamed of living on a ranch when she was little, I told her.

"Well, shoot," Carmen said.

Word for translated word, the Hanna Story began to unfold. It took us almost two hours and three TV breaks to cover it all. I thought our family story was quite common, a tale of yearnings wagered and lost, but Carmen told me that it wasn't.

"I think your parents are the kind of people we'd be friends with," she said. "They sound like regular people who aren't regular."

Since Mom and Dad couldn't come visit us, they sent something important in their place: authentic American food. "Let's see what your host brothers thinks about Kraft Macaroni & Cheese," Dad wrote. "They don't get many opportunities to try the food we actually eat in America."

In all, we sampled American peach tea, dried Idahoan mashed potatoes (my host brothers gave this a seven out of ten), Kraft macaroni and cheese (a six out of ten), several packages of Top Ramen (Asis junior: "*maybe* a five out of ten"), and chocolate Jell-O pudding ("*¡Joder tío!*" Adán raved. "I want this in my mouth!").

To showcase the food for my host brothers, I made "American college food" for lunch. All in one sitting, we doubled our daily fat intake and plowed our way through the mac and cheese, Top Ramen, and Jello pudding. A few weeks later, we finished off the rest of the *comida americana* at our second All-American Cookout (they marked this event on their calendars and looked forward to it). When we were about to eat the mashed potatoes at our second cookout, Asis junior had a question. "You put olive oil on these *patatas,* right?"

"Usually we just eat them plain."

He took a bite then cringed. "*¡Aí tío!* I don't understand why you Americans don't use olive oil."

"That's because it's *comida rápida, hombre.*" Adán told his brother in between a forkful of mac and cheese. "Americans do everything fast and cheap—they're like the Chinese. That's why they make all this fast food—they're always in such a hurry." He looked at me and took another bite. "*¿Sí o no?*"

While my host brothers weren't crazy about American *comida rapida,* they were amazed to learn that you could buy Top Ramen for ten cents a pack. "In Spain, this would be at least eighty cents," Adán said.

When we had finished all of the food, the three of us sat around the table and leaned back in our chairs, our bellies stuffed from running one leg of the American triathlon. "I feel amazing," Asis junior said. "Like I could bang ten women. *Tío,* someday I'm going to come to America and visit you and all the women in LA."

"Let's start with Penelope Cruz," I said. "She's right here in Spain."

"*Sí,* but first you've got to go to Italy and give me a report on those *guapas,*" he said. "When do you leave?"

"Tomorrow."

"*Ten suerte, tío.*"

Tomorrow my friend Devin and I would fly to Italy to visit a certain graveyard, among other things. This would be an important trip, my host brothers said. "Lots of women to see. You better get ready."

I began packing my bags. Tomorrow, twenty days of Spring Break were about to begin. I shoved the remainder of my clothes into Dad's hiking backpack and readied it for use. Before the sun came up, I would be gone.

Weeks 12-13

Italy

By six in the morning we were headed for the cemetery. The sun hadn't risen yet and by the time the city woke, Devin and I were across the Mediterranean, in Italy. We stood on the edge of the known world, thought of the only images of Italy we'd ever seen in the Olive Garden menu, and took off for the unknown. I thought of every Italian restaurant I'd ever been to—the olive oil, the spaghetti, the chefs with the tall white hats and the dark-curled mustaches, the pretty waitresses. Any images I once had of the rolling vineyards of Tuscany would be immediately replaced upon arrival with scenes of overturned fields and grass creeping through sidewalk cracks. Before the cemetery and before Italy, however, several things began to happen.

It started with the cemetery. We'd heard about it in a guidebook that listed the Milan cemetery as one of the top things to do and immediately knew that we'd struck gold. How often was the city graveyard the coolest thing to see? We'd grown tired of looking at cathedrals and the graveyard became part of a larger concept.

Our thinking was this: in eight days we would visit eleven cities. For twenty-one year-olds, we didn't really think it was that ambitious of a plan since it only averaged to 1.3 cities a day. We could do that. Two months ago in cooking class, Devin had asked me if I wanted to go to Italy for Spring Break. After class and a Mau on tap, we began hatching plans while poring over Google Maps with beers in hand. We would visit Florence, Venice, Rome, Milan, and since we were going as far as Milan, hell, why not, we'd even make it to eastern France since it was only a three-hour train ride. We planned big—somehow it would all work out. I thought so anyway.

But Devin was a different sort of traveler than I was; I had learned that much in the past two months. He was a great friend, a man of dripping conversation and a fellow overachiever and law school prospect. He was also fiercely independent, although I wouldn't learn that until later. And while he hadn't originally planned on going to Morocco with me, I figured that might be a good thing. Between the two of us, one of us needed to have some common sense, even though he didn't look it. Devin was a curled blond who looked more like a Californian surfer than an Oklahoma City suburb boy. He was a fan of emo Death Cab for Cutie and worship music, pastel green tees and Converse shoes, v-neck shirts and tight pants. He didn't wear an old 1970's hiking backpack like I did because he didn't need to: he'd bought a brand new one. He liked Buffalo Wild Wings and grew up in a gated neighborhood. But even though everything looked perfect on the outside, Devin said, it certainly wasn't, and he never went to church "until the end of high school." Then he had his conversion experience. Before that, he'd smoked a lot of pot and done bad things with lots of girls. Things they did in dirty movies. "I can't believe I used to do that."

On a chance trip to youth group with a friend, Devin met the Lord and turned his life around. He'd never been the same since, and neither had I. We were both determined to live life larger than life itself—to shoot the whole pig and go for it, a vivacious abundant life with plenty of pork to spare.

"What worries me about this trip is us," Devin said. "I've been on trips before with people and by the end of the trip, we ended up hating each other. We're friends and I really don't want to hate you."

"We'll be fine," I said. "What's the worst that can happen?"

"I don't know," he said. "Well, let's get back to planning."

Under the mood lighting of Devin's bendable desk lamp and the glow of our laptop screens, we poured over digital maps and booked hostel reservations. Each week we would meet to discuss the trip and get more and more excited as Devin's room became our sailing point. It was the sort of room you could spend hours in. Chairs were strewn with magazines in English and Spanish waiting to be read ("I've been meaning to get around to those," Devin would say), and books lined his upper closet shelves. In between glances at maps, we would talk about Lee Strobel's *The Case for Christ* and *Un Gato y Una Gaviota* from Spanish class. Our conversations could go anywhere, and one day Devin asked about my testimony.

"So what's your story, man? I mean, if you don't mind me asking."

"That's a long one," I said. "Do you want the whole thing?"

"Of course."

Well, you know what he discovered—there's more to this cowboy than meets the eye. Devin learned the story about the farm, my stint in juvenile lock-up when I was fifteen, and my quest to change my life from living with a single mother in a forgotten version of Seattle. I told him the whole truth, so help me God, the good and bad parts. I told him how my parents had divorced and how I had spent most of my early years with my mother and how every night I would watch her sit at the kitchen table and cut coupons out of coupon books while listening to praise music. During the day, she cleaned rich people's houses, and when I would get home from school, she would let me play with my friends for an hour or two, then we would run errands and go to ten different stores so we could save ten cents. That was in the days of one dollar gas, I reminded him.

"But your mom wasn't normal," he said. "She taught parenting classes, and yet you ran away from home."

I told him the things she did or I thought she did, now it didn't really matter. What mattered was that long ago, she did everything in her power to prevent me from seeing Dad, even going to the point of threatening her own breakdown if I ever left her.

"She told you she would die of a broken heart if you ever left her?" Devin asked. "Like she would actually die or …?"

I didn't say much more. My mother was always a believer in tough love, love that hurts.

"That's a lot, man. Wow." Devin went silent for a moment and leaned his arm over his desk. In the warm light of his lamp, a yellow glow illuminated the shadows of an Owen Wilson Oklahoma face. "I mean, wow. That's a really cool story. You put yourself in lock-up to set yourself free."

"I guess it's easier to talk about it than it is to actually live it." I looked down and saw that my shoes were untied. I reached over to tie them. "What about you?"

"Man, I was so far off the mark, I don't even know where to start." Devin leaned back in his chair until the front legs were off the ground. He braced his hand on the wall behind him to steady his tilt.

"Growing up, my older brother and I, we could do whatever we wanted—I would ask for something and get it. When my brother went off to college, my Dad paid for the whole thing. He was a doctor, but he smoked a lot of pot. Both him and my mom did. But when they had me, they decided to stop. They weren't believers, though. 'We have to quit this,' they said. 'We have to set a good example for our children.' I've always grown up respecting people and learning to say the right things, but when you come home from school one day and learn that your dad just cheated on your mom with a nurse, it tears your family apart. That's what he did. He cheated on her. I didn't know what to do. Now my brother, he hates my Dad, and I still like my dad, but I wonder every single day why he cheated. I guess part of it is acceptance, part of it is forgiveness, and part of it is learning to tell the difference. Believe me, I'm still trying to figure all of that out."

Conversations like this, they defined us. I may have had a hell-bent Moroccan spirit in me, but I still longed for this. Over the past two months, Devin and I had become good amigos, which meant that we were connoisseurs of late-night talks on castle ramparts as often as we frequented karaoke nightclubs. Sometimes he would wonder about a girl and come and ask me about her. I'd do the same. But deeper still, we tried to figure out what this mess of studying abroad and living in another country was supposed to mean. In Italy, we would figure that out. That was our issue, we determined. Everyone had to have "an issue" and this would be ours. We would finally find out what this whole travel thing was about, what it all boiled down to. "That's why I'm worried about this trip," Devin said. "We think we know each other, but maybe we don't. I'm worried that we might push ourselves too hard and lose it."

Eleven cities in eight days. By departure time, we decided to scrap France and aim in the general direction of three places—Milan, Florence, and Venice, and the rest, surely, would unfold—as long as we endured. Starting in a cemetery in Milan, we were about to find out.

Hovering above Milan like a lost soul, the cemetery sat silently behind a black wrought-iron gate. Beyond the gate, tombs were marked by elaborate entrance towers that were painted in red and white alternating stripes, colors that usually represented courage but that in cemeteries began to embody the opposite effect. Beneath the towers, open-aired walkways were lined with gray statues, as if a moment of celebration had suddenly been turned to stone and joy was frozen in place. The paths were of gravel and the sound of scraping footsteps was the only noise in the graveyard. There were no fountains.

"This is pretty eerie for ten in the morning," Devin said.

"Thanks for being obvious," I countered.

"Shut up." He saddled his pack over the shoulders of his white v-neck and strode towards the entrance. "Let's split up," he said. "I want to spend some time alone." We'd only been in Italy for one day.

"You're going to make me brave these tombs all by myself?"

"All by yourself."

"Man." I shouldered my pack and took off.

Devin started walking and lowered the brim of his Quicksilver hat over his forehead until it angled slightly away from me. He put on his headphones, and with his bright orange coat, he didn't look ready for the seriousness of the cemetery. I didn't understand how he could use headphones in a place like this, where the silence was not quite so obvious. By now, he had his back turned to me.

"Why do you have those headphones on?"

"Because I want to think." He turned back around and waved his hand at me. "Remember, *you* dragged me in here, because *you* wanted to see the cemetery. I'll forgive you though, because hopefully it will be important." He did an about face and disappeared through the black gate.

Now alone, I headed toward the red and white towers. Underneath the towers ran a series of arches and I passed through them to enter the cemetery. Not a soul stirred inside, but there was a presence to the place, as if someone was there. An Eden to the deceased, the graveyard at midday was alive with an odd sense of lingering death clinging to still life. Other than plants, there was no movement, even as a massive city unfolded in front of me.

Along the gravel lane on either side, a row of dead marble storefronts shadowed the main walkway forward. Brooding in silence and awaiting entrance, two-story tombs with glass doors peered into the path. Names were inscribed above the frames, and when I peered into the first tomb, I saw a gated stairway that descended into a dark pit. I hurried past. As I moved, a crow split the air and cawed, tightening the spell of the place. I jumped and repositioned myself in the middle of the path. There was no sign of Devin.

Ahead, a massive tower of sculpted dead loomed in the distance and I began making my way toward it. Along the way, I passed a rotten cherry and a crucifix, along with a bouquet of dead flowers and a skull suspended on a platter above a grave, hanging from a chain. Over another sepulcher, a faceless statue of an angel gripped the pommel of a sword as it bore the blade towards the ground, ready to defend the crypt.

While I didn't know the exact name of the cemetery, the City of the Dead seemed obvious enough as hundreds of buildings and statues extended in every direction as far as I could see. While I walked in the shadow of dead storefronts on the main avenue, I passed other streets just like it that ran through the city, crisscrossing and cutting between tombs and rain-washed stones. Unlike I had expected, there was no manicured grass or comfortable plots of inset graves. Instead, weeds grew at the foot of tombs as a pattern of names became steadily apparent. This wasn't where the nameless lived. It was a cemetery for the best, the rich, the famous and the once-famous—who all now happened to be dead. As I pushed onwards, the tombs continued to shade the path around me, crowding out all sense of space. It was a cemetery that was more gray than green.

I continued working my way through the first portion of the city until I arrived in front of a wall of names that looked like a ten-foot marble checkerboard. Inscribed on each square of the wall was a name, an insignia, and a thrush of wilted flowers. Woven together, the wall represented an entire family through the generations, every father, every son. Whether the family had died from a lack of promise, I couldn't tell, but the family line had ended and all that remained was a marble reconstruction of a simple family tree. For the rest of time, this wall was all that people would remember the family by. No matter what price had been paid long ago to try and keep the family together or grant it a future, it would only be remembered as long as the line endured. Because just being family was never good enough. The story had to survive, even if you didn't.

"When I need to think about something important, I go to a graveyard," Dad said. He was dressed in his black Sunday slacks and a blue plaid fishing shirt as Paul and I walked on either side of him through the grass. We were young then, but not so well dressed in our mismatched action figure shirts and stiff jeans that rubbed against our ankles. If I remember right, I was fourteen and Paul was ten. On all sides of us, flowers and May buds blossomed pink, even as we walked among the sleeping dead. "Look at all these names," Dad said, pointing down at various gravestones. "And to think that we don't know a single one of them."

Dad called our attention to the births and deaths of Robert Freedman and Martin Bowman and other names that we would never know as we walked by graves that stretched before us in gray-dot symmetry. "When I was young, I used to come to graveyards just to think. I'd wonder, 'what do my decisions mean in the long run? What really matters?' I thought about that a lot. I tried to figure it out, and for awhile, I never had an answer."

Dad kept walking forward, oblivious to the fact that as soon as he started talking, Paul and I decided to dodge the oncoming lecture and venture off to look at gravestones on our own. We wandered through the endless, lulling grass for half an hour or so, then Paul split off to be by himself. He was always a thinker, even though his long dark hair and young face never looked it. Paul was sensitive to things that mattered, Dad used to say. He knows a lot more than he lets on. I hadn't made up my mind on that yet, but he was my brother so he always got the benefit of the doubt.

After I'd thought and thought about nothing for what seemed like forever, I found Paul at the far end of the cemetery and I told him that we should go and find Dad. When we found him, he was sitting with his back to a tree and his hands clasped in his lap, his eyes closed. Paul said he had a question, and Dad slowly opened his eyes.

"Dad, will you ever be buried in a graveyard?"

"What makes you wonder?" Dad asked. Birds chirped in the tree above us and the main entrance gate was visible a hundred feet away. I watched an old woman get out of her car carrying an American flag and a basket of flowers.

"I just didn't know." Paul looked at Dad and blinked several times.

Dad placed his hands on the ground and began to push himself up. "Guys, I won't be buried in a graveyard."

"What?" I asked. "Why wouldn't you do that?"

The old lady with the flowers weaved in between gravestones, walking in a direct line steadily away from us. I watched her reach into her coat pocket and pull out a handkerchief as she came to a stop in the middle of one of the rows. Her face dropped.

Next to me, Paul shuffled his feet and lowered his voice. "Then how will we find you if you're not buried here?"

"That's just it. You won't find me. But you'll always know where to look for me." Dad put his hand over his heart and closed his eyes.

"But you'll be gone."

"Yes, maybe for a little while." Dad knelt down to meet our eyes before a tender smile smoothed across his graying face. "When I die, I want you to scatter my ashes on the farm we're about to buy. Someday on the Home Place, we'll have our own graveyard and we won't need somewhere to be buried."

* * *

"What took you so long?" Devin asked an hour later as he got up from where he was sitting on the dirty grass and dusted off his butt. "I've been sitting on this patch of grass forever."

"In your words, 'I just needed to have some time to myself.'" I ran my hands along Dad's backpack and fiddled with the straps, trying to read-just it.

"Well, you should do your thinking somewhere else, somewhere where I don't have to wait for so long."

"You could have explored the cemetery," I tried.

"I did. It was boring."

"Oh." I had spent a lot of time planning our cemetery visit, but Devin didn't really care. "Well, on to the next town."

We went on to the next town. For the next three days we hiked be-tween six coastal villages in the Cinque Terre and ate dinner with two girls from South Africa. We both liked the prettier of the two, so that became a bit of a problem. Then we bought some real Italian sausages and spaghetti to cook at our hostel one night, only to find that they didn't have a kitchen to cook it in, so it got moldy and we threw it out. One thing after another, things began to go south. Every night, Devin would wander off to stare at the Terre surf with his headphones on, watching it beat endlessly against craggy, cloudy rocks. He needed some alone time, he said, he was figuring out what traveling meant. Accordingly, I learned that traveling with Devin also meant that he liked to slow down and take a nap in the afternoons, usually right about the time I wanted to climb a mountain or do something interesting. When he would opt for a nap and tell me to wander the mountains by myself, I would return with stories and he would counter with jealousy and the cycle would begin the next day.

Cities began to roll by. Our time was short and our days were spent mostly on trains. When we'd arrive in Florence or Pisa or whatever town we were in, we would have just enough time to spend several hours wan-dering about taking pictures of anything noteworthy before going sepa-rate ways. Then we'd get back on the train and Devin would plug in his headphones and I would stare out the window.

Together we went to Catholic Mass on Easter, but we prayed alone at the church, fought over food and hostel details, then rode a taxi to the next town where we did it all over again. Oh, we had some good times in there, too. We hiked the Cirque Terre trail and cracked a few jokes. We made a fire on the beach and watched the waves crash next to us in the dark. A few days later we saw the leaning tower of Pisa, but Devin didn't want to take a lot of pictures in front of it, so we resorted to looking at the tower while arguing about which restaurant to eat at. By Florence I was getting tired of wandering nameless towns and being told to do things by myself, and by our final stop in Venice, I was really starting to hate Italy. It wasn't the rolling vineyard Olive Garden we had dreamed of; it was becoming far more than that.

In the eleventh city, in Venice, our journey came to a close. "Aren't you hungry yet?" I asked Devin when we arrived on a water bus.

"Not really. Why don't you grab something for yourself?"

In front of us, a beautiful scene unfolded. Sprinkled in warm spring air and pastel hues, white airplanes drew streaks across the sky, carving lines into the horizon. Murky canal water reflected dual images of the burgundy and beige buildings that began to fold into view, bent four stories high around the water's reflection. In front of us, a classical-style church stood in greeting, and next to it, a leaning tower, another Pisa. All around, people walked and talked as they moved in and out of glass shops where you could buy a duck, a dog, or your very own model of Venice in fluorescent blown glass. We didn't quite know where to begin.

Since we hadn't eaten in four hours, I suggested a nearby cafe and Devin reluctantly agreed to a window seat so we could watch the boats move along the channel. Outside our window, a gondola peacefully made its way through the water as the driver calmly lifted his long black oar and steered a young couple towards what was likely their honeymoon suite. I wanted to watch their faces and see their olive hair and Mediterranean jewel eyes light up as they turned to each other for a kiss under the arched bridge, but as I shifted my weight on the seat, the sun burned into my face through the window. By the time I shifted back, the couple was gone and in their wake, a lovely, dirty canal.

"Let's split a pizza," Devin suggested. A minute later our waiter came over and Devin ordered a wrap, smiled at the waiter, and folded his arms in front of him on the table. "Well, I guess I'm having a wrap."

That did it.

Conflict ensued. Bickering and you-said, I-said dominated the conversation landscape. We watched happy people paddle down the canal as we fought, until water and gondolas were all but forgotten. At the end of eleven cities, perhaps we had reached for too much. Devin got up to leave. "Why don't we split up for awhile?"

We parted ways, letting the water and our suspicions sit between us like silent canals. Who was this rich-boy son of a doctor who could go hours without eating, who would disappear for hours on his own, then suddenly begin a conversation as if he hadn't ignored you for the whole day? And, from Devin's perspective, who was this Steve Hanna—some stubborn guy with a hick accent who wanted to do everything together as if it was some sort of brotherhood experience? That Baker kid, he was a wreck—that was for sure. He never wanted to be alone. Well, he'd have to go off on his own now, see how he liked that.

We split ways that evening, and the only thing that brought us back on good terms was when I ate something disgusting and threw up after midnight in our hostel and woke everyone else up. At two in the morning, I huddled in a bathroom stall with yellow walls that in Spain would have symbolized sickness. I was on my knees, alone, in front of the toilet, giving it everything I'd eaten. Devin walked in. "Are you alright?"

On our final day in Italy we sat on a tiny island, hung our legs over the edge of a concrete overhang, and watched the boats move up and down the main channel in front of us. Cargo boats made it look like the battleship game we used to play as kids, and at first, we didn't say anything. The conversation could have happened anywhere, but here with this setting, amongst canals, bridges, bus boats and all sorts of ships, here in this backdrop maybe it became more real. It's not that you need or exactly search for a backdrop like this, but when it appears or when you find it, you can't help but enjoy it. I don't remember everything we talked about, but I remember what I forgot about.

Three feet over and next to me, Devin tilted back a forty and took a drink from his beer. He'd already peeled the label off it. I don't even remember what it was called; it wasn't that good. Sitting in his orange coat with his legs swinging over the edge of the concrete, Devin leaned back on his arms and the wind carried his blond, tangled hair across his face, even though it was mostly held in place by his backwards hat. "Everything that has happened in Spain, you know, it all really came down to this. Hanging our feet over the edge, yelling at each other and drinking a beer."

"I guess," I said before pausing to watch a water taxi load and unload a group of passengers. "But isn't this supposed to be more than that? The time of our lives, I mean. Something grand?"

"That's what they say." Devin took another drink. "Well, it's been anything but that."

"You're right. But what about studying abroad? I mean, we were going to figure this thing out, find out what it really meant."

"Thirty thousand dollars of student loans is what it meant … and I wish I could say it was worth it."

"Yeah."

A ways in front of us, a boat with a crane began burrowing into the canal, sifting rocks on the bottom, digging.

"This is fun, don't get me wrong," Devin said, "other than us bickering like old wives." His eyes turned to follow the crane. "But the truth is, I could have gone to Hawaii on a national exchange and had just as much fun."

"True."

"But I also would have smoked a lot of pot."

"Also true."

We laughed and looked over at each other. "Okay, you're right. This is all I ever dreamed of. And eventually, maybe a girl."

I looked away and across the water. It was so distant, all the way to the shore. "Someday, you'll find her."

"I don't like someday." Devin took a final swig and sat down his now-empty forty. "I swear, sometimes we live our whole lives for someday.

'Someday far in the future, your life will mean something.' That's what they tell us in school. Pay the price now, make the hard decisions, sacrifice, and maybe someday, it will mean something to someone. That's what life is, right? We live our lives for a day we'll never see, on a promise we may never fulfill."

I looked out across open waters and my vision blurred to blue-gray. "Someday though, can mean an awful lot." The crane began digging deeper and pulled up a load of dirt and gunk from the ocean floor. "When I was little, my Dad used to tell my brothers and I that someday, we'd get to see miracles. And when I was young, I used to believe him. Funny enough, in Morocco a few weeks ago, I began to believe him once again. Well, I probably believed him all along, because you have to, don't you? You have to believe in a better day or else life becomes too hard, even though our lives would seem pretty good to most people. All I know is that miracles are never what we're told to watch for. Like these boats, they come and go, depart and then arrive, and sometimes we only get to glimpse them for just a moment. But if one of them appeared, I could live my whole life for it. I could live my whole life waiting to see something unbelievable, if it was big enough to be believed in, even if it was just a promise to myself."

Devin looked over and threw his arm out in playful jest. "Stop it," he laughed. "Now you're making me a believer!"

"But it's true, isn't it?"

"Yes." He looked away. "So true that sometimes, I wish it wasn't."

In that final moment, the pieces came back together. No wonder fireworks had been flying yesterday. It had been eight days of hard lessons, of testing, learning, and enduring. And there were more ahead in that canal in front of us. We would find a boat, cross to the mainland and find our way back to the airport. Somehow, we'd been through this many times before: now it would be easier. I knew this. We had crossed the divide, sat on the island with our legs hanging over the edge and completed our training.

For all of this, this was what the Pact meant. It meant that even though someone long ago had paid the price to set my family free, I had to go to the edge just as they had done so many years ago. There was no other way to learn. Over the last few weeks I'd brought myself to the edge of a table and rusty chain, the edge of waterfalls and mountain fissures, the edge of a swimming pool jumping to my father, and the edge of a canal in Venice to learn the same lesson. Here under this blue sky sitting amongst a sinking city, I didn't think of the Pact, only that since being in Europe, I hadn't wasted a second of my time and didn't intend to. I had learned some valuable things and for the first time, I knew that I had either luck or whatever it took to carry on. Because lurking behind the story of the Pact was also a promise. One day, one of Vaclav's descendants would return.

I looked over at Devin, my knees bent, rising. I swung Dad's mountain backpack that had now earned international status over my shoulder. Devin glanced up at me, his Quicksilver trucker hat cocked over a sunburned Owen Wilson face from Oklahoma. "Let's go."

III

The Return

WEEK 14

EL CAMINO DE SANTIAGO

MIDNIGHT—THE TRAIN. It's dark inside and outside; the windows have fogged in places from heads leaning against them, breathing. The only light in the car comes from vagrant orange reading lights plated above each seat, just enough to give the car an eerie glow. Other than a dark-haired man sitting across the aisle from me, everyone else has their heads bent forward, hanging in the air as they sleep; the seats aren't very comfortable. The man across the aisle eyes me suspiciously, his face malicious. He looks down and makes note of my hiking boots. *El Camino de Santiago*. In a moment he knows where I am going and what stop I am getting off at. Sarría.

The captain walks down the aisle, looking down at the passengers and reaching above someone every so often to check the fading lights. *¿Todo está bien?* I feign sleep. We have been through this before. I am still scared, but this time I know how to handle the situation.

The door shuts behind the captain and it's just me and the lingering man. He looks over again, slits his eyes and reaches his hand into his coat pocket. He mouths something to me, something I'd like to run away from, but I slit my eyes and do the same, reaching into my pocket for the latch on my knife. The other passengers look asleep enough to be considered dead. The man looks around again, his eyes like dark pools of water that shimmer ominously, hiding something. A ruse, he relaxes back into his seat, willing to bide his time until I fall asleep and he can have what he wants. By dawn, six hours from now, I would be on a road I didn't know, walking. He knew this—there was plenty of time to rob me. Would he follow?

The train brakes to a stop. I look over my shoulder to determine the man's intent. No trace of movement. I press my face against the window to discern the name of the town we are stopped at. There is no sign at the train station. We are in a no-name town without a sign to mark where we are or where we are going. There won't be any sleep tonight.

Several minutes later, the train pulls out of the no-name station. I grab my bag, stand up with conviction, walk by the dark-haired man as if I don't see him as a threat, and make my way to the coffee car. My suspect eyes me warily, but doesn't make any sudden moves as I walk out in my black coat, blending into the night. I would ask for directions later, from a source I could trust. For now, there is a long way to go until Sarría and Carmen's home in Santiago.

FINDING CARMEN'S FAMILY

"You never went back home?" I asked her. "At sixteen, you just got up and left?"

Wide-eyed, Carmen looked straight at me. Her eyes were open like bowls *tan largos* to hide her customary blue eyeliner. "It was the only thing I could do."

The week before I boarded the train, the full story began to unwind at a table of wooden barstools down the street from our apartment. As the nine o'clock April light began to wane, palm trees swayed in the wind outside the window, while inside lights hovered above tables like glowsticks. Across the table from me, Carmen sat hunched over her *vino blanco*. She didn't drink, she claimed, but she did occasionally drink white wine—

water. She lifted her glass to her lips and took a sip. Asis sat next to her, distractedly reading the paper, *un periódico*, and sipping a Mau from tap. In a week, I would be going to Carmen's hometown and hoped to visit her family. I sat across from them with a beer in hand and listened.

"*Hace muchos anos ...*" Carmen began as the full version of the story unfolded. Her father had never liked her. I already knew that he used to beat her, but that was beside the point. "Estif, the problem was that he loved my brother far more than he ever loved me." When you love people at different levels, she said, you have to differentiate; you have to make sure they know they're not equal. That was how it felt anyway, at the beginning. Then twenty years ago, her brother had married *la loca*, a crazy woman who had turned a good man ("ok, an alright man") bad. "*¡Aí, la bruja!*" Carmen said. "That little witch-bitch!"

One of the first things the new wife asked Carmen's brother to do was take over the family estate. Several years later, he did just that and didn't ask Carmen for permission. Of course she wasn't *amargura* about that. It was impossible to be bitter, really. He'd simply never told her about it. One day she returned home to visit her parents, but when she tried to walk into the front door of her old house, a family she'd never seen before was eating dinner. They jumped and Carmen scrambled out the door. *Dios mio*, that little shit had sold the house! Even worse, he'd taken all the money for himself. When she confronted him about it, he claimed that he had tried to let Carmen in on the sale, but his wife told him to keep the money for themselves, so he hid it all away.

"*Las chicas son más peligrosas que serpientes*," Asis interjected, momentarily looking up over the paper and the rim of his reading glasses. Girls were more dangerous than snakes. He winked at Carmen and she lightened up a bit. "Oh, they're dangerous alright. The *brujas* are."

Right before Carmen's parents died, her sister-in-law poisoned them against her, too, and when Carmen returned to visit her parents on their deathbed, they didn't want to see her. "The only one who would have believed that I was a good *hija* was my grandmother, but she died long ago." Since then, her parents had wasted their lives away in a government-assisted nursing home where the crazy wife and the corrupt brother had abandoned them for good. Eventually, the bruja even convinced her own husband, their favorite son, to stop visiting them. Not only had the bruja won control of the estate, she had subverted the family in the process and now Carmen's brother only went to visit their parents twice a year, even though he only lived fourteen kilometers away. As for her brother, well, Carmen hadn't seen him in years. "Do you think I want to get screamed at?"

Carmen wasn't the only one alone—there wasn't any family left on Asis' side either. An only child, his most vivid memory growing up was of his father dying when he was barely a young man. Years later, his mother died on a visit to Alicante, and any rag-tag cousins that he might have been related to were scattered all over France, leaving him and Carmen together with no one but each other. Carmen, an abused girl, and Asis, a lonely child. "So we're all we have," he said, putting down the newspaper and adjusting his reading glasses on his nose. He crossed his arms on the table. "You, Adán, Asis junior and eleven years of American kids we'll probably never see again—you're all the family that we have."

Carmen and Asis didn't live normal Spanish lives; their immediate families had never been close. They'd lived through many hard and lonely years, and they worked hard in the present. When they came home from work, they spent their nights talking to American students who half the time couldn't understand what they were saying, and they spent dinners explaining simple things like how to say orange, *naranja*, in Spanish. They laughed and made jokes that only the two of them were able to understand. Then they would explain the same things about Alicante twenty-two times to twenty-two different students and have the same conversations in front of the TV in their living room (*"la parada del autobús está aquí, el Mercado Central está alli …"*). By the time an *hijo* finally learned enough Spanish to joke with them and share dinners with their Spanish friends, he would have to leave and another would take his place with little to no understanding of the language, and the process would begin all over in four-month increments. Semester after semester, they were teaching Spanish and building a family one son at a time, but it was harder than raising real kids. With real kids, at least you got to enjoy the fruits of your labor. Instead of raising more of their own kids, however, they preferred to spend their time raising study abroad sons who would never forget them, but who nonetheless would never be able to come to their thirty-year wedding anniversary or eventually, their funerals.

"We pray for you kids every day," Asis said. "It might not make any sense, but somehow, all of this is going to be worth it."

Asis was right, sacrifice didn't make any sense. Not at the time anyway, at least not to the one who had to do the sacrificing. But in some histories, hard lonely lives have a way of leading to surprising turnarounds, even if they do come one hundred and twenty-five years later.

One hundred and twenty-five years ago, Vaclav washed himself in what was probably a dirty washbasin as beginnings rinsed in ruddy mud, clay, and forgetfulness—that was how I imagined it anyway. In a town that most people drove their horses by and forgot, in a house that was desperately falling apart, and in a family that no one said would ever amount to anything, a young boy washed himself in a simple pail of barely-heated water. The walls of the shed-house were stripped bare; there was nothing left. No music, there was only the soft *sop-sop* of water sloshing against the side of the basin as Vaclav quietly moved a rag across his body in the dim evening light. With each rag-stroke the water dirtied. In the morning, he would be at work again, herding geese and chickens, and his life maybe would regain some sense of meaning. From birth, he knew he would have to work to help his mother make ends meet.

It wasn't all bad though, he must have told himself. For a boy, herding chickens was fun. He believed that. You got to run and play and chase little yellow and red chickens and hold them in your arms as they struggled to get away, *cluck-cluck*. When their beaks would bob up and down in his arms, his mother would laugh at times. Now she was in the kitchen somber, cooking dinner. Living with them were probably other family members, but we never knew their names.

For being the one the Pact would later send to America, Vaclav Belohlavy certainly didn't look the part. Born a bastard child to a young woman, his birth was supposed to be forgettable in a no-name 1857 Bohemian town. In the early years of his life, it certainly was. He went to school in the summer and worked the rest of the year. Playing with friends was probably rare. As soon as he was old enough to work, he dropped out of the third grade and started herding geese and chickens full-time. By eleven, he began herding cows to support his working mother and by twenty-seven, he met a girl, Marie Jimel, and they got married. Whether or not he had many friends, I don't know, but the letters suggest otherwise. Even at eighty-six, he never knew who his father was.

The scene shifts to the night of the Pact when Vaclav stood beside his mother and new wife as they gathered around the candle-lit table. Inside and outside, it was dark as a mantle descended on the hovering light of a single waxed flame. As hands reached into the middle of the table to drop coins that clanged in a pile beside the candle, Vaclav reached into the center and gave everything he had earned from cow herding. That wasn't the only price he paid.

When all of the money was gathered and when the Belohlavys put their hands together and sealed the Pact for good, he would be asked to pay the final price. Like the other young men of the family, they asked him to draw lots to become the one they would send to America, at least that was how I imagined it. As if on cue, the rest of the family backed away from the table, leaving Vaclav and several other young men huddled around the orange light. An old man appeared from out of the shadows and placed a lot of straws on the worn surface before disappearing once again. One by one the men drew lots, but the man next to Vaclav was selected. He was frightened. Winning the draw and becoming the One meant that he was now destined to leave everything he knew behind. His family—his father and mother, his wife and children—everyone he held close would disappear, at least until he could send for them. Even though he didn't have much else, he was being asked to sacrifice his immediate family in order to save the extended family. It was a heavy cross to bear, and even though he would have the opportunity to change family history, he realized that he couldn't do it. He wasn't strong enough.

When he backed away on the day of departure, he gave Vaclav the train ticket. *Maybe you'll know what to do with this,* the other man said. Vaclav nodded. Perhaps it helped that he didn't have a father to cling to.

In 1885, a lonely cow herder left for America, leaving his pregnant wife in the process. He would send for her, he said, but he didn't know when that would be. By the time he had raised enough money to buy her a ticket to a better life in Nebraska, their newborn son had died. He found out the day she arrived in America.

The train pulled into the station. It was still dark outside, but unlike the other towns along the road to obscurity, this one was faintly marked. The word *Sarría* beckoned and hung suspended from a barely-visible sign-post next to the tracks. Sarría was a town with a name, and that pointed toward an imminent destination.

The pilgrimage would start at dawn. I checked Dad's mountain pack to make sure it was still holding up. The bag was good, but my boots weren't. A week ago I'd bought some boots at a *zapatería* for "a bargain" at twenty-five euros, but I learned that you got what you paid for: the soles had already cracked and my boots were filled with water from the streets.

I went into a nearby café and changed into my tennis shoes while several hikers began to materialize. They carried large, internal frame backpacks and wore raincoats and thick Gortex boots. Like most serial hikers, they also had ample facial hair. *¿De dónde sois?* I asked. *Argéntina*, they replied. They went up to the counter to order a cup of coffee, then sat at a table to wait for the sun's first light. It would be a long walk in tennis shoes and blisters, but the end of the road would be telling. Ever since she was a little girl growing up in a village near the cathedral, Carmen had memorized the legend of Santiago, and appropriately, she had passed it on to me.

"In Santiago, there is the tradition of St. James," she explained the night before I left. "When I was a little girl, I used to go to the cathedral and place my palm in the handprint of the apostle inscribed on the main pillar and pray."

The story of Santiago meant that you could pray for five things—one for each finger. When you placed your hand inside the apostle's, you were supposed to come with five requests. "Only five," Carmen reiterated. "It's spiritual discipline, but I'm not always good at that part."

When she would tell me the story, Carmen would usually grab one of her plastic crosses and hold it in her hands as a prayer charm. "I usually pray for *trabajo* and *salud*," she said, "because work and health make life worth living. I would sometimes pray for *dinero*, but if you have work, it usually means that you have money, so sometimes I leave that part out."

I nodded.

"But in Santiago," Carmen's voice hung suspended in the air. "Prayers are different." She got up from where she was sitting in the living room and moved over to the china cabinet and a picture of her sons. "When you get to Santiago, there's something I must ask you to do."

THE ROAD TO SANTIAGO

Early light began to filter across the horizon. A soft April chill hovered in the air, clinging to leafless trees that lined and sprouted along a winding, uncharted road through the countryside. Moss clothed trunks in fur and ivy draped from branches that overlooked distant hills turned golden as the sun collided with morning fog. Ahead, a dirt path stretched beneath two hills and continued further ahead. Beyond the hills, swampland and grassy plains unfolded with each step; all of it Spain's last frontier, an east-west Manifest Destiny that sang of birds and snowmelt brooks. Frozen in time, the Camino was ageless and golden in the early morning. Inching on towards the cathedral in Santiago, the road beckoned.

"*Hola*," I called out to two middle-aged women as I neared them on the road ahead. "*¿Qué tal?*"

They responded in Italian and turned to face me. The taller of the two had a ball of tangled auburn hair that struggled above her forehead, held at bay by a red headband. The shorter of the two had a tighter haircut that clung to her ears as if they had been pruned. Both of them looked like they were coming undone by their hair; they were teachers. That didn't matter though, they told me. Work was not what we were going to talk about. They were hiking the Camino to finally do it, they said. "And to stop cooking and being Italian women, at least for a week."

For the first few hours, we walked together. Every now and then along the side of the road, one-room churches from a thousand years ago would appear on the horizon and the road would sketch its way towards them.

Carved in stone and as tall as low trees, we would enter unchanged chapels to the scent of alter incense and the image of an age-worn crucifix. Wooden benches lined the center floor and we would kneel and pray before greeting the old parishioners who guarded the guestbook. From the locals, we'd collect stamps in our *credenciales* to chart our progress along the Camino, then we'd continue on our way to the next stone church. The rhythm of the road, it went on.

Several hours passed until we reached the first decision point. For the past hour, we had been following roadside stones bearing the imprint of the yellow conch, the symbol of the Camino. We hadn't seen the conch or its complementary yellow arrows in a while, but we weren't worried. Then we arrived at an intersection. Right, left, or ahead, the path was unmarked. We stopped in the middle of the crossroads where trees grew on every side, obscuring any sense of bearing. On the Camino, you didn't carry a map—you weren't supposed to need one since the road was generally marked.

"Which way?" the short-haired woman asked. "There's supposed to be a marking, a yellow arrow, that's supposed to point us in the right direction."

I took off Dad's backpack and began examining the rocks and trees along the side of the road. Somewhere a sign would indicate our way forward. I ran my hands along tree trunks and turned over rocks and fallen branches, but I couldn't find anything in the undergrowth. Thorns pricked my hand as I dug into the ground looking for anything. I found nothing.

I went back to stand in the middle of the road with the Italians and we crossed our arms and stood silent. It had to be here. I went back into the bushes and searched our surroundings again. On my fingertips, the Camino carried the dingy feel of dirt rubbing and somehow slipping through your fingers.

As I ran my hand across the jagged edge of a rock and reached to pull a branch away from my face, I uncovered a faint yellow arrow. Barely visible and drawn long ago, it pointed vaguely in one direction. I waved the Italians over and they nodded. We turned to the right and followed the arrow.

✳ ✳ ✳

On day two of the Camino I met the Germans. Rain misted over an early foggy morning as I lumbered up a hill in three layers of coats while dodging mud puddles to keep my shoes from getting wet. Dreary enough, the route ahead was looking hard.

"*¡Buen Camino!*" came a sudden greeting call behind me. "*¡Buen Camino!*"

I turned around to find two military men walking toward me. I'd seen them before. Last night while checking into the *albergue*, a pilgrim's shelter where Camino walkers stayed each night, I had overheard two men in camouflage talking to the hostess in Spanish. There was something confident and sure in their demeanor, the way they stood straight and walked in straight lines even as they talked in circles. I don't know quite what it was, but I knew I needed to find a way to meet them. Direct indirectness—it was a rare character trait. Now behind me, they called out in greeting. I turned and waved.

The first thing I noticed was that they both wore army boots, but were of surprisingly different heights. Daniel, the shorter of the two by more than a few inches, had a short military haircut and looked more Eastern European than German, his face slightly pulled back. He introduced himself first. "I work at a cell phone store," he said.

Next to him, the taller of the two had longer, fluffy hair that crawled across his forehead and suggested a traveling playfulness uncharacteristic of a military man. "I'm a baker," he said as we shook hands. "Lu." More than names, these were people defined by what they did.

I introduced myself the American way. "I'm Steve," I said.

"Well, what do you do?" they asked in English.

"I'm a student."

"But your accent—you must be from America!" Lu exclaimed.

I nodded.

"I've been to Vegas," Lu began in between breaths at the top of the hill. "So many casinos, so many beautiful women!"

As we crested one hill and began working our way down another, Lu told me about his trips to Vegas and America. "I usually lose most of my money in Vegas, so someday I want to do a road trip across America," he said. He had friends in Miami, and someday they would go on an American Road Trip like in the movies. "That's what you do in America, right? You go on road trips?"

As for his own travels, he'd already road tripped across Europe, seen the pyramids of Egypt, gone on safaris in South Africa, and walked the Great Wall of China even though he still lived at home with his parents and worked in the family bakery. That was the permanent part. "For more than three hundred years, every man in my family has worked in the bakery. Destiny, it's inescapable sometimes."

As we reached the bottom of one hill, the path wound through a grove of pine trees. Hanging over the path, dangling needles brushed our coats with a soft wicking sound as we lowered our heads. Lu led the way as Daniel and I walked behind, side by side.

"So you've grown up your whole life knowing you'd have to work in the bakery?" I asked. "Is that easy?"

"Decisions are, at least," Lu said, glancing over his shoulder at me, his face bent somewhere between a smile and resolution. "But there's conflict too."

What he really wanted to do, he said, was live life like the Camino— constant travel, life to the footsteps of forward motion. But then there was the bakery. He liked it well enough, the art of baking and growing a business that was rooted in a definite place in time, but he also loved movement—travel—two goals that were unfortunately opposed. Each year, he said, he worked seventy hours a week in order to spend four weeks away from the bakery and Germany. In the coming year, however, he would inherit the business and travel opportunities would come fewer and farther between. Since his younger brother played the piano and didn't have a head for business, Lu was the obvious heir now that his parents were going to retire. That led to another problem: unless he was to somehow find a girl and get married, he didn't have anyone to share the bakery with ("and we all know *that* will be a long shot"). As much as he wanted it, marriage would mean settling down, and adventures and stories would probably have to come to an end. As it was, this was his final adventure with Daniel. "That's because Daniel's married," he jested.

"I am," Daniel said. "And I wouldn't have it any other way."

"Rub it in," Lu said.

"I will." Daniel looked over at his friend and pulled out a cigarette. "Light my medicine stick," he jested. Lu pulled out a lighter and lit both of their cigarettes as we continued walking.

Ever since they were kids, Lu and Daniel had grown up together in Glauchau, East Germany, perhaps better known as "the German Democratic Republic," as Daniel was fond of saying. "I still fly the old GDR flag in my basement," he said. He didn't want anything to do with West Germany.

In the same small village where their parents and grandparents and great grandparents had lived and died, Lu and Daniel would remain to tell the rest of their families' stories.

For Daniel, it was time to settle down. Unlike most Germans, he had gotten married at twenty-four, and had two kids by twenty-six. A third child was on its way, and he was glad that his wife had allowed him one last trip out of the house like old times. But while she was nice enough to let him go, his job wasn't nice enough to pay him for the time off. Even if his life depended on it, he would never escape the cell phone store, he said, working full-time for six hundred euros a month. "It's hard enough to have a family. But even harder when you can't afford one, and even harder when I know that I'm not educated enough to get a job anywhere else."

I looked over at Daniel and asked about their camouflage. Even that wasn't a choice, he said. In Germany you either joined the civil service or joined the army, so ten years ago they had both decided to join the army. Ten years later, they decided to hike the Camino.

We reached another unmarked intersection. This time open low-grass hills rolled for miles, bordered in the distance by a faint line of rusted trees. An abandoned village loomed to our right, and nestled between two hills was a collection of stone foundations where ivy and moss had sprouted between cracks. Ahead and to the left, the sky stretched above trees and a stony brook. "Where to?" Lu asked. "We followed people at all the other intersections."

Like before, I searched the nearby undergrowth and found a yellow arrow faintly inscribed on a strip of rotting tree bark. I pulled the plants aside and nodded to Lu and Daniel, and they nodded back. We would follow the arrows.

Over the next four days, three nights, and ninety kilometers, we walked through forests, farms, thousand year-old villages, and the largely un-populated northern parts of Spain as *peregrinos* bound for Santiago on the most famous pilgrimage route in Europe. In the words of the patron saints, the Camino was "a way." It was the way to the bones of Saint James and the road to Finnisterre and world's end, the westernmost point in the Old World.

Along the way, yellow arrows marked our progress and pointed us to-ward Santiago. Etched into rocks and carved into trees along the way, we looked for *la flecha amarilla* to point us in the right direction. The arrows appeared in a number of predictable places, but they were not necessarily in the same place every time. Obvious signposts bearing the arrow were placed every so often, but sometimes we would walk for hours without seeing an arrow. It became a journey of trust, a journey of beginnings and endings.

Each day began and ended at a different stage: the Camino was di-vided into thirty-one *etapas*. Each stage required a day to complete and ended in a covered shelter, an *albergue*, where pilgrims would rest and recover in sleeping barracks before the next etapa began. Stages varied from fifteen to thirty-five kilometers per day, depending on the terrain. The weather was usually rainy, and back in Alicante, a volunteer at the local *oficina del peregrino* had advised me to pack a raincoat and water-proof pack cover. "It can rain for days on end," he said.

The thought of rain defined our daily routine. Every morning at six o'clock, all fifty of us in the albergue barracks would wake up early to check the weather. Someone, usually an old person, would run to the window and give us *la lluvia* report, and we would adjust our routine accordingly. If it was raining, people would get ready faster, talk louder, and complain more, but if it wasn't, the fifty of us would wander around and slowly cycle through the one communal bathroom with four toilets, three sinks, and three showers, making small talk until the albergue staff kicked us out to begin the next etapa. I tried setting my alarm the first night, but after it went off and I woke everyone up, I realized that alarms were a bad idea. On a pilgrimage, you didn't need them.

The Camino, then, became more defined more by the things we didn't have than by the things we had. We didn't have more than three changes of spare clothes. We didn't have the news, TV, or cell phone service. We didn't know what was going on in the world outside of the Camino and we didn't have anything to do but walk and talk. Other than my loaf of bread and jar of peanut butter, we didn't even carry extra food. It wasn't customary to listen to iPods as we walked to add music to monotony—after all, the point of the road was to learn how to deal with monotony. At first, we didn't even know the people we were travelling with, but the Camino assured us that we would have twenty-four hours a day to learn about our fellow pilgrims and why we were travelling together. On the Camino, there was a reason for everything, even a reason for absence. When something was absent, it meant that it couldn't be a distraction. When something was present, it meant that it was there for a very distinct reason.

As such, I began to get to know my fellow travelers. Bound together on an ancient route across northern Spain, the other pilgrims hailed from Korea, Venezuela, Australia, Mexico, Italy, Scotland, and Germany. A divorced woman from Australia clutched her walking stick and talked about days gone by as if the air in her lungs was the last thing that remained. A woman from Valencia complained of constant tiredness, but found strength in the soreness—her husband had left her and that was just how life was. A group of Venezuelans had traveled across the world to complete the pilgrimage, but they had left their families behind in order to do so. They would see them again soon enough, they said, but long walks with empty thoughts were hard. Taken together, we were all that we had on the road.

At first I talked to everyone, but after learning that the other pilgrims were either forty or twice-married and divorced, I travelled the rest of the way with Lu and Daniel.

"I don't know why we're here, but I know that for some reason we have to be here," Lu said one morning. "One of the German celebrities wrote a book about the Camino, so of course that meant we had to do it."

In the mornings we would eat together before starting the next etapa. I usually ate two peanut butter sandwiches for breakfast ("American food," Lu called it), then we would put our coats on and be walking by eight o'clock. Usually by nine, Lu, Daniel, and I were sweating so hard that our coats had come off (if it wasn't raining), and by eleven we had passed most of the non-Spaniards along the way, who had stopped to take their first major eating break. We never stopped for a full lunch. Since the Camino was in Spain, it revolved around the Spanish eating schedule, which meant lunch at three or four that coincided with when we would arrive at the next village and the next albergue. Upon arrival, we would usually loot a grocery store for sandwich material and beer.

While eating, we'd hear stories from other travelers about life on the road. Two German girls told us about how they'd tried to hike an alternate route across the mountains, but along the way they'd run into snowed-in albergues and foaming wild dogs with skin that clung to their rib bones. Stranded in the middle of the mountains, the girls had to fend off the dogs with sticks. They didn't sleep for two days straight, they said. We heard other stories, too, like stories from an Italian, Matteo, who had started the Camino in France and walked for days on end through flat wheat fields. He spoke of the driving monotony and the listless wind.

In exchange, we told them our stories. Daniel would usually talk about the German Democratic Republic, Lu would usually talk about one of his road trips, and I would usually talk about Morocco. That always got a reaction. But when people would express disbelief at my story, Lu would defend it. He'd been there before, he said. He'd seen what happened in Morocco. After all, he was a fellow Morocco survivor and he'd be damned if my story wasn't nearly true.

After travelling stories, a light dinner, if any, followed at eight, then it got dark and we went to bed. In the morning we would wake up, put on yesterday's sweaty clothes, and do the whole thing all over again, five days in a row, with each day becoming harder and longer than the last. If you started in the south of France and did the whole Camino, the routine repeated itself for an entire month. The process, we were told, was supposed to build spiritual fortitude.

I don't know exactly what spiritual fortitude was supposed to look like, but the Camino began to exhibit a strange effect on us. The rest of the world disappeared. Past and future turned to nothingness and the present became a kaleidoscope of rolling hills and the occasional Spaniard driving herds of gaunt cows through crumbling villages with a whipping stick. One-street towns passed by the hour, and villages that a thousand years ago had boasted one hundred inhabitants now struggled to find five. But while the world around us remained mostly forgotten, the road ahead was in good shape as a series of yellow arrows pointed us steadily forward through villages strewn with the sound of wandering, pecking chickens, through forests and whispering swamps and distant hills, through someplace vaguely familiar, someplace we'd never seen before, but that nonetheless we'd known all our lives in a delicious, soft spring way. The only thing we ever knew while walking was how many more kilometers till the next albergue.

It was an incredibly freeing feeling. I forgot about the Pact and the Dream. You could physically see a weight and a burden being lifted from people's faces, even as our packs bore into our shoulders and the road challenged every leg muscle we had in us. There were no deadlines and no obligations, no paperwork to do, no errands to run, no bills to pay, no distant goals to worry about, no cell phones, text messages, email, stores, or shopping; no promises to make or fulfill. It was just you, your fellow pilgrims, three changes of clothes in your pack and the road stretching on further ahead.

The effect began to spread. Day by day, you could feel the changes the Camino was making. Even though we were just putting one foot in front of the other, *poco a poco* the Camino began to make little changes. We laughed more and had more time for others. We talked to random strangers on the road and took part in their lives. We took an active interest in each other and had more grace for the slow walkers or the early snorers. With nothing to worry about, our priorities shifted. The pressures and burdens of the world began to fade away until all that we were left with was a process that would change our lives forever, like Jesus' famous words, "pick up your cross and follow me." I didn't understand it at the time, but as we followed the path laid out for us in yellow arrows, I discovered a spent, lovely sense of peace. "For my yoke is easy and my burden is light," says Jesus, even though He ultimately calls us to carry our cross and die with Him. But if peace is like a river, it also pulses steadily in one direction, flowing toward a definite end.

On the third day, we made a rest stop in the early morning and I poured half a water bottle into my mouth. Droplets clung to *boca* canals as I swirled my tongue around to collect what gathered and tasted like rain dew. I capped my bottle and looked over at Lu and Daniel who had found a roadside bench to sit on. In the time that it took me to take three swigs, they had already sloughed off their packs and stuck medicine sticks in their mouths. Under the brims of their army hats, the tips of their cigarettes glowed orange in the early light.

Lu took a puff and reached into his backpack for what I expected would be a water bottle. Instead, he pulled out a six-pack of Estrella Dam and set it on the bench. I laughed.

"We're Germans, what can we say?" Lu held his medicine stick between his fingers as a white line of smoke drifted lazily in front of his eyes. "But at least we're integrating—this is Spanish beer." Lu and Daniel cracked open cans that hissed and fizzed before looking each other in the eyes and raising their beers. "*Prost!*"

I sat down and unpacked my jar of peanut butter and loaf of bread. Lu and Daniel laughed.

"You've got America with you and we've got Germany with us," Lu said, pointing first to my sandwich and then to his beer. "Between us, we're like the Cold War."

"No, we're like the German Democratic Republic," Daniel cut in.

"Right," Lu said. "So let's talk about the Cold War."

In our conversation, Lu told me that the Russians were actually the good guys in the Cold War. "I swear, what do they teach you Americans in your history books?"

I also discovered, among other things, that 9/11 was a plot hatched in secret by the U.S. government. "The evidence is mounting," he said. "Of course they'd try to cover it up."

Our conversations went back and forth, and we went from talking about the government to talking about golf in no time. The two were, in fact, connected, and I learned that in Germany there were lots of regulations. If you went to a golf course, you wouldn't be able to golf until you had passed a golf certification test to show that you knew how to correctly handle a golf club. After all, golf clubs were dangerous. You could hit someone with the fat end. "If there was a Camino in Germany, you'd need a license just to use a walking stick," Lu said, before chucking the butt end of his medicine stick into the grass and stamping it with his foot. Walking sticks were dangerous too. You could poke someone's eye out if you didn't use it properly.

"You better find yourself a stick," I said. "They're still free in Spain."

Lu went back to comparing American and European economic and social conditions. "We're getting distracted," he said. "This is important. The American system is fairer: you get out what you put in and you can make your own decisions, but the German system works better. Everyone gets the same thing. And while I think you have to work harder in America, you get the chance to make your own life. Over time, you get to choose who you become."

On the Camino, we were choosing. As the day drew to a close, I told them about the life my family had made in America since leaving Bohemia many generations ago. Over those short four days, we were becoming friends and that meant that our friendship would continue beyond the end of the Camino, Lu said. "If you ever get the chance to visit Germany again, you should come visit us. We live near Dresden, two hours from Prague and old Bohemia, the Czech Republic."

Two months ago on my third week in Spain, I had seen my study abroad director's poster about the Camino and wondered what would happen on the twisted, dirt-covered path that wound through valleys and forests, where two paths converged and in Frost's immortal words, I would have to choose a path. Unlike real life, the Camino would reach a definite end, urging forward with each yellow arrow towards a certain end. Months ago, my director Luis had told me that I should undertake the journey and for some reason I had agreed, though I could never put a finger on exactly why.

In the story of the Camino, there was a reason. Long ago, after Saint James was executed in Palestine, his disciples Atanasio and Teodoro fulfilled his dying wish and carried his body back to Galicia, Spain to be buried. Centuries after them, a Catholic bishop in Galicia decided to take a walk in the woods. He wasn't sure exactly why, but he felt compelled to take a walk. While walking in the forest, he stumbled across the tomb of Saint James. Immediately he called the king from León, who became the Camino's first pilgrim and built a cathedral on the original burial site. Almost overnight, thousands of people began to follow in the king's footsteps to see the body of the Saint at road's end, all from a simple walk in the woods.

The Apostle's remains, however, were now only visible on the tenth year, the Holy Year. On the tenth year, *El Puerto Santo* would be released and the Holy Gate that was normally closed would creak open for the crypt and the *restos* to become accessible. It was the tenth year.

At the end of the fourth day, we passed the final yellow arrow that I could remember. A steep hill and a long climb awaited.

"You again?" Lu said, looking up at the hill.

"Yep, you again," I said.

We started up the hill. Lu and Daniel draped medicine sticks from their lips, then halfway up the hill decided that smoking was a bad idea. "Don't ever start smoking," Daniel said.

"It'll kill your soul like marriage," Lu said.

"Shut up," Daniel fired back.

It was a lovely climb, really. I'd like to say that clouds broke at the top, that fresh air and heaven descended and hit us with a second wind midway up the stretch, but all I remember was that the hill was a long, winding climb. At the top we reached a metallic modern cross, but we were so tired that we didn't bother stopping. At sunset it would have been a nice view, but with hunger pangs, we pressed on to the albergue. When we arrived and discovered that there were no private restaurants, we resigned ourselves to the food that was in front of us.

"You really should come visit us," Daniel said as we sat at the counter eating sandwiches. After finishing the Camino, this was our last meal together. In the morning, our paths diverged.

"My father always told me that you get to see everyone in your life at least twice," Lu said when we waved good-bye. "We just don't know when we'll see each other next."

The following morning I arrived at the cathedral of Santiago to complete my journey and fulfill Carmen's wish. In the cathedral, I would place my hand in the hand of the apostle and pray for five things. Carmen had asked me to pray for work, health, and money (in that order), and I would do it. Her other request was that I abandon the search for her family. "They're not really worth finding anyways," she said. What was worth it, she reiterated, was the tradition at the cathedral—to pray for *cinco deseos*—the five things you wanted most. "Estif, I am only asking for one prayer from you. The other four—they must be your own."

Outside the cathedral an iron gate hung above the entrance to the Puerto Santo and the holy crypt. Inside would be the silver chest with the remains of Saint James. Coincidence or not, James also happened to be Vaclav's name in Czech. It was the tenth year and it was decision time. I tucked my head under the gate and headed for the crypt.

THE EDGE OF THE WORLD

While the Camino technically ends in Santiago, another road begins that leads to Finisterre. Literally, it means *el fin de la tierra*, the end of the earth, and that's exactly where I picked up the trail when I arrived in Santiago. In the days of old, pilgrims would continue to Finisterre to see the sun set over the ocean at the western-most point in Europe, the end of the known world.

At world's end, there is a lighthouse. A slight, white-paved path leads the way to the end of the Camino across breaking cliffs and a flush horizon where a square, white building stands. It's not a normal lighthouse. On top, a bronze dome houses what looks like a bell and the stillness in the air feels like the bell should toll. Along the path to the lighthouse, a lone white cross stands on the edge of the rocks, looking out across what is to come. Near the cross, a stone bears a yellow conch and reads 0 KM. At the lighthouse, the Camino ends.

I tried the door to the lighthouse, but it was locked. A dirt path curved off to the right and disappeared behind the square building. I followed the path. On a cliff to the right of the lighthouse, rocks broke and cracked below me as radiant surf bent and sparkled in perfect light that crashed endlessly against craggy rocks and green-sea outcroppings. With each wave, the past and future collided in endless precision, rhythmic, almost a blur. A sift of wind brazed my cheek and I raised my head to probe ahead further still. On the last stretch of cliff and hidden a little ways behind the lighthouse was a tall metal tower, a smaller version of the kind that held up power lines. Anywhere else, a metal tower would have been an unwelcome sign of modernity, but at the end of the Camino, it was more foreign than familiar. Hanging on the angled pieces of the tower's silver frame was a line of charred shirts, and near the tower, a burning stake.

Just as the first pilgrims had done so long ago, I stood at the burning point. It's an ageless feeling that defies space and time. The ocean spreads out like fire even in the middle of the day, vast, endless, impossible to comprehend, and it's even more difficult to comprehend that once there was something else, another continent waiting to be discovered. Vaclav had crossed this ocean years ago and six generations later, his descendant had returned.

As the pilgrims before me had done, I took off my shirt, gathered some brush, and burned them both at the stake. The tradition at Finisterre is to burn some of your hiking clothes to symbolize the parts of you that have melted away on the road. At the edge of the cliff, the flames licked and curled around wrinkled branches that slowly gave way and sighed.

Once more I looked out across the burning horizon until the sky and sea became a blue form of one. In the silence of the expanse, the fire next to me died down. The wind stilled. I took a breath, turned away, and stepped back from the edge of the cliff. With one last look over my shoulder, I began walking away, slowly at first, until I picked up the pace and started running back the way I had come. It was time to return home.

WEEKS 15-18
ALICANTE, SPAIN

WHEN I ARRIVED HOME MID-AFTERNOON, Carmen and Asis were already in front of the TV. Just like usual, Dior bounded down the shadowy hallway to greet me, but this time he didn't pee. He licked me, of course, but quickly shook his curls and bounded back down the linoleum floor toward the living room. Carmen and Asis were in there.

I heard a faint buzz coming from the end of the hallway and I walked toward it. As I passed the trinkets on the dresser, I heard my footsteps echo. There wasn't much noise, not like usual. *"Estif,"* Carmen called from the room at the end of the hallway. *"Por fin, ¡gracias a Dios!"*

When I entered the living room, Carmen and Asis turned their heads from where they sat on the couch with their feet crossed. *"Mira,"* Asis said, and pointed to the flatscreen TV in the corner of the room. Across the thirty-inch diameter, we watched a black cloud of ash erupt from the cone of a snow-covered mountain. I thought it looked pretty cool, like wonder and horror all at the same time, the sublime, but the reality of the situation was actually quite dire. Carmen and Asis sat static.

"How was the Camino?" Carmen finally asked, while she stared at the screen before a new series of images began to play.

The ensuing scene was new and familiar all at once. We watched the same *Icelandía* volcano explode again, but this time the footage was from a different angle. Then it erupted again at another angle, a helicopter clip, then once more as a close-up. Over and over, the image of a European Mount Saint Helens replayed within the black outline of the TV frame, confined to Iceland but reserved for Spain all the same. In the words of the Spanish announcer, it was *grande, oscuro y malo*, which translated to the end of Europe as we knew it for at least the coming week.

Not only had a volcano erupted in Iceland and halted all air travel for the coming week, but *Grecia ha caido*. On box-model television screens across the continent, riots rocked the streets of Athens as the Greek economy tumbled to the ground on the back of debt and retirement reform. Through restless volume and alarmed faces, picketers and thieves swarmed city streets, protesters and Greek derelicts halted traffic, and bystanders donned gas masks to protect themselves from the police. Men in swat jackets held clubs over pedestrians, and anyone with a camera trying to document the violence was taken out. Protesters filled and fled the screen, and at once, almost without warning, everything was suspect. It was a strange way to end the Camino.

While Lu, Daniel, and I had been hiking the Camino across Northern Spain, we certainly knew that Europe was on the edge of its chair, but we had no idea that it was about to tip over. Almost overnight (or so it seemed), we returned to a world where the dollar was worth almost as much as the euro and where the European economy had reached its newest low since the Great Depression. Insulated from news access by the Camino, we didn't hear anything until it was already well-known.

When we returned to the normal world's rhythm of televisions, the Internet, cell phones and news reports, the word was everywhere. *Get to the airport quick or you won't make it out in time.* The day before we finished the Camino, we heard from a roadside shopkeeper that a volcano had exploded in Iceland, but we didn't think it was really that big of a deal. When I arrived at the Santiago airport to fly back to Alicante, the first announcement over the loudspeakers silenced the pull-cart air. *Tomorrow the airport will be shutting down.*

On the last day of open flights, I boarded a plane back to Alicante. My German friends who had bought tickets for the following day, however, were not so fortunate.

Getting lost, they hinted at later, had never been more necessary.

Stranded in Santiago, Lu and Daniel made their way to the bus station, where they learned that all outbound bus and train tickets for the following week had already sold out and that all flights within Europe had been cancelled.

"We couldn't give up, but we had to get back, so we found a way," Lu wrote when they got back. "Along the way we saw so many people give up and admit defeat. Everywhere around us, people sat on the floor of airports and bus stations, crying or yelling at people on their cell phones. After the Camino and actually being nice to people, it was naturally a bit of a shock."

But surprises and interesting things had a way of happening at the beginning and end of Caminos, Lu reassured me. When they were standing in line at the bus station, a man in front of them happened to have two tickets to Barcelona that he needed to get rid of, and without asking them for money or their names, he gave them the tickets and walked away, no questions asked. Seventeen hours later, they arrived in Barcelona with no idea of how they were going to make it to Germany, only that now, they were closer. In Barcelona, a chance encounter with a Norwegian journalist in another ticket line led them to a taxi cab and a car rental store in France. And in France, the rental store happened to have one car left that needed to be delivered to Dresden, just two hours away from their home. There were several stops along the way, of course, like Paris, but they only added to the sense of adventure. "I will never go to Paris ever again or deal with the damned French," Daniel added.

"Me neither," said Lu. "God, the French!"

Five days and several scavenged meals later, they arrived home, right about the time the Norwegian journalist's article appeared in a local newspaper about two Germans he'd met on "the Real Camino."

"Pretty cool, huh?" Lu said. "It took us just as long to get home as it did for us to hike the entire Camino."

Of course I heard all of this via email, but Lu wanted to tell it to me in person. He was that way, really. "I didn't realize the truth about the Camino until after the volcano," Lu told me. "Just when you think one Camino is ending, you find that the real Camino is beginning. And you know what? It's never what you thought it would be."

Anyways, he implied, I wouldn't be able to get the essence of the adventure without the personal flair, the ambience, and maybe a beer or three and a medicine stick. "The bottom line is that you should come visit us and hear all about it."

I wrote back and told him no. It was a dead end, really; I had other plans. Plans that might hinge on what happened with the volcano.

Eleven weeks ago on the verge of a potential quest to find my family in northern Germany, my friend Aaron and I had booked tickets for a trip across the Swiss Alps. Our plane would leave in two weeks, and we would arrive backpack-ready to absorb as much or as little of the mountain trek as we wanted. It would be like the red light district in Hamburg and the Red Gate all over again, we told ourselves, only this time without hookers. If the volcano's ash cloud cleared the skies in time, we would be ready.

But eleven weeks ago, Aaron had also said some memorable words that I forgot and then remembered again in convenient times and places. With the threat of a long-term ash cloud, now was such a time. "All roads eventually become dead ends," he said. "The question is, which road do you take when the road you're on ends?"

While Lu and Daniel worked their way across Europe by car, train and foot, newscasts showed hundreds of thousands of people just like them. European airlines lost $150 million per day and the European economy lost billions from displaced workers. It was worse than the BP oil spill.

Safe at home, I cast myself across the couch in the living room with Carmen and Asis. In a silent row, we huddled in front of the TV while footage of the volcano eruption replayed by the hour. Images of people lying shoulder to shoulder on the floor of major airports were burned into our brains. Airports became homeless shelters as air traffic halted for the week. News cameras showed fights breaking out in bus stations as the fortunate fought each other for last-call tickets and the unfortunate sat on the floor without food. I remembered being detained at the port in Morocco for eight hours and sleeping on the floor, and now I was watching an entire continent do the same thing for a week straight.

While the newspaper headlines warned that Spain was in serious trouble, nobody seemed to pay any attention to it. Alicante's sun-dusted restaurants and street cafes were still full, and the palm tree beach was still filled with the tanning jobless. There was the usual *crisis económica*, of course, that spelled twenty percent unemployment and a line of two hundred people in front of the welfare office, but even when the *crisis del volcán* arose, it was hard to notice that anything else was amiss. In front of the TV, I learned that there wasn't really a crisis.

"Usually in Spain, we just take out loans to solve the problem," Asis said, while we watched a special about how the government was spending tax dollars to throw a fiesta in Seville. I told him that our government in America did that too, but he didn't believe me. "Well, it can't be as bad in America as it is here."

More news poured in by the hour. The ash cloud was steadily migrating south, and within days it would blanket most of the continent.

In spite of all of this, I heard plenty of good news from my Spanish friends. With the economy as bad as it was, there was no better time to run Spanish triathlons, especially university sponsored ones. This week on campus, *la universidad* celebrated the Spanish tradition of paella with La Fiesta de Paella. What this really meant was that we got to celebrate the noble ideals of drinking, skipping class, and generally having a good time. All told, it was like Spain's version of Warped Tour where 20,000 students got to party in the school parking lot while talking in Spanish and singing American pop songs in English. After the school party, I asked some of the Spaniards why we were having a fiesta when the school was losing money, but they assured me that there was no better time to party. If the world was going down, then *de puta madre tío*, we've got to party like there's no tomorrow!

"*Madre mia*," Carmen said when she heard someone at the *supermercado* say something similar. "*Qué terrible*."

I couldn't fault the Spaniards, though. You didn't have to look much

farther than the country's leadership to see where the mentality origi-
nated. "We can finally see the light at the end of the tunnel," proclaimed
President Zapatero in a newspaper headline. However, the *periódico* also
reported that in a demonstration of national leadership, King Juan Carlos
II and Queen Sophia were about to embark on a month-long vacation to
the Canary Islands.

My Spanish professor Don Juan said that on royal outings, it was normal for the king and queen to invite a bunch of their friends and charge
one million euros to the Spanish taxpayer, even during times of crisis. "If
you're royal, well, to hell with you. I guess you have to be royal," he said.
He had been invited on one of their private jets before, but he claimed
that he had refused it. "I had romantic plans that night."

In Don Juan's class, we took a critical look at recent news. Even as
President Zapatero tried to encourage people to spend money, we learned
that Spain's economy had recently been pegged the second-worst in Europe. And if that wasn't enough, Valencia's mayor (the one who hosted
Las Fallas a few weeks ago) had been charged with money laundering.
But there was some good news in all of this: wine was only one euro at
the *supermercado*!

Compare this mentality to that of my Bohemian great grandfather.
There is a famous story of when Grandpa took his father out deer hunting
many years ago, after the Great Depression. After they had been walking around all day with no luck, they finally spotted a deer. "Shoot it,"
Grandpa told him when he had a clear shot.

Old Joe Hanna raised his rifle but wouldn't shoot. "I wouldn't want to
waste a bullet if I missed."

THE FAMINE OF 1894

If the Great Depression was hard on the family, the Famine of 1894 had
been even worse.

Years earlier when Marie Belohlavy arrived in 1885 Nebraska without
their infant son, she knew Vaclav would be disappointed. I imagine that
as she stepped off the train, an engine lulled behind her, a throbbing,

sputtering sound. She must have stood on the platform, suitcase in hand, looking for her husband; yes, there he was. He was dressed nice in his best work clothes, but when they made eye contact he looked startled. His eyes tore away to the industrial, mechanical background, then back over her, searching. He looked to the left and right of her, behind her and in front of her, but there was no sign of what he was looking for, only the sign of a suitcase and the blank satchel that she carried, like the hopeful, emotionless look on her face. "Where is the little one?" he must have asked right away.

"He's dead," she said.

It was the first time he heard the news.

"Life is one experience of first joy and then sorrow," he later wrote in a letter. The entire family had saved up money to send him to America, and as such, he had to build the next generation. He needed his son, but now, perhaps more than ever, stoic resolution. No matter if his children died or how bad things got, he had to make the best of it and find a better life, no matter what was about to happen. He reached for his wife as she stepped off the platform and pulled her tight. All of this—the loss of their son and possibly more—they would overcome it.

That's my interpretation anyway, but even with their embrace, the scene was tinged with a sense of loss and the open-sky weight of a sinking dream. Nebraska was not what it was supposed to be. And there was no going back, even as things continued to get worse.

It began with the drought. The summer of 1894 saw less than three inches of rain in Boyd County, Nebraska. Coupled with a heavy frost and a late May freeze, there were no crops that year, and no reserves left from the year before. Vaclav, his wife, and their three young girls began to starve. By the fall, newspapers on the East Coast were already publishing accounts of the drought and relief aid was being sent to Nebraska. From what the records show, everyone got the help they needed—except the Bohemians. In what local historians describe as the lowest, poorest, neediest people on the Nebraskan plains, the Bohemians were pushed aside by the other Nebraskans who were more forceful at claiming their share of the rations. "Then we knew what it meant to be really poor, worse than in Europe," Vaclav wrote in a letter back to the family in Bohemia.

But as poor as they were, there was always the Belohlavy solution. Once again, they would make a pact to see them through.

On a dark night when the moon was probably full, a group of Bohemians slowly gathered into a sod house. On the dirt floor in the middle was a candle and one by one the group sat around the flame, just like before. Vaclav sat in front of the flame, sterile and resolute, his face barely breaking with the flickers of the tallow wick, his beard and face long and drawn, his arms around his daughters on either side. Between one daughter and the next, Marie Belohlavy wrapped her arms around the other children and silently stared into the flame. She'd been there for the original Pact. Across the flame from her, a ragged blond woman suckled a baby under her blouse as her husband sat silently next to her and stared at the floor, his hands marred black in the light. Together, the young and the old gathered around the flame, bound this time not as family but as survivors. Starving and with little hope, Vaclav and the other Bohemian settlers pooled their money to ask for help from a Bohemian colony far to the north. Once again they placed their hands into the center to seal the pact, and once again an old man appeared and placed a lot of straws near the flame. Lots were drawn and a new man was selected. This time, the group's fate rested on the shoulders of a young man charged with riding a horse to Minnesota in the dead of winter.

In restless memory, the scene continues in black and white before slowly fading to the sound of hooves padding into the snow. While I don't know how the scene actually played out, this is my best guess. What I do know is that several weeks later, against blizzards and other odds, food and planting seed arrived by train from the Bohemians in Minnesota. They would make it through the coming year. Like Vaclav's successful entry to America, the horseman had conquered the frontier and they would survive.

For the next eight years, Vaclav and his wife worked as hired hands on nearby farms, making enough money to support themselves, and eventually they were able to get a homestead and have a place to call their own. It wasn't much more than a sod house with a dirt floor, but they had a place, a plot of land, and for the first time ever, somewhere to call home, even if it meant nothing to anyone but the Bohemians back home. To them, I imagine that Nebraska was paradise. For the first time in Belohlavy history, we finally owned something. In the open, wheat-covered plains and under a rolling, breaking sky, the landscape was finally able to capture the size of their Dream. It was vast, impenetrable, and formed in a land where there were no mountains. Nebraska—Indian for flat water.

Little by little, their situation began to improve. In no time at all, they began trading chickens and household supplies with the Indians. They built and rebuilt their sod house. They had several more children (all girls) and laughed and played with them. They had a house, a dirt floor, and the American Dream. They'd done it. They'd made it. But right when things started to improve and they were about to have their seventh child, a son and heir to the Belohlavy name, Vaclav's wife died in childbirth. The baby survived, but without Marie to nurse him, he died two weeks later. After twenty years of marriage, Vaclav became a widower with no heir to his name and six young girls to raise all by himself. The loss of his wife was devastating. Not only had he loved her, but he had sacrificed for her in ways that she would never know, even if she ultimately may have held it against him.

Genealogists and cultural historians report that the nearest town from 1894 Boyd County, Nebraska was thirty to fifty miles away from Vaclav's settlement. Like lots of other Bohemians when they first arrived, Vaclav didn't have a wagon to drive forty miles into town, let alone enough money to buy a loaf of bread. But while he didn't have the luxury of gaining anything in the New World, he had the luxury of being able to forget whatever he wanted to leave behind. That included his wife.

"Just leave Marie behind," the other Bohemians told Vaclav when he first arrived at the Bohemian settlement in 1885 Wilbur, Nebraska. "Just leave your wife behind and she'll never know that you're still alive." That was one of the only concrete memories we have of Vaclav—when everyone told him to abandon Marie in Bohemia for a newer, younger, prettier Bohemian-American girl. It was simple enough, the other Bohemians pointed out. All he had to do was throw away any signs of his marriage and then Marie wouldn't exist anymore, back home or anywhere. If he didn't like her or wanted to upgrade, he could get rid of her.

"I was lonely," Vaclav wrote many times, but he kept his wedding promise and remained faithful. He had grown up a bastard child, and he knew what it meant to be abandoned in the worst sense. "I was very lonely," he wrote again in a fragment of an old letter we found preserved from his early days in Nebraska. He missed her. Instead of looking for another wife, he began working harder so that one day, he would be able to send for her. But she didn't know this because he never sent her a letter.

Six months later and without any prior word of his survival, Vaclav sent money and it was Marie's turn to come to America. In those days, when someone sent for you, you had to go, but I imagine she left with a sense of mixed feelings. Not only had their baby died, but Vaclav had left her while she was pregnant and she never forgot that. At a Bohemian train station, he had left her to pursue a Pact and something like a future. She knew this. But she also knew that her husband was a man of vision, even if he wasn't a man of much else. He was resolute. He was determined. And he would turn the family around, if no one else could. Perhaps she had married him for that reason.

When her train pulled into the station, a husband and wife embraced, holding between them the weight of trust and death and the promise that they would work things out and that somehow, either now or later and certainly with God's help, they would find a way. It turned out to be much harder than they had thought.

When Marie died in childbirth, Vaclav didn't know what to do. And when his newborn son survived the birth only to die two weeks later, he didn't know what to do. *How do you go on when you've lost everything?* seems like a perfectly philosophical, well-meaning question, but it's really quite basic. You go on because you have to.

To this day, I don't understand how Vaclav found the will to keep going when bad thing after bad thing should have torn him apart. In a life that started with a bastard birth and a difficult childhood filled with work herding chickens, things only got worse for my great ancestor. He never spoke English. He was never rich or even close to middle class. His children never went to college, and his grandchildren didn't go to school, either. Years later, Bohemians like him wouldn't even shoot a deer for fear they'd lose a few pennies if they missed the shot.

I think Vaclav did all he could in spite of the circumstances. Suicide wasn't an option, but putting one foot in front of the other was. Maybe that's all it takes. He had already made two pacts that had saved the family, but perhaps his greatest action was simply his own resilience.

"I was lonely," Vaclav wrote many times over the years. "I was lonely." Would his loneliness ever amount to anything? Had he survived his wife's death only to be lonely and only to feed his family and bring his daughters into poverty and that was that? Four years after Marie died, he tried remarrying but his second wife died of cancer. "Life is one experience of first joy and then sorrow," he wrote. There was nothing to do except continue on, but in the ensuing years, two of his daughters died, and in his lifetime he had to bury two wives and three children. At life's end, it would be hard to say what it had all been worth.

He may have pursued the Pact, but he'd failed the family and failed to provide an heir to continue the Belohlavy name in Nebraska. Without a son, he'd also failed at the Return and wouldn't have anyone to send back to Bohemia. Perhaps it was better that way. The night of the Pact, their sacrifice had been worth so much and there had been so much promise. Since then, everything had fallen apart. They didn't need to know how badly he'd failed them.

Nevertheless, he would press on. One day, somehow or someway, someone would be able to complete the Return. His daughters or their children, perhaps. On cold winter nights, he would pass on the story of their eventual Return and then go quiet. *I will come back.*

Plans began to fall through. Ever since I visited Aaron in Germany, we'd been planning on "doing Europe," you know, backpack style, no showers, across the Alps, that sort of thing. The ash cloud had finally lifted and I was getting ready for the trip when I got a call from Aaron. "I'm not going to be able to make it," he said. Strike one.

Strike two. I now had about a week's worth of vacation after school let out and suddenly no plans. My Spanish friends couldn't travel because they had finals, and my American friends couldn't travel because they had to go home after finals. Portugal looked like an option, but it would be a long and expensive bus ride to get there and I was running out of money. Strike three.

"You could just stay in Spain," Carmen said. She was right. I could, but something lay heavy on me and I didn't know quite what it was. Had I missed something? Doors were closing in front of me, and there was only one real option left. I wrote to Lu the next day. "Can I take you up on your offer?"

Dresden is two hours from the Czech Republic. *I will come back.*

Week 19
Glauchau, Germany

In a valley that most people drive by and forget, a woman tends a pharmacy in Nepomuk, waiting for someone from long ago. Her store has just opened and her staff has just arrived. She wears her white lab coat and her long, brownish-blonde hair falls across her upper back, parted in the middle of her forehead, just enough for her glasses to sparkle when she catches the light just right. But even though there is life in her eyes, her building is medical, the walls are white and sterile with product brochures and boxes of vitamins and pain pills. A customer comes in the door and she asks him how he is doing. *Fine, thank you*, he says in Czech. He doesn't hand her a prescription but instead tells her exactly what he needs. She nods, then asks one of her pharmacy technicians to go and get it for him. He pays her in a jumble of korunas, then leaves the store where another customer takes his place and orders a different prescription. She goes and gets it for him and again he smiles and thanks her before leaving. She nods her head and smiles back, but really, the day is like most others. She dispenses some products, thanks her staff, and at the end of the day locks the door and goes about her way. All of it is fulfilling, but there lurks something more. She is waiting for something to happen.

Across the world in a valley that most people drive by and forget, a father
and his brother build a fence while waiting on word from afar. In desperation, they send a final email with instructions. "If you can make it to
Bohemia," Dad writes, "please go." For eighteen weeks, he has faithfully
delivered his call to action. *This is my last plea.* Working alongside him
is his brother Ken, the last one to venture forth to Europe. Years ago, he
wanted to find the family, but was unable to do so because of the after-
math of the Cold War. As they string and restring sections of barbed wire
fence, they talk about those days and others. Years later, they will do so
again.

They end the night in the same camper they have slept in since the
seventies when they were boys. Together in the camper, Dad writes the
final email. If there is any chance at all of finding that other forgotten valley across the world, he would give anything for it.

The day before I leave for Germany, I receive his final plea, but I am
resolute. I will not go and find the family.

When I board the plane in the early morning, a pharmacist opens
and closes her door and a father sleeps across the world. Two hours and
a country later, I will be in old East Germany. I board the plane and fall
asleep.

On a landing strip in the middle of a rapeseed field that most people
will never know, I stepped off the plane into a small military airport set
between rolling hills. It was not where I expected to land. Before the
flight, Lu assured me that he lived near Dresden, population 800,000.
There would be plenty of stuff to do. But in place of Dresden, I discovered
several things: a sign that read Altenberg, a one-story air terminal with
one departure desk, and a single yellow plane on a lone strip of runway.
Beyond the runway, country fields began to expand like memories while
a parking lot waited for travelers. There were no taxis, but somewhere in
the parking lot, Daniel was waiting.

I stepped onto the concrete wearing my usual ensemble. Since our last outing, I looked mostly the same and retained my black euro-jacket, worn tennis shoes, and Dad's old hiking backpack as evidence of our pilgrimage together.

Standing next to a sputtering maroon car in the parking lot, Daniel recognized me immediately. *"¡Buen Camino!"* he called as he held up his hand and waved.

Just like before, he wore his camouflage military jacket, but this time around he looked a little more James Dean as he leaned against the car with a cigarette hanging out the side of his mouth. His hair wasn't slicked back (it was too short to feather), but he had a relaxed East German look that acted like everything was fine, even though his car wasn't starting. Direct indirectness—it was a fine trait. He raised his eyebrows as we shook hands.

"I heard you had quite the time in France," I said as I loaded my backpack into the trunk.

"France," he took the medicine stick out of his mouth and exhaled a thick cloud of smoke. "Don't even get me started with the French." He shut the trunk with a metallic thud before putting the cigarette back between his lips. "The worst part was that I had to tell my wife that Lu and I were in France together."

"How'd that go over?"

"Not well. She thought we were lovers."

I laughed.

He winked. "No, she was fine with it." He opened the car door and was about to get in. "Really, life goes on much as it always has—we're just waiting for our next child to be born, which is another way of saying that we're waiting for something to happen. Something big."

We drove off to find Lu.

A half hour breezed by as we worked our way through conversations about France, the Camino, and other exotic places as we wound through the East German countryside. At one hundred and thirty kilometers per hour, yellow flower fields extended on either side of us; Daniel called them apps—little budding rapeseeds. The farmers mostly harvested them for oil.

In addition to the suburban nature of the countryside—its sprawl—
I learned that Lu and Daniel didn't actually live in Dresden—they just
said Dresden so that people would know where they were on the map.
"We're in the German Democratic Republic, of course," Daniel reiterated
before clarifying further. "That's kind of a nice way of saying that we're
about two hours from Dresden by train." He rolled down his window and
tossed out the butt end of his medicine stick. "Sorry if that was a bit of a
mix-up."

It wasn't a problem, really. The only thing I needed in big cities was a
steady supply of English and Spanish speakers to talk to, but Daniel assured me that I would be fine. "Everyone speaks English here. Since we're
not the GDR anymore, we have to learn English in school instead of Russian."

"You learn history, too, right?"

"Yeah, history. GDR history. *Real* history."

"Real history," I said.

"It's so real," he said, "that some people still speak Russian."

I nodded. This was going to be interesting.

We arrived in Glauchau ("Glau-ho," Daniel enunciated) mid-morning to
a slight drizzle. Daniel had to work at "that damn cell phone store," so he
dropped me off in front of Lu's bakery. It was a bakery that was perhaps
best defined by what it wasn't than by what it was. Across the street stood
an eighteenth century castle with turrets and high windows. In the sunlight, the fortress would have been impressive, but in between rain drops
and a clouded sky, the castle looked cold. In contrast, Lu's cream-colored,
plain-walled bakery would have looked bland in summer light, but in the
misty rain of a dreary day, the walls carried the hue of a cream frosting. I
stepped inside at once.

The door opened inward to a display case of cakes and pastries arranged by size and color. Behind the glass case was a squat older man.
He had the same face as Lu and the same fluffy hair that could have folded under itself, but he was a rounder, older version, and he wore a gray
apron. "Hullo," he said.

"Hullo," I said, as Lu appeared from a doorway behind the counter.

"You again!" he said. "When I heard that voice, I knew it was The American!" Lu approached with a small cake in his hand. "Try this," he said. "It's like the Camino, but better—it won't take you all the way through France."

I tore off a corner of the white, crumbly cake and ate it. "You're right, amigo, it's better than escargo."

"Snails." He shook his head and reached to shake my hand. "Steve, this is my father," he said and pointed to the man across the glass.

"Hi again," I said.

He said something back in German that I didn't understand, followed by an awkward silence. I shook my head vigorously, as if that would somehow communicate my enthusiasm for meeting him. He looked at me blankly.

"Well, no matter. Let's go meet the rest of the family!" Lu said. He led me through a space in the corner of the room and we moved behind the display case and into the next room—the kitchen. It smelled of sausages and of Germany. "We smell like Germans and we know it," Lu proudly declared before pointing to a case of beer sitting on the floor. "That's the other smell of Germany."

In the kitchen next to an industrial-sized oven, we found his mother wearing a white apron and whispering in his younger brother's ear. Like Lu's father, both of them were rounder than they were tall, but unlike Lu's father, they had dark hair that curled over their ears and glasses like fur. "My mother wants him to help a customer," Lu said. "That's not usually his specialty."

I learned that in the Ullmann family, everyone had a role. Lu dealt with the customers and did the accounting and general management, his brother handled the German sausages and the cooking, his mother ran the restaurant, and his father baked most of the pastries. Everyone knew how to do everything, Lu clarified, but he personally preferred not to cook. After all, it was far more efficient to have one person do one thing and another person do another. And since he didn't like all of the work, well ... someone else should do it then. That was how they had survived communism, Lu said. They had worked together for the common good doing unequal work. "It's all basically fair," he added. "If you believe in that." He was quick to whisper in my ear *don't tell Daniel I just said that.*

I put a finger to my lips. I wouldn't tell.

Lu explained more about the bakery. His family didn't just own a bakery and a restaurant; they also managed a hotel. "Germans are notorious businessmen, but I was able to talk my Dad into letting you stay for free," Lu boasted. "Most people don't get to stay for free."

We exited a door at the back of the kitchen and arrived in a small courtyard. A series of doors lined the courtyard walls and Lu reached into his pocket to produce a hotel key. We worked our way through hotel stairs and hallways to arrive at a door marked 217. "This is your room," Lu said. "I hope it's alright."

We opened the door to a white room. The walls weren't white, but a pallid shade drawn across the window created a bright waft of light that played across wooden walls. "For over three hundred years, my family has owned this business," Lu said as he looked out the window and down into the courtyard through the transparent cloth. "Your country hasn't even existed for that long."

I set Dad's backpack down in the corner. "No, I guess not. We Americans have a pretty recent history," I conceded.

"But it is still *a* history," Lu added. He brushed the shade away from the window and the whiteness in the room disappeared. "Your family— are you going to go and find them?"

"I don't think so," I said.

"Well, if not, you can always go see Prague."

"Yep, there's always Prague."

Lu sat down on the edge of the bed, then promptly stood up as if he'd suddenly remembered something important. "I just remembered," he exclaimed, "We need to compare watches."

"What?"

"What do you mean *what*? I mean compare watches. You know, make sure we're both working on the same time table."

Lu got up from the edge of the bed and held his wrist next to mine so we could both watch the second hands slowly turn. He studied the minute hand on my watch until it crossed the twelve.

"This is kind of a new concept," I said. "German time. Well, you know the Spaniards."

"Yeah, and where did their Camino time get us? Sore, that's what." Lu touched my watch, a German way of saying that he wanted me to change it to the correct time. "You know us Germans, we're notoriously on time."

"You're notoriously ridiculous."

Lu started for the door. "I get off at five everyday, so … you're free to wander till then. At 5:07, though, it's fun time. That means beer time."

"5:07." I repeated and checked my watch again.

"See, I've already got you thinking like a German," Lu said, before closing the door behind him.

Over the next few days a certain routine developed. By five o'clock each morning Lu would begin working in the bakery and wouldn't get off until five o'clock that evening. Since he had little time for lunch breaks, I was mostly on my own during the day. By night we would drink, visit the "beverage store" (a supermarket-sized store filled with every conceivable type of German beer), then drink again. For an average meal, Lu claimed that the average German needed at least a six-pack to wash it all down. Another German we met at the beverage store heartily agreed, although he felt sorry for himself. Of the 3,600 different kinds of beer in Germany, he'd only tried sixty of them. Even for a beer drinking country, it was easy to get stuck in your ways.

I discovered this same sense in the streets: it was easy to get stuck in them. Streets wandered and bent and twisted and turned, and one moment I was on top of a hill and the next I was at the bottom of a larger hill, looking up. It was a town of roses and pastels where buildings were differentiated only by shades of pink and beige, even though all of the houses seemed to carry the same black metal roofs. It was a town that catered to the bicycle, and on the official Glauchau tourist map, bike paths were labeled as official city streets and properly named in German. However, this posed a problem. I had neither a bicycle nor the ability to speak German.

By day, I wandered cobbled streets and sampled sauerkrauts from street vendors I couldn't speak to. I visited the Glauchau tourist office, but they only spoke German and maybe Russian, and they nodded their heads whenever I said anything, so I left. I ordered a kebab at a Turkish restaurant, thinking that perhaps I would find company in the presence of foreigners, but quickly learned that they only spoke German, too. Through all of this, it continued to rain. A Monday drizzle quickly turned to a Wednesday downpour, and other than the sound of falling rain and the guttural voices in the street that I couldn't understand, I heard only silence. For most of the waking day, I was very lonely.

Then night would come and Lu would take me to his Tuesday night poker group and we'd celebrate German patriotism with a hand of cards, a fresh pint of beer, and a cheers called *prost*. I joined in on the festivities using my limited German abilities. *Ine bier, bitte.* One beer, please. That made the locals laugh. They couldn't understand anything else I said, though, so I played a silent poker face the rest of the night while everyone else was laughing. "That was fun, wasn't it?" Lu said when we left. I nodded.

On another night, we drove out to see Lu's "garden," a one-room cabin in the countryside that he had inherited from his grandma. There weren't any plants on the property except for a hillside of grass, but Lu kept calling it his garden. He was very proud of his garden so I didn't bother to tell him that it wasn't actually a garden, per se. "Someday I'm going to build a fire pit here," he boasted. "Then we can roast sausages and drink beer and stuff."

We spent some time with Daniel, too, but he had to work long hours during the week, and it soon became apparent that I needed to find something else to do during the day. I looked into a two-day trip to Poland, but Lu dismissed the idea. "It's too boring," he said, and suggested I go see Buchenwald concentration camp. "There's nothing to see in Poland anyway."

Maybe Lu was right about Poland, because whatever it was, I couldn't shake the feeling that I needed to go to Buchenwald. I had to—I felt compelled to go. It's strange to write this, but as I boarded the train, and as we began to move from standstill to full motion, and as the countryside began to blur gray-green as forests and dark clouds meshed into one, my heart began to speed up and keep time with the train. Maybe I was excited, or maybe it was something else, but out of nowhere, I felt a soft nudge. It was almost imperceptible. Whether I knew it or not, something was about to happen.

In a valley that most people drive by and forget, a woman opens and closes the door to her pharmacy shop once again. The walls are sterile. Her pharmacy coat is white and spotless like always, her hair is brushed and falls across her back. Products line the walls of her store and she arranges a display of vitamins that have just arrived. Customers appear and enter like they always do; no, there's nothing new here. But in all of this, there is a light in her eyes. She fills prescriptions and enjoys it, even as something lingers and tugs at the back of her mind—she's barely aware of it now because the days go on and on. Tomorrow she will return, and hopefully, whether she knows it or not, a promise will be fulfilled. She closes the door to her shop and heads home.

In another valley across the world, a father and his brother gather the last of the willow branches to burn in a nighttime fire. They have finished working on the fence for the day, but there is still work to do. Once the branches have been gathered in their arms, they place them in a small pile next to the river and burn them; the outlines of their cowboy hats are barely visible in the orange glow that dances across rippling water. In low tones, they talk. But what is there to talk about? they ask each other. Someone getting a divorce? They have been through all of this before and yet somehow now, in the light of the flames, maybe something new will happen, something they've always wanted. They gather more sticks for the fire.

As the fire grows with sagging branches, they sit on rotting logs and think of someone they both know who is traveling across the world, so close and yet so far away from their dream. Whether they know it or not, they begin to pray that maybe this time, maybe somewhere across the world, their yearning might be fulfilled. They continue burning.

In a third valley, a train churns its way steadily forward. In all of this, there is a unity. A young man is asleep and in a few hours, he will wake. The Dream will be revealed.

BUCHENWALD CONCENTRATION CAMP

Like lost spirits, fog descended early in the morning and wrapped its fingers around trees, spreading branches like tentacles. Around the bark there was a sudden viscous cold, a feeling almost supernatural, as if attuned to a place of frequent death. Pine needles parted themselves and stuck intrusively into the air like pins that had fallen onto the floor and stabbed tender feet. The air was ghostly, too, hesitant in expectation, thick with the sound of cawing birds and branches that moved and disappeared.

In my customary black coat, I stepped off the train and into the gloom. Like everyone else who disembarked, I held my hand in front of my face and waved it through the air—a test. The fog did not give way. Ahead, I could barely make out the brown hair of the person directly in front of me, and further ahead I could discern the faint outline of more pine trees and an abandoned shed. That was it.

The path into the concentration camp led through the forest and I found myself walking behind a father and his two daughters. As long as I was behind them, then at least I wasn't alone. But the woods crept in, and as I followed the floating strands of their dark hair that wisped in and out of gray space, trees began to appear in front of me and on either side, as if out of nowhere. At first, the apparitions were manageable, but as we advanced further into the camp, trees became sudden fences of barbed wire that cut the stillness in the air. I imagined blood on the wires, but there was none. I continued to follow the family in front of me, but when they stopped to examine the fence, I pressed on alone.

Fog enveloped either side of me. The scene was bare. Other than my black jacket passing through a murky forest, there appeared to be nothing else. Every now and then, however, there was. Ruins of decrepit buildings would suddenly creep out of the fog like hallucinations before disappearing two steps further down the path, as if they had never existed. Several buildings appeared and disappeared until I reached the entrance tower. A clock was affixed above an iron gate, but the clock's hands didn't move. I checked my watch. It was early in the morning, but the hands on the clock tower read 3:15. It wasn't even close to the afternoon. I passed through the gate and entered the main compound, expecting to find barracks, but inside, there was nothing.

In the olden days the barracks used to line the inner camp, but after the camp was razed, the barracks had been completely destroyed and the fields of Buchenwald were reduced to a ruined, hollow ground. Most of the buildings had long since been razed, but the horror of what they had once housed was still present, perhaps more so in their absence.

To a gray background, I walked across an endless field of gravel. Other than a few people marking space in the expanse, there was nothing but the silent crunch of rocks and the soft wicking sound of my coat. For what seemed like miles, no plants grew. There weren't even stubs of grass, just rocks and the subtle outlines of bricks to mark where the barracks used to be. The air sagged, as if it had been deflated across a field of nothing. While I had expected to see pictures of people dying and starving, I hadn't expected to experience how bleak it must have felt. I continued on.

As I crunched through the gravel field, two buildings appeared out of the fog. A sign outside one of the buildings said it was the crematorium, and I looked up to find a dark cloud coming out of a smokestack. Like long ago, the crematorium churned out a continuous cloud of smoke to remind the prisoners that they could be burnt next. The Nazis re-engineered the crematoriums multiple times during the life of the camp to maximize the number of bodies that could be burnt. Buchenwald wasn't Auschwitz and it wasn't a death camp, but it fulfilled the same purpose as a work camp.

The building next to the crematorium housed the disinfecting stations and examination rooms. In the examination rooms, doctors would call patients into empty rooms to measure their height. Cut into the measuring device behind the patient was a slit in the wall where a Secret Service guard would have his gun trained at the patient's exposed neck. While the physician measured the patient, the guard would shoot the person through the slit in the wall and the body would fall to the floor. The guards didn't want to look their victims in the eyes.

I followed a group into the basement and we entered an empty room with one noticeable feature: yellow-stained walls with a row of hooks bolted to the ceiling. When the doctors and guards weren't able to kill people fast enough, they brought the rest of them into the basement where guards thrust the hooks into their necks and hung them to die, torturing them while they lived out their last moments. A present to an especially faithful Nazi captain was a lampshade made of harvested human skin.

I tell you this because the experience was bleak and because it was moving me to action. In the final 140 days of the camp, over 100,000 people died. In addition to the tens of thousands of Jews who lost their lives, people from Russia, Romania, Hungary, Poland, Italy, France, Slovakia, Spain, and Czechoslovakia had been killed in the inspection building. I paused over the funeral sign and closed my eyes. One word stood out: *Czechoslovakia.*

A sinking feeling crept over me. They might have been here. I wondered if our ancestors had paid the price long ago to set Vaclav free, only to die years later without ever hearing word of the Return. It was certainly possible.

In that moment, Buchenwald became strangely personal. Whether it was true or not, I saw my ancestors being here and being burned in the crematorium or being hung from the hooks in the inspection room. I saw them being beaten and starved, lying like boards in the barracks at night, their skin pulled tight across poking rib bones, their eyes like reclusive animals.

On the side of a path in the middle of the forest, I sat down on a bent and twisted log and rested my head in my hands. All of the history and all of the death only added to what I was feeling. The gloom and the forest and the loneliness of Glauchau—I was miserable.

On that bent and twisted log, I decided to go to the Czech Republic and find my long-lost ancestors. If it wasn't for Buchenwald, I probably never would have ventured forth, but after seeing all of this and after being left alone in Glauchau and generally feeling sorry for myself (perhaps more than I should have), I needed a story to believe in. Once again, I needed a quest and I needed a purpose for being here. Almost immediately and almost without thinking, my heart began racing towards the original Home Place. I remembered all of Dad's pleading for the past eighteen weeks, and I was finally ready to fulfill my charge. I would go and complete the Return.

Huddled around the table that night in Daniel's house, Lu, Daniel and I began making plans. We didn't know what, exactly, those plans would entail, but in a black and white vision, we rested our elbows on the grains of the wooden table and leaned in. Above us, a light bulb dangled over a collection of bottles that we'd already finished. Light glanced off the glass and reflected back at each one of us. Outside the house, the rainy streets had fallen asleep and grown cold. Daniel had put his children to bed and his wife had gone to sit in the living room. It was just the three of us under a single orange light, almost like the original Pact, only this time the mood was more rugged, as if we were heading out West on the Oregon Trail, even though we were, in fact, heading East on a different sort of Manifest Destiny. Tomorrow, I would venture forth with a map in hand and journey to Dresden, then change trains and continue on to Prague.

"I'm excited about this," Lu said. "Think of it! One hundred and twenty-five years and now you're going to find your family. They won't even recognize you."

"Well, it's not quite that exciting, nor is it that simple," Daniel added. "We don't even know where Nepomuk is. It's not on our map." He reached into his pocket and unfolded a pocket map of East Germany and the Czech Republic. He placed the map in the center of the table and we peered over it.

"See, it really is like the old stories," Lu said as our eyes wandered across the map. "We have no idea where we're going."

Of course we had no idea where Nepomuk actually was, but that didn't matter to us. We would just find it.

Like any good western, our coats clung to our shoulders and dark bottles hung from our mouths in limpet sips. Low light pooled and clung to the insides of Lu's eyes, lighting up the rest of his fluffy hair and square chin even as the rest of his body was shrouded in shadows. Daniel bore a look of determination, but he raised his hands to make a point.

"OK, we have the basic plan, but now what? How will they know you're a Belohlavy when you actually find them?"

That was the one detail we hadn't considered.

I scratched my head. For all the Bohemians knew, I could claim to be anyone.

I took a swig and a slight drizzle of beer ran its way down my chin, but I was undeterred. "I have an idea," I said. "I could write them a letter."

Lu nodded. His face was blank, but I suspected he liked the idea because it adhered to the classic principle of adventuring: if something could be done in an outdated fashion, why then, you had to do it. A simple letter would have to do. I would write Vaclav's story and by that one simple act, they would know that I was his descendant. In Prague, I would then get the letter translated into Czech so that the Belohlavys would be able to read it. The plan—it was foolproof.

Lu stood up to get another beer. "You realize that this whole find-your-family thing is something we Europeans can't quite comprehend," he said as he used two beers to pry open the top of his fifth doppelbock. "I mean for us, we've never really had to find our families."

Daniel took a drink from where he sat at the table and stared off into the wall behind me. "When I grew up, there was no question about where I was going to live. The answer was always just … Glauchau. I don't regret it, but sometimes I wonder why I didn't do anything more."

"Maybe you did," I said. "You just didn't know it."

"Maybe," he said. "But the days of the GDR are long gone."

"Communist," Lu said.

"At least we had work back then. And free beer."

"OK, I'll give you that much," Lu conceded.

As they squabbled about the GDR and other issues from twenty years ago, I thought about the rest of the plan. Since he was working during the day, Lu wouldn't be able to travel with me to Nepomuk, but the plan was that he would drive over and meet me in Prague later that night. If Lu didn't hear from me by dark (and this was our worst-case scenario), he

would drive directly to Nepomuk and come get me. Since we'd both survived Morocco, we knew that we needed an escape plan. We also knew
that (a) the search had the potential to be dangerous, (b) the language
barrier was formidable, and (c) the trains in the Czech Republic were
notoriously late. If I missed a connection on the way back, I would need
Lu's help to get back to Prague. It was a dangerous prospect, staying in the
Czech Republic alone.

"Do you guys realize what's at stake here?" I asked, cutting into their
conversation about the GDR.

"Of course we do," Daniel said. "What's at stake is you finding your
family."

"Well, right," I said. "But it could get worse than that."

"The Bohemians and the Moravians have always been pretty bad," Lu
said. "Is there anything more to that story?"

I told them about Great Uncle Leonard and how he once thought
to visit Nepomuk while fighting in World War II. He was wounded in
France and sent back to the United States. Since Leonard, I was the first
one to make it this far and the first one in a position to attempt the Return. It was a story of pacts and promises, I told them.

"It's probably strange to hear me say this," Lu said, "but I think you're
going to find your family. After one hundred and twenty-five years, you
have to."

Daniel rose and gathered the empty bottles before reaching to turn
off the overhead light. The night was about to be over, but tomorrow the
search would begin. "Well, amigos ... *¡Buen Camino!*"

WEEK 20
THE CZECH REPUBLIC

THE JOURNEY INTO THE CZECH REPUBLIC began with a series of coincidences. The first—I boarded a train bound for Dresden and took a window seat. After a few moments, a certain girl with eyeglasses and a book in her hand began walking towards me. She was blonde and beautiful, and although I never quite got her name, I was able to gather one small detail.

"Hello," I said.

Her head was buried in her book as she sat down next to me, but she lifted her eyes up to mine. They were sapphire and she had a ponytail, too. I looked down. "Hullo," she said. "You're an American, aren't you?"

"Yes," I said, looking back at her and then down again. "Loud and proud."

She laughed at that, then tucked the book that she was reading into her purse. "So what are you doing here?"

"Do you want the long or the short version?" I asked.

"It's a train ride—the long one."

"Then I hope you're one for stories."

I was setting out to find my family, I told her, as I recounted the Belohlavy Story—the Pact, the Dream and the Return. The story wasn't finished, but I was going to see it through to the end.

She folded her hands in her lap; she couldn't believe it. "What you're doing isn't supposed to happen in real life," she said. "It's like the cinema because these things don't happen anymore."

"Well, I haven't found the family yet."

"True," she said. "But you're looking."

The train slowed to a stop and she stood up and gathered her book. She pointed at it. "If you find them," she said, "you should write a book."

A moment later, she was gone. On the seat next to me, a soft ray of sunlight beamed through the window and onto the spot where she had been sitting.

The second—when the train pulled into Dresden, I arrived full of purpose but with plenty of time to spare. In seven hours, I would take the connection to Prague. Between now and then, I had no idea what to do, so I reverted to normal tourist mode and began wandering the city. By the fifth hour, however, I happened to meet a group of people who revealed a certain piece of information.

The scene this time was at the top of a bell tower that overlooked the city. It was a beautiful, lovely view, something perhaps more fit for a honeymoon than a single guy with a balding spot on the back of his head. Standing on a lonely platform at the top of the tower with my arms spread across the railing, it felt like I didn't really belong there all by myself, like I was hogging the view. A flutter of doves dashed in front of me and made cute noises with their beaks. The sky extended forever until it met hills and finally sparkled with a glimmer in the distance, almost like a whisper. As if on cue, I heard a whisper, then voices began to climb the stairs behind me. They were speaking in English.

I was curious, but tried to play it off, so I looked out again over the red roofs and the square yellow rises. I saw a river and an ancient bridge connecting two parts of the city: old and new. I saw destroyed buildings that in recent times had been rebuilt, and I saw pastel finishes on stone foundations, not all of this from the air but some of it from street memory. With a bird's eye view of the road ahead, it was easy to see where one street ended and another began.

The voices climbed the stairs and reached the lookout platform as a group of German biology students came to lean over the railing next to me. I overheard part of their conversation that shifted from school and specimens to the history of the city itself. *Dresden wasn't always like this, you know.* During the war, the churches had been destroyed, the houses razed, the war itself an eviction. *It wasn't always like this.*

"You guys speak English?" I said.

"Of course," they said. "We're science students."

A long-haired guy standing next to me squinted his eyes. "Why do you ask?"

"Other than my friends and a girl on the train, you're the only people I've been able to talk to."

They laughed. "Really?"

"Yeah."

"Well, if you ever need to talk to someone, find a doctor or maybe a pharmacist—someone who knows science."

That line—it didn't seem important at the time. I asked another question.

"So why were you talking in English just now?" I wondered. "I mean, you definitely speak German."

"That's a good question," one of the guys said. He looked down and then out across the city where the streets merged and converged below us. "You know what? I guess it was just on a whim."

The third—two hours later as I boarded the train to Prague and the country of my ancestors, I happened upon two people from the city of my birth. As I was walking through the train peeking into various cars and looking for a place to sit, I noticed a couple wearing sweatshirts that said *University of Oregon.* I couldn't believe it. "Where are you from?" I asked them.

"Eugene," they said. "You?"

I held my breath inside my chest before releasing. "Oregon. I was born in Eugene."

I sat down across from them, and we began talking about home. As we talked, a slow beam of sunlight floated through the window and landed on the seat next to me. It felt strangely warm, almost like a glow.

East, to Prague

The strange glow continued as darkness began to descend on the city, even though the warmth couldn't last. I stepped out of the train station to clouds rolling over a trash-strewn street and menacing glares from people doing cocaine on the benches outside the station. Wild cats licked plastic lids that floated with occasional gusts of wind and stray dogs wandered in and out of the building that looked like it was ready to implode.

In my mind, I had a fairly romanticized image of the Czech Republic. For one, I imagined the country as a series of unending farms and not as a city. I imagined open fields that rolled endlessly instead of a post-industrial landscape. The place I imagined was where people were happy, where they wandered and worked on farms and had lots of kids, a place where people were generally friendly. It was a land where everyone had a home. I was expecting to find the land of my forefathers in an almost mythical sense, but instead found a city that largely didn't care what I was there for, much like its people. It was easy to wonder where the glow had gone.

One man in particular summed up everything I noticed about the Bohemians: he stood motionless in front of a graffitied wall with his head down and his back bent, as if he had been beaten and somehow become accustomed to it. The history of Bohemia was rife with inconsistent and inefficient leaders, and it made sense, then, that the people had developed a glazed complacency and apathetic attitude. In fact, if you had raised your hand and slapped the man across the face, he probably wouldn't have noticed because, well, that's just what life was: another blow to the face.

I proceeded out of the train station and into the city. No one spoke

English, even though they had supposedly learned it in school for years. A trail of sex shops lined half a city block as boarded up buildings and wary glances unfolded with high rises on every side. Since it was getting dark and I didn't have a map, I hailed a taxi and directed the driver to a hostel that Lu had spoken of. "They always have rooms there," he said.

But this wasn't a normal weekend, I learned upon arrival. Something special was going on (the staff wouldn't quite tell me what it was), and all of the other hostels would probably be full that night—strangely enough, just for a night. "I'm sorry," the attendant said before turning me away. "You're on your own."

By now it was nine o'clock and darkness had fallen. I stepped outside and saw people huddled in rings blowing smoke out of joints and sniffing things, and I saw women dressed like prostitutes stick their black boots under faint streetlights. There was a murkiness to the street, as if it was lying in wait and ready to pounce. I put on my hardened Morocco face that looked like I was ready to kill someone and hit the street in search of another hostel. The next hostel was also full, so I took another taxi to the hotel district and knocked on every door until I learned that all of them were full too. I looked at my watch. It was ten till ten and everything had closed except for one travel agency that I happened to pass by.

Upon entry, the walls were empty. For being a travel agency, there were no pictures of palm trees on beaches or moonlit cities or the Great Wall of China. The walls were white; the only desk in the center of the room was scratched, faded and bare. A woman sat behind it with a clump of blond hair tossed atop her head. In America, we would have called that a mop.

"Are you looking for a travel agency?" she asked. "Because you might be in the wrong place."

Instead of booking trips to China, she explained, she booked hotel rooms for foreign workers. "No one wants to go to China, anyway."

I told her it sounded like I had found the right place.

She referred me to a sign on the office door. "See? NO VACANCY." She explained that for some reason—again, she didn't know why—all of the hotels were booked, and all of the rooms she had to offer were full. The phone rang and she answered in punctured Czech.

I waited until she hung up. "You're just in time," she said. "Someone just called and cancelled their reservation." She had one room available for 1,200 korunas—all of the money I had. "We're closing in ten minutes," she said. "You better decide fast."

It was decision time. I didn't have enough money to buy the hotel room and a ticket to Nepomuk, so I had to choose one or the other. I wanted to find the family, but I didn't want to sleep on the streets and risk my own life in the process. Maybe I was overthinking it, but in my wildest dreams I had never envisioned sleeping under a bridge in the country of my ancestors. I reached into my pocket to hand her the cash.

As I was about to hand it to her and seal the reservation, the agency door opened and five high school students from Thailand appeared. Just like me, they also needed a place to stay that night. I put my money back into my pocket and reached to shake their hands.

Together we split the cost of the room and the lady at the travel desk asked us to follow her into the hotel. She didn't have any blankets or mattresses, she said, so she recommended that we break into one of the other rooms and steal some sleeping supplies. "Most of our customers don't use all of their pillows, anyways."

We left the office and followed her around the corner of the building and into a small back door that led to the hotel. In place of a lobby or front desk, there was an empty hallway that led to a brown staircase that creaked and groaned as we climbed two stories. On the third story, the lady from the travel desk pulled out a rusted key and opened an occupied room, sticking her head inside for a sneak peak. "Good, they're not having sex," she said when no one was there. She led us across a tumble of clothes on the floor to a supply closet sitting against one of the empty walls. She reached inside and pulled out two bed mattresses and several pillows and sets of sheets. "Now for the paperwork."

She handed the mattresses to the Thailand kids, and asked me to follow her back to the travel office to finalize the reservation. I wrote my name on a torn scrap of paper, then she handed me the key, turned off the lights, and asked me to follow her to the street corner. "It's dangerous outside," she said.

Barely lit by the glow of distant streetlights, the road was mostly dark.

Three of the four stores across the street from us were boarded up, but after the surprise arrival of the Thailand kids, I didn't feel threatened. There was a vulnerability on the street that night, as if both the woman and the road were daring to reveal something about the true character of the Czech Republic. She pulled out a handkerchief and blew her nose.

"I probably shouldn't tell you this," she said, "but my husband left me."

"What?"

"Yeah, one day, he just walked out. Gone. He's a boarded up building now, just like the ones across the street."

The orange light from one of the streetlights caught her forehead just right, and for just a moment, a line appeared and disappeared across her face.

"I don't know why I told you that about my husband," she said, "but thank you for waiting with me."

A taxi pulled up to the curb and she stepped forward to get inside.

"I'll be back at seven in the morning," she said. "Come see me if you need any help."

As it turned out, I needed a lot of help. I needed a letter translated.

In the wash of low lights and dirty streets, my eyes followed the rear lights of the taxi until they folded away and disappeared.

I returned to the travel agency the following morning with a letter and a question. "What does Belohlavy mean?" I asked.

The woman's hair was again a mop, her desk again faded and brown. Over a stack of papers, she looked up and said *ahoj*. "Belohlavy, huh?"

I nodded. To me, a lot was contained in a name, and before venturing forth to find the family, I wanted to learn what our name meant. From the time of my birth, I had always assumed that it meant something special.

"Belohlavy is a common Czech name that means 'whitehead,'" the lady at the travel desk said, emphasizing the word *common*. "For your equivalency, it's like being called Smith or Jones in America. Right now, for instance, there are probably two hundred people on this very street named Belohlavy."

I couldn't believe it. After the Pact and after everything we had endured, there was no luck or magic to the name—we were just like everyone else. I looked around at the bare walls and the scratched and faded desk. With nothing to lose, I handed her the letter.

While she agreed to translate the letter into Czech, she had some serious doubts about my odds of success. "I just want to know one thing," she said. "There are hundreds of Bohemians walking around Prague right now with the Belohlavy name. I just hope you're not going to go up to each and every one of them and claim to be their family."

Again, I didn't know what to say. All the way to Bohemia I had imagined that somehow the Belohlavys would instantly recognize me and welcome me into their arms. I had never imagined that they might never be related to us.

"I hate to tell you this," she said, "but you're probably not going to find them."

In the back of her voice, a predominantly Czech belief lingered. *Life was just going to knock you down and you might as well not even get your hopes up.* Her husband had left her long ago, that slob. *Life was designed first for suffering and then for failure—you were going to get both.*

"People," she sighed before agreeing to translate the letter. She told me to leave the letter with her and come back to get it later.

Several hours later when I walked back into the travel agency, she handed me the Czech version of the letter and something else—an eight-by-six paper sign. I held it up in the air in front of me, but I couldn't read it. She pointed. "It says, 'I am an American looking for my family that left Nepomuk in 1885. Do you know Belohlavy?'"

I set the sign down on her desk and thanked her. "You didn't have to do this."

"You're right, I didn't." She looked away and off into the street behind me towards the boarded up stores, thinking about something. "I can't shake it, but for some reason I feel compelled to help you. I just have to." She lost her thought again. "I'm giving you this because you won't be able to talk to anyone in Nepomuk on your own. You're going to need some serious help."

I folded the sign and tucked it into my pocket. Her eyes were still trained on the stores across the street, so I turned and looked over my shoulder before asking one final question. "Is there anything else I should know about Nepomuk?"

"It's the birthplace of a saint," she said before sighing. "But nowadays, that doesn't mean much anymore."

I thanked her and headed onto the boarded-up street once again. Juxtaposed against the boards of nailed up lives, I saw a new side to the Czech Republic. It was a country of desperate dreams, and I fit right in with the rest of them.

Armed with little more than a torn piece of paper that bore a message in a language I didn't understand, I had nothing more than the story of a lonely man named Vaclav to depend on. I didn't know where his family lived, what they looked like, or even if the Belohlavy name had endured over the years through multiple marriages. Other than the story of the Pact, I had no proof that I was related to him, and after all, anyone could tell stories. But we were not in a country of manufactured stories, we were in the Czech Republic, a country of desperate dreams, and somehow—I don't know quite how—I began to believe.

Armed with this belief and little more, I set out to find one person in a country of ten million people—a person who didn't even know that I was looking for them. The odds were about to get even bigger.

At the train station several hours later, I learned that there were, in fact, *two* Nepomuks. One village was more south of Prague and the other was southwest from the capital city. Since I had only one day to attempt the Return, I would have to choose one or the other. I asked the lady at the train station which Nepomuk she thought was bigger. She wrote the number 300 on one piece of paper and 3,500 on another and drew stick figures next to each of the numbers. I pointed to the one with 3,500 people. When she handed me my ticket, I glanced down at the times and realized one critical detail: because of the intermittent train schedule, I would only have six hours in Nepomuk before I had to return to Prague later that night.

After I left the train station, I tried to mitigate my odds by buying a Czech phrase book. I would learn this language. I studied my essential Bohemian survival words like *nero zumeem chesky* ("I don't speak Czech") and *guday'ya la schkola?* ("Where is the school?").

The plan was simple. Like the story Dad had always told me of the man who had found his long-lost family with the help of an English teacher, I was going to arrive in town, find the local high school and ask the English teacher to help me find my family.

It all sounded good until I found out … there's no high school in Nepomuk.

FINALE

On May 24, 2010, I jumped on a series of trains that would take me to Nepomuk, and as far as I knew, I was the only English speaker on the train. Wearing a gray Idaho shirt to represent the state that the Belohlavys eventually settled, I tried to appear as obvious as possible. Strapped across my back was a small pack with three items: the translated letter, a picture of our family on the farm (so they would know who we were), and a picture of my Spanish home in Alicante (so they would know how I had ended up in Europe). The sign was folded in my pocket.

While I may have looked prepared on the outside, I had no idea how to navigate the train system since all of the signs were in Czech. And since Nepomuk was just a tiny stop along the way, it was hard to figure out which train I needed to take because Nepomuk didn't appear on any of the main signs. But just like before, I happened to find the right people each step of the way. At my first junction in Plzen, a man next to me directed me to the right connection. On the ensuing train, I held up my sign and began walking down the aisle. "Nepomuk?" I asked each passenger in slow, enunciated English. "Nepomuk?" They either shook their heads or turned away, at which point I proceeded to the next cabin. At one of the cabins, an old man said Nepomuk in response, so I sat across from him and showed him my sign.

"Old Man Belohlavy!" he began to say, as if he recognized the name. "Old Man Belohlavy!" After the second or third time of saying this, however, the old man fell asleep, then woke and shook himself off, then began talking gibberish, not even in Czech. I asked him about Old Man Belohlavy, but he began to stare at the wall as his eyes spun in circles.

About an hour later when the train came to a stop, his eyes stopped spin-
ning and he abruptly stood up and announced "Nepomuk!" I didn't see a
sign to verify this, but I decided to follow him off the train. As soon as we
stepped off the railing, the train churned away and was gone.

Dust gathered behind us until the train platform went quiet. Other
than three or four noticeable buildings in the distance—a ticket office,
a restaurant, and a general store—there wasn't much else. I tried to talk
to the old man one last time, but he raised his hand as if to dismiss me.
With his back to me, he wandered down the dirt road towards the general
store.

As I stood still on the train platform, I noticed something about the
village. Nepomuk was the sort of town you could inhale in one breath,
but that took several minutes to exhale. Set beneath rolling hills and fields
of yellow flowers, it was a quiet, lonely town, yet somehow very familiar, a collection of once-memories and experiences. Just like the second-
hand store where objects and senses from different lives were arranged
on shelves for display, Nepomuk was a collection of memories and frag-
ments that I'd known my whole life and suddenly found gathered between a set of tracks and a dirt road. I had known the town all along,
long before I arrived and long before I was born, through a patchwork
of oral history and through the glimpse of dreams. Dreams were fleeting
though, and time was running out.

I glanced down at my watch. Not only did I have less than six hours
to find the family (the train had arrived late, of course), but in less than a
week, I would be gone for good. I left the train platform, reached into my
pocket, and unfolded my sign.

First the ticket station. I said *ahoj* to the ticket lady, then held the
sign up to my chest and said, "Belohlavy." She shook her head. Next the
restaurant. Whether people were eating or not, I approached them like
a used car salesman and showed them my sign. In response, they shook
their heads and said things I couldn't understand. No one said anything
about Old Man Belohlavy. I went into the other buildings that lined the
street, but still no luck. The last building I tried was the bakery.

Inside, a line of about five people formed in front of the counter. I
started at the back of the line and showed my sign to each of the people

in turn, getting a no each time. When I reached a man near the front, he pulled me aside and told me something to the effect that I wasn't even in Nepomuk. When he saw my expression plummet, he pointed out toward the road and said one word—*follow*.

I left the bakery at once and began following the dirt road. I didn't know if he was right or wrong because there weren't any signs, but at this point I had nothing to lose. For probably a kilometer, I kept walking. Squat houses lined the road on either side of me and weeds grew in the yards; I didn't see anyone and the place looked abandoned.

At the top of a slight hill, a sign said *Nepomuk 5* with the picture of an arrow. For another five kilometers, I followed the arrow and ended up walking alongside what appeared to be a major paved highway, but no cars drove on it. Green fields rolled in either direction and wooded hills walled in the valley. I kept walking.

The highway bent around several hills and corners before the road forked and an entrance scene unfolded. On a bent signpost, a highway sign bore one word: *Nepomuk*. Tall trees that were the Czech equivalent of oaks lined either side of the fork, and I watched the road continue ahead under the shade. Just like before, there was a subtle familiarity to the scene, as if I'd been here before. The Nepomuk sign was made of the same green highway metal like the road signs back home, and with the slight bend in the post, it reminded me of Baker. The trees, too, could have been exported to Main Street, and I followed them into town.

On the way into Nepomuk, an English-speaking archivist was walking home for lunch and our paths crossed on the side of the road. My heart jumped when I said *ahoj,* and he responded with hello. I showed him my sign, and immediately I could feel it—*this was the man who was going to lead me to my family.*

He brushed me away and told me it was lunchtime.

"Can you please help me?" I asked. "This is like history—I'm looking for my long-lost family."

"But it's lunch time," he repeated, before turning away.

The road continued and I passed a series of apartment buildings, the local hospital, and finally, a pharmacy. Nothing caught my eye, so I continued walking.

But as I passed the pharmacy, something began to tug at me. I didn't quite know what it was. I looked at the pharmacy again. The building was white and nondescript, and with its green cross and *Lékárna* sign, it could have been anywhere. I kept walking. Further up the road, something tugged at me again as I remembered a line from Dresden that seemed forgettable. *If you ever need to talk to someone, find a doctor or maybe a pharmacist.* That line—it didn't seem important at the time. I doubled back and walked into the pharmacy.

In a small valley that most people drove by and forgot, a woman tended a pharmacy next to the side of the road, and I stepped inside to meet her. The pharmacy had just opened and just like the outside of the building, the walls were medical and nondescript, a sterile shade of white. Lined with brochures, vitamins, and pain pills, the edges of the store were defined but the inside awaited arrival: there was no one in the pharmacy except for two people—the pharmacist and myself. Behind the counter, she waited. Her brownish-blonde hair was parted in the middle and it fell long across her back. She wore glasses and the light glanced off of them. Her face was open to a smile.

I reached into my pocket and slowly unfolded my sign. In the silence of the room and the space between us, I moved clumsily, unfolding the paper crease by crease, turning it in my hands until it made a slight crisp. I moved to where the pharmacist stood at the counter and held up my sign for her to read. "Belohlavy?" I said.

She adjusted her glasses along her nose and looked intently at the sign. I watched her eyes read and reread the words as they moved back and forth across two simple lines. *I am an American looking for my family that left Nepomuk in 1885. Do you know Belohlavy?* She paused and rubbed her forehead, before looking at me again and reading the sign once more. Her face began to light up and she was silent until she said … "Belohlavy!"

As if on cue, several other women appeared from the back room and came to stand next to her. With their sudden appearance, I didn't know what to do, so I said "Vaclav!" and started telling the story. The pharmacist listened intently and nodded, her face rising with emotion, a vibrancy beginning to overcome her whole being. When I had finished telling the abridged version of the story, she looked at me and said, "I go help you find family." In English.

Before I knew it, all of the women were on their cell phones calling people across town. There was something about the Belohlavy name, and I heard it in almost every one of their Czech sentences. One call led to another, and within minutes the pharmacist (her name was Anna) took off her lab coat and told me to run around the back of the building and jump in her car—I had to move quick. We were going to find my family and she was going to take time off work to make sure it happened. She didn't know where the Belohlavys were, but just like the old man on the train, she mentioned Old Man Belohlavy. She didn't know who or where he was, but her English professor would know more, she said. She hadn't understood my entire story, but with his help we would be able to figure the rest. Her English professor was the only one in the region, and he lived ten kilometers away in the nearby village of Prádlo. "It's a bit of a drive," she said.

During the drive, Anna told me that she'd taken her first English class just three years ago. Every week since then, she'd been taking night classes, but it was only for one hour per week to learn basic English. "I speak so bad," she said, and shook her head. "I'm sorry."

She had never taken any English classes growing up and she had never used it for science. In fact, she didn't even know why she had begun taking the classes in the first place. "I took English classes just because," she told me.

When she ran out of words to say, Anna began to laugh, and I began to laugh with her. Hills zipped by us as we dipped and rolled through the landscape. Along the way I tried to tell her more about myself, but struggled to find the right words to say; it was easier for her to gather the gist of what I was saying than to follow the conversation word for word. When it was my turn to leave things hanging, we would both laugh again, but it was hard not to laugh in spite of the circumstances.

The very idea of what we were doing was numbing. Ten million people had, in the matter of an hour, been narrowed down to 3,500 people in one of the two possible Nepomuks. *Velmi vám dekuji*, I read to her out of the Czech phrasebook. *Jsem vám velmi vedcny*—I'm very grateful to you.

When we arrived in Prádlo, we saw an old woman cutting grass on the side of the road with a scythe. The village had only three dirt roads and several hundred people, Anna said, so we took the first road until we arrived at a large yellow house. Anna motioned me out of the car as a tall, white-bearded man stepped out to greet us. It was the English professor, and accordingly, he wore large thick-rimmed glasses. "Hello!" I said, excited to meet him. Before he replied, he bowed his head and apologized— he didn't think his English was very good.

"That's alright," I said. "All we have to do is find Old Man Belohlavy." I launched into the story about Vaclav at once.

When I finished the story, the English teacher translated the story into Czech for Anna. Her face lit up and she looked at me with new eyes. "You came all the way across the world for some Bohemians?" she said in broken English as her cheeks swelled and became flush. The story and the quest—they were becoming hers.

But Anna's English teacher was not as excited as either of us and there was good reason for it. Old Man Belohlavy, he told us, was dead.

All of the sudden, Prádlo became still. Anna's eyes peered at me over the rims of her glasses. My face dropped, but I refused to believe it. After all of this ... he couldn't have just died and not left an heir. "Tell us more," I said.

Legend had it that Old Man Belohlavy had lived in Nepomuk many years ago, but for some reason or other, he had decided to move his family to nearby Prádlo where he wanted to live out his final days. "He's been dead for over ten years," the English teacher said. "He died with his wife in a nursing home."

Known simply as Old Man Belohlavy to everyone who knew him, I learned that my great ancestor's first name was a mystery, but he had two daughters who were now married and well on their way to being dead, too. Both daughters had changed their names, and one of them had left town years ago. The other daughter, who went by the last name of Rokytova, was somewhere in Prádlo, the English teacher was sure of it.

Anna's teacher translated the information into Czech. Now armed with the full story, she would be able to tell anyone who I was and who, exactly, we were looking for.

When I asked the English teacher where we could find Belohlavy's daughter, his help began to dwindle. He raised his hand above his eyes and sized us up in the midday sun. "You'll have to ask around. I have no idea."

We left the house of the English teacher and drove back the way we had come to ask anyone we could find about Belohlavy's daughter. The first person we found, of course, was the old woman cutting her grass with a scythe, so Anna pulled over and asked if she knew anything. The women looked at Anna and then looked at me, before pointing back the way we had come. A man down the street knew something, she said. Back and forth, we crisscrossed the three streets of Prádlo, traveling by rumor and word of mouth until we received the final lead. In a two-story house with a locked green gate, we would find Belohlavy's daughter. I was so excited when we heard the news that I wanted to leap over the gate, rip down the front door, and barge in with a hug one hundred and twenty-five years in the making. It was not to be so.

Midday sun stretched across an open sky as we approached the final house in Prádlo. We'd been all across town and now, at its end, the Return was about to be fulfilled. In that moment, I wasn't sure what I was thinking. Momentous would seem an easy word to use, but it misses part of the simplicity. I had no idea what was going to happen. As it was, several things had already happened. The wind had stilled. Anna and I had begun talking in lower voices. The woman cutting her grass across the street with the scythe had turned to watch, and the clouds it seemed, had cleared from the sky. There was a lingering stillness, almost a sacred sense of haunting, and as Anna and I climbed the steps one by one that led to the house, time seemed to evaporate. Even though I was approaching a house that was, in a sense, my own, each footstep felt strangely distant, as if all the years between us had only worked to drive us farther and farther apart.

Perhaps the feeling was a product of the hillside. The Rokytova house sat at the top of a slight hill, and it was a house best defined by its ability to keep watch. Not only did it command a two-story view of the surrounding landscape, but it also had a balcony built into the second level and a green gate at the top of the stairs designed to prevent entry to the yard.

Anna and I followed the stairs to the entrance gate. I tried the handle, but it was locked. Across the yard and thirty feet away, the front door to the house was open. They were here.

"Belohlavy!" I yelled across the front lawn and into the empty house.

"Belohlavy!" Anna yelled, before trying several sentences in Czech.

No one appeared.

We waited a few moments, then began yelling again, this time louder and faster. No one appeared. We yelled again and again, and the air swallowed our words and spat them back at us, leaving us breathless. Anna turned to me. Maybe we should just go.

"No," I said. "Let's give it a few more minutes."

We waited and the wind didn't pick up. I yelled again, but no luck. Anna signaled me to give up the effort, and right as we were turning away, a heavy-set older woman materialized in the shadow of the front door, filling the frame with her body. Her cheeks were old and sagging, her hair thinning, her teeth cracked and her smile broken. She waddled outside the front door and began talking in angry Czech. It was Belohlavy's daughter.

"What the hell are you doing here?" she asked.

I said Belohlavy and she pointed at me and said something that sounded nasty in Czech. I didn't know what to do.

I had imagined a glorious homecoming, where Belohlavy's daughter bounded across her yard to hug me, our hearts racing inside at the vulnerability of all of it, but real life doesn't always work that way. Instead, she stood stoically, frowning twenty feet away, barely outside her doorstep, looking for any reason to dismiss us. We were bothering her.

"She thinks you're a liar," Anna said. "The woman keeps saying, 'they came back, they came back'—I think she's referring to the Belohlavy's. She's trying to say that Vaclav never stayed in America like you're claiming."

"Oh, he stayed all right," I said. "And I'm here to prove it!" Of course that proved nothing, but I felt vindicated.

When my attempts at persuasion failed, Anna took over. *You might not know who this boy is,* she said, *but you should at least listen to him. He came all the way across the world to see you. Would he do that for a lie?*

My quest had become her quest and she was not about to give up. Perhaps for her, the story had become personal, and I wondered if maybe some of her relatives had gone off to America, too. I didn't know what her background was or what motivated her, but Anna was clearly determined to get this gate open.

As Anna continued to argue with the old woman, something finally began to give way. The old woman hung her head low and stopped talking. At about the same time, I decided to shut my mouth and stop claiming to be a Belohlavy. I took my hands off the gate and put them in my pockets. From thirty feet away, we stared at each other across the gate in silence. Our lips didn't move, our eyes didn't waver, and if the scene had panned to the left or to the right, neither one of us would have moved. One, two, three, you could count the seconds and see them drip away, until finally, after all these years, the old woman began walking across the lawn to open the gate. As soon as she opened it, I met her at the entryway and gave her a hug that was long in the making. I'm not sure she knew what to think at first, but soon enough she wouldn't let go and I wouldn't let go and we were locked there in the front yard, embracing both sides of the family as Anna watched from afar. One hundred and twenty-five years ago the Belohlavys had sent one person to America on the wings of a desperate pact, and one hundred and twenty-five years later, the Belohlavys had sent one person back to fulfill it. The Pact was now complete.

When we released, the old woman walked back into the house and returned to the yard with a photo of her granddaughter, Petra, and a piece of paper with an address and the word *anglicky.* She wanted me to write to Petra because she spoke English. I gave her my contact information, but didn't expect to hear from her.

I reached into my backpack and pulled out the letter I'd had translated into Czech. When I gave it to her, she revealed her name for the first time: Marie Rokytova. In the middle of her front yard, we hugged again and said goodbye.

* * *

When Anna and I arrived back at the pharmacy, all of the staff gathered to celebrate. The walls became more than white, the building more than simply medical, the feel more than sterile. Even though there was a line of customers running halfway through her store, Anna asked them to wait for a moment. Something special had happened and we were going to take a picture. The whole staff gathered around Anna and me in the middle of the pharmacy, and one of the bewildered customers offered to take the photo. What was this crazy American doing with all of these Bohemians? A camera flashed and sealed the moment.

Anna ran behind the counter to find something to give me as a memento, but all she could find was a roll of strawberry vitamins. I told her that she didn't need to give me anything, but she gave them to me anyways. "It's nothing," she said, "I wish I could give you something more."

"You already have," I told her. People didn't usually drop everything for a complete stranger with nothing more than a sign and a story. I never saw another person like her in all of Europe. Who was this person who would do something like that? This was what I expected the Belohlavys to be like. I expected them to be excited to see us.

I stayed in the pharmacy a while longer that day, but customers began getting impatient. Orders had to be filled. Painkillers needed to be prescribed. Anna went behind the counter to help a customer, but when I told her that I was about to leave, she ran into the middle of the store and gave me a lingering hug. "I won't ever forget this," she said.

She wouldn't. Because like Lu said, you see everyone in your life at least twice.

It's getting to be about sunset. For the rest of the day I have wandered the city of my ancestors, scouring the names of old tombstones in the graveyard, visiting the church of Saint John of Nepomuk, and eating goose in restaurants. I have received strange looks, and other than the archivist and a certain pharmacist, I have spoken to almost no one. It is the end of the day, and at last my watch tells me it's time to go. I arrive back at the train station.

A searing orange ball tears the horizon in flames. A distant castle on a hill becomes illuminated and a certain magic envelops the sky in a warm, fuzzy glow, as if it's being held in the palm of a larger hand. Because across from me on the other train platform, Anna appears once again.

There's a catch though. Anna only sees me because my train has been delayed for twenty minutes. She doesn't know this, even as she yells across the platform, *Steve!* I run over and give her a final hug. Above us, a plane streaks across the sky and the tail of its smoke stands out like tunnel vision because there's another catch, too. The American version of my last name, Hanna, used to be Hána in Czech.

As we're about to say goodbye, I write down my address for her and she points to my last name and says, *is that your last name?* And I nod and say yes and ask, *what is your last name?*

Hána, she says, *just like yours.*

I look at her more closely this time and notice something that hasn't occurred to me before. We have the same slightly rounded faces, the same foreheads and the same thin lips—our smiles are the same, too. I think to myself, *this is impossible, isn't it?* But then one thing tugs at me, and as crazy as it seems, it all comes together.

Whether it's true or not that Anna and I are related … I'll leave that for you to decide, but what I know is this. We Hannas have always believed in miracles.

The story goes that over the years we lost track of where the Hannas came from. While Dad had been able to trace the Belohlavy line all the way back to the beginning, he'd never been able to figure out what happened to the Hannas before a small band of them left Prague in 1870. Dad's research had narrowed them down to somewhere in Bohemia and he knew that there was a Hána River in the Czech Republic. Since Dad didn't know where to find them though, we hadn't even attempted to look. After all, their story wasn't nearly as interesting—there wasn't a pact involved. But interesting things had a way of happening to families that didn't make pacts. In 1870 our family name was Hána, but when our ancestors left Prague for Nebraska and Indian Country, they wanted to sound more American, so they added the extra *n* to the name and dropped the Czech accent mark to go by Hanna.

Together, Anna and I stood on the train platform and laughed. It felt soft, rich and deep all at once, all over my soul. For if the woman who led me to my family also happened to be family, then we didn't know it until the very end. There was a reason she had taken my quest to heart. Long ago, part of her family had left for America, too, and with each ensuing generation, the story had been passed on. She had never forgotten it.

A soft glow hung between us. The connection and the story—it seemed almost too unreal to believe.

Moments later, the train whisked me away to Plzen and Anna's wave disappeared from view as the train pulled forward and then turned out of sight. As quickly as the story had unfolded in six hours, it was gone, but next to me on the train sat Anna's daughter (also named Anna). She was heading back to college. Cousins or distant cousins or whatever the relation might have been, we sat next to each other as family. There was a lot of catching up to do.

Laugh at the craziness and irony of it all, I had come to find the Belohlavys, but I may have ended up finding both parts of the family. And from what I gathered, it sounded like the Hána side of the family had moved to Nepomuk within the last few years. I asked my distant cousin why, but she didn't know. I asked her if she knew why her mom had started learning English, but again, she didn't know. Then I asked her what her dad's name was. "Vaclav," she said.

In a small farming town in rural Bohemia that most people drive by and forget, two families were reunited after one hundred and twenty-five years, six generations, and two world wars. Here in Nepomuk, in the middle of flowering fields and under a plane-streaked orange sky with low-hanging clouds, here in the middle of a small village and the birthplace of a saint, here is where we made the connection, cast the line against all odds and found the family. Even as the countryside passed by at a steady blur, I could still make out the tiny silhouette of Anna waving as the train pulled away from the station and began rolling away. Like so long ago, part of the family had been sent away once again, but this time it wouldn't last forever. In a valley that most people drive by and forget, two families would never forget.

WEEK 21
ALICANTE, SPAIN

BEGINNINGS ARE ALWAYS ENDINGS, and endings are always beginnings, though we don't always know it at the time. For the last time, I returned to the shadowy hallway on the fourth floor of a certain apartment building. The door creaked open and Dior padded over to greet me. The sound of the TV buzzed from down the hallway, the space heater sat in front of the living room door, and the air, as always, hung still. If my guess was correct, two people would be waiting in the living room.

"*¡Estif!*" Carmen exclaimed when I stuck my head in the door. "*Dios mio*, you're back!"

"*Siéntate,*" she said. Her hair was once again pinned to the top of her head like a China doll with a red sweatshirt, and Asis sat next to her on the couch in his baby blue pajamas. It was the middle of the afternoon.

"It's been a hard day," he said. "Lots of TV specials."

Carmen patted her lap and Dior jumped onto the couch. "What happened in Germany?" she asked. "*Cuéntanos.*"

Since they had no idea that I had ventured into the Czech Republic to find the family, I started the story with Lu and me in East Germany, then told them the story of the Pact and the Return. Asis turned the TV to mute and they sat in rapt attention.

"*¡Qué terrible!*" Carmen pronounced about the Pact.

"*¡Qué fuerte!*" Asis added. How strong they must have been!

While he thought finding my family made for a great story, he wanted to remind me of one little detail. He pointed to Carmen and himself. "Just don't forget about us."

When there were five days left in Spain, Carmen and Asis asked me to take a walk with them down to the *puerto* and watch the boats set sail. *Hace mucho calor,* they said as the sun burned across our skin and lit up a blue sky perfect for boats to sail off into. We walked around the boardwalk and Asis poked fun at *los ricos* who could afford elaborate yachts. "Who would want one of those?" he said. "I've got a Mercedes."

We talked about everything and nothing in front of a line of endless boats that arrived and then departed, much like the lives they watched. Well, you'll be off soon enough, they said. A new student will take your place. We'll try to teach him some things, but we'll never forget the boats that we helped set sail. "Like our Mercedes," Asis said, "we own you and you own us, too."

If family means six generations of problems and promises like I learned in Nepomuk, it also means that we are bound together by these dreams and desperations, even as we try to cast them off. Like the Bujans, we can't choose our families, and in some cases like the Belohlavys, we may not fully know them, but in everything they leave an imprint on us that endures through space and time. For all the deep wounds that family can bring—and there are many—family are also the source of life's greatest joy.

When we returned from the walk, Carmen and I sat on the edge of my bed. As our eyes wandered across the walls and all of the memories they contained, a life story began to unfold, a story that included Adán in his second grade picture and Asis junior and his third grade classmates. On the closet door there were the UNLV and University of Arizona stickers, too, that marked the presence of sons and students from semesters or years ago; all of it telling the story of a mother and a father in a small apartment on the fourth floor of Calle Alona, Alicante. When I gave Carmen a silver-framed picture of all of us that we had taken earlier in the semester, she began to cry before leaving the room. "I need to be somewhere alone," she said and shut the door to her room.

I wasn't entirely sure what to do, so I wandered back to the beach where the sky drew shapes on moving water and illuminated the whole of the world in an orange and red glow, a glorious fade before the transition to nightfall. Like that sunset, the final days came to a rose-colored close. They would be reborn again.

We were transitioning from Idaho to Ohio. My last three days in Spain marked the coming of a new study abroad student, and Robert from Ohio came to live with us. The day Robert arrived, Carmen cooked a big Sunday welcome dinner, complete with a healthy dose of culture-shock: snails. "I haven't eaten snails in four or five years," Asis said as he piled a heap of shells on his plate, while we eyed them warily before taking nibbles and first bites. Roberto (as Carmen and Asis began calling him) had never been out of the States before, so on his first day we introduced him to snails, topless European beaches, 100% Spanish, blazing hot weather, 10:00 p.m. dinnertimes and the siesta. I think it was a little much to take in. "I'm not quite sure what to think," he told me in English before heading to bed. "There are lots of changes."

The following day I showed him around town and we went to a museum. I showed him how to do the little things, too, like how to get cheap food when he would starve between prolonged Spanish mealtimes. We talked a lot while we were out, but he didn't speak much around the house and Carmen couldn't figure out why he was so quiet. *"Estif, Roberto es muy quieto."*

"Está aprendiendo español," I told her. He was still learning basic Spanish.

Roberto's first days were a neat look back to where I had began and a snapshot of how much I had learned in my short time here. "How do I catch the bus?" he asked me one night. Five months ago, I was asking the same question.

* * *

"Are you ready to leave?" Roberto asked as we were eating lunch the day before I left.

His question caught me off guard, and I didn't really have an answer. "I thought I was ready," I said. "Leaving is just like coming to Spain, except it's worse."

Months ago, I had heard something about this. *It's harder to return than it is to arrive*, the study abroad office had told me. I didn't believe them. How could it be harder to leave than to arrive? You got to go back to your friends, family, and regular life! But that was exactly why it was so hard to go back, because in the process of returning to something, you had to lose something.

The whole family gathered to say goodbye, Spanish style, and two hours before midnight we started our *fiesta final*. In the living room we ran two parts of the Spanish triathlon, lots of good food and drink, and in the gathered fellowship of the whole family, it was the right way to say goodbye. Asis junior changed his work schedule to be there, Adán arrived home early, and Carmen cooked up a final meal that was the exact same as our first—a black skillet of paella.

If I could have scripted the moments that followed after dinner, we would have embraced as a family as if we'd never see each other again. There would have been tears, a slow walk to the bus station, our eyes locked through the glass of a disappearing window, our hands waving as the midnight bus pulled out of the station. What the goodbye actually was, however, was a stressful occasion of last-minute packing and marathon sprinting so I could catch the bus on time. There was no long, sad hug; no tears, only a quick embrace as we laughed at how ridiculous our rush to the station had been when the bus arrived a half hour late. "*España*," Asis laughed. "You never change."

Ending Where We Began

I began my journey in the Philadelphia airport and I will end it in the same place. On January fifth, I sat in the airport listening to people speaking in foreign tongues and I was nervous and scared to death. Life as I knew it was about to be over, and as it turns out, I was right about that. Five months later in the same Philadelphia airport, I sat reading a copy of *El País* and listening to salsa music, and suddenly, I was the foreigner. What was the deal with everyone speaking English here? After five months abroad, English seemed foreign and all I wanted to do was speak Spanish again. But the flight announcements were called over the loudspeaker in English, and soon it was my turn to board the plane. There was no family to wave to as I stepped aboard, but I wasn't worried. Mine would be waiting soon.

When I arrived home I received the first email from the granddaughter of the Belohlavy family. Petra wrote back, overjoyed at what the Return meant and how good it felt to finally be connected again. "I always wanted a big family," she wrote, "I just never knew that I already had one."

Petra and I have begun writing to each other. A lot has happened in the span of one hundred and twenty-five years, and somehow a four page summary letter can't even scratch the surface. It's a warm and altogether strange feeling to be related to someone you've never known. Growing up, Dad always used to tell us the story of John Wesley and how he famously said, "my heart has been strangely warmed" when talking about his first encounter with the heart of God. I'll just say that it's a now-familiar feeling.

Piece by piece, Petra revealed the rest of the story. Several years after Vaclav arrived in America on the price of the Pact, his mother and brother were sent on a mission to find him and bring him back to Bohemia. The whole family missed him.

"They came back," Belohlavy's daughter kept telling me when I stood at her gate and she refused to let me in. "They came back to Bohemia," she insisted. And she was right. They did come back—his mother and brother returned to Bohemia empty-handed because they were unable to persuade Vaclav to abandon the Dream. A few years after they had returned, the brother's wife gave birth to a son who became the father of the woman I met. So we were related, Petra said, through the relationship of Vaclav and his brother (who I had never heard about until Petra told me the story). While it was nice to know that we were related, it didn't surprise me one bit. We Hannas have always been believers.

There was one final detail. After the brother returned to Bohemia, Vaclav and his brother wrote a series of letters back and forth. "We heard from him until about 1947," Petra told me, but they hadn't heard from "the Americans" since then. Vaclav died in 1947.

And that is the Belohlavy story. Petra signs her letters to us, "with love from the family." Even her grandmother, the sour old woman, began to open up and get excited about the history. What a wellspring that is! And to think I never wanted to find the family in the first place! Through it all, something larger was going on.

In final moments, a pool of memories unfolds in black and white fashion, beginning and ending with a Father standing in the pool with his arms outstretched, his hair wet. As if a slow motion film is set to mute, the rest of the scenes play: a vase is shattered at my feet, Adán pounds a wall and fights Asis over the sweater, an old man crosses his arms and blocks a door in Morocco, waterfalls thunder and I jump, Lu says *¡Buen Camino!* while climbing a muddy hill, Mary Rokytova calls me a liar before the Return is complete. This was either all of it or part of it, but as the thin strip of memory creaks away and finally recedes, one thing is certain: there was direction. One night long ago in Bohemia, a Pact was sealed that set things in motion. For one hundred and twenty-five years, it propelled our destiny, bound us to our fate, and gave birth to the Dream, but perhaps not entirely on its own. The Pact was complete, but if Lu was right, we wouldn't need it anymore.

"Remember what I said about how you see everyone in your life at least twice?" he asked as we had said goodbye for the final time. "Well, we've now seen each other three times. And you know what that means—your family might be closer next time than you think."

If it's true that we will see everyone in our lives at least twice, then it's time for a new pact. Only this time, under new circumstances, there's one slight difference.

It will be a promise.

IV

THE PROMISE

"I will signal for them and gather them in, for I have redeemed them, and they shall be as many as of old. Though I scattered them among the nations, yet in far countries they shall remember me, and with their children they shall live and return. I will bring them home..."
Zechariah 10:8-10

One Year Later
Baker City, Oregon

In a valley that most people drive by and forget, Lu and I are running, herding cows. Across yellow fields we run, chasing two-ton animals in front of us that scatter and disperse as we yell *hiyah!* and flap our arms like scarecrows. "This is so much fun," he says in between breaths. And even though he's not holding a rope or wearing spurs, we realize that you don't really need those things anyways. "I feel like a cowboy!" Lu says.

Between the banks of a frozen river and worn irrigation ditches we run. This could last forever, but it won't. Above us, snow clouds foretell a coming storm, but we brush it off for now, at least for another hour. Because if it's true that you see everyone in your life at least twice, I have now seen Lu four times. This year he came to visit for New Years. We went on adventures and caught up on old times. We showed him the Tame House and the Home Place, but he preferred the Home Place and herding cows. Dad was with us too, driving the truck to keep the cows moving in the general direction, laughing to himself. It was fun to see Lu be a cowboy.

But it couldn't last forever. The storm clouds would break, the road would call, and Lu would have to drive his rental car south to Las Vegas where he would finally get to lose all of his money before he flew back to Europe. "I've never been so excited in my life," he said. And he finally got to do the Great American Road Trip. "It's everything you said it would be," he said before adding, "When you have to drive in the snow, that is."

Baker's familiar ring of mountains loomed over us, protective and peaceful all at once. They didn't stick their noses out often, but when they did, they meant it. Under their watch, we hugged and said goodbye.

When Lu arrived back in Europe he wrote a letter about the rest of his time in Vegas. Without spilling too many details, it sounded like he thoroughly enjoyed himself.

We receive other mail from Europe, too. Carmen sends long letters signed *besos* with every conceivable detail about her life: new trinkets and Asis junior's love life. She likes Adán's new girlfriend, she says, but she really wants to see me again. When am I coming back? Other family members ask that question too, and just like long ago, letters from the Hannas and the Belohlavys begin crossing the Atlantic. A postcard arrives from Anna the other day, and Dad jumps at the opportunity to write her a long letter about the history of the family in America. Petra and I continue to write back and forth and she tells me that she was recently accepted into law school at the university in Plzen (about an hour from Nepomuk). Coincidentally enough, Anna's daughter also attends the university in Plzen, but she doesn't know Petra yet. Until a year ago, they didn't know they might be connected.

Petra constantly asks, *when are you coming back, when are you coming back?* And I tell her soon, in just a little while, hopefully next year. It's a promise; we will return once again. As it stands, Dad and I are already making plans with the rest of the family, because this time I want to bring everyone back. After all, it was always their dream to return, not mine.

Speaking of that dream, Dad and I embarked on a round of summer visits to tell "the Czech Story" to the rest of the Hannas and Belohlavys in Idaho. When we told the story for the first time (it was more Dad talking than me because he was so excited), Dad's parents—Grandpa Hanna and

Grandma Belohlavy—sat across the table from us.

"Of all the places in the world where both sides of the family could have been, they were in Nepomuk?" Grandma exclaimed. "And they didn't even know it?" She couldn't believe it. "Arley," she said, turning to Grandpa, "this sounds like a familiar story!"

Back in the 1800's, Grandma said, both the Hannas and the Belohlavys left Bohemia and without knowing it, both families ended up settling fifty miles apart in Nebraska. "They lived next to each other for fifty years without knowing it," Grandma said. "Can you believe that?" And then, for some reason or another ("at about the same time"), both the Hannas and the Belohlavys decided to move to a small town called Emmett, Idaho. They still never knew each other. When my grandparents got married ten years later, the two families met each other for the first time. Sixty-five years later, they would be reunited once again in a small town called Nepomuk.

"Strange, huh?" Grandma said.

Dad smiled. "Well, I don't think strange is quite the right word."

Other things happened, too. For years, Grandpa had developed a feud with his older sister. They didn't like each other much, but when we sat both of them down together to hear the story, something finally gave way and they've been slightly better ever since.

"Did you see what the story did?" Dad pointed out later. "Redemption."

Perhaps we had our own redeeming to do too, and Dad began speaking more openly about his dreams once again. When we had moved to the Tame House he had grown quieter, but he always had a lot of dreams, he said. One, of course, involved the Bohemians, but that dream was now fulfilled. His other dream revolved around the farm. "I want our farm to be the Home Place," he was always fond of saying. "Years from now, I want people to talk about our farm as the Old Hanna Place."

The whole time that my brothers and I were growing up, all he really wanted to do was build a place for us to come home to. And maybe, at its end, that's what he and Mom ended up doing, even though we never really had one. As you know, their dream was deferred, and to this day, we still haven't fully reclaimed the farm. But through a lot of work, we may have reclaimed a home.

Paul had a term for the work we'd do on the farm. "Poverty Camp," he called it, but that only described the summer when Dad, Paul, and I lived in front of our own house in a borrowed RV camper and worked all day long in hundred-degree heat. Eating utensils were limited to one per person, or better yet, non-existent. We'd microwave frozen food on slabs of cardboard that we'd rip from barn boxes, and we weren't afraid of mosquitoes getting in our food. It was either work or rest, and we were tired of both. But somehow the idea of Poverty Camp stuck and came to define the next several years. Life was about the Dream, the dream of the barn and other dreams, and if living in front of them was the closest we could ever get, then we'd live in front of them every day.

While we still haven't moved back to the farm yet, we're getting closer to it each day, close enough to where it hurts.

A year ago when I was twenty-two, Dad left the farm in the Conestoga truck. As was our usual habit in my post-college days when I was living in Boise, I'd drive over to meet Dad in Baker, and home became a point that was halfway in between us. I'd drive over from Boise and he'd drive over from the Tame House and instead of going fishing or hiking or going to play sports like other fathers and sons might have done, we worked. Twelve-hour days were a start, heat and mosquitoes aside. We'd sleep in a camper that my uncle had hauled over and that we'd somehow never found a way to get rid of. There was something about it, being twenty-two years old and sleeping right next to my dad. We weren't snuggled up together and each of us was in our own sleeping bag, but the feeling was there. Dad would turn over at night and roll into me. I'd roll into him. I remember lying on my back and staring at the lid of the camper where paint peeled from the ceilings and crinkled like cream-colored snow. This was what I'd lived my whole life for—right here, to lie down at age twenty-two next to my Dad and just be with him, yet never hold him. We didn't hug until the end of that weekend, after I'd been frustrated with the barn job and after we'd both gotten frustrated with each other and all the work left undone.

"Well, I'm about to go," he said.

"Alright, bye," I said. And that was that.

But as Dad bent a slab of sheet metal into the canopy shape of a Conestoga wagon and tied it to the back of his unwashed truck, and as he drove off into the distance with a cloud of dust trailing behind him, and after sleeping in the camper and working and living next to each other for years, after all of this—being apart for so long and everything else that we'd been through, I ran to the edge of the fence to watch him go. I waited, of course, until he was just out of sight so that he wouldn't see me watch him go, but suddenly everything that I thought mattered disappeared and only one thing remained. Either we'd been branded or we'd been doing some branding ourselves, but it hurt me down in my soul. It hurt to have my father love me.

As the truck slowly made its way down our driveway, and as Dad stopped periodically to look at the cows or the fields, I dropped the fast food cup I had been holding and climbed on top of the fence. I'd never watched a car leave our driveway and follow it all the way to the end, all the way to the highway. Not even when I was a kid. And yet here, at twenty-two years old, wearing the same cowboy hat I'd had since I was sixteen when he'd pronounced that I'd "earned the spurs," here I was, sitting on a fence that I had helped him build, crying for my dad. I watched the truck turn left at the end of our long gravel driveway, then northwest, towards the next town and towards away, and I was left sitting on the fence in front of Dad's dream—our dream—that we never seemed to be able to fully own. I felt the tug of the strings of love then, and it felt *good*, good down deep in my soul. It felt so good to have him with me that weekend; it was all I ever really wanted. What Paul used to call Poverty Camp—us working on the farm and sleeping in my uncle's camper—had become the thing I loved most. Home wasn't in Baker. Home wasn't in Spain. Home wasn't in Nebraska. And home wasn't in Bohemia. Home was somewhere in between, somewhere between where we were and where we always wanted to be, somewhere off in the distance just beyond a cloud of dust and a truck, always in sight, but barely visible. Home was sitting on a fence watching a Conestoga truck and in a heart's moment being everywhere and nowhere all at once. Home wasn't here and never would be, but the tug of the strings of love always reminded me where to look for it.

I sat on the fence awhile longer, then took off my hat and walked back to the barn to shut the doors. It was time to go. I drove away that day not too long ago, but I would be back again some time later, ready to work alongside him, because at its end, it was never really about the Bohemians. It was about somewhere in between, building something that we'd have forever, somewhere called home.

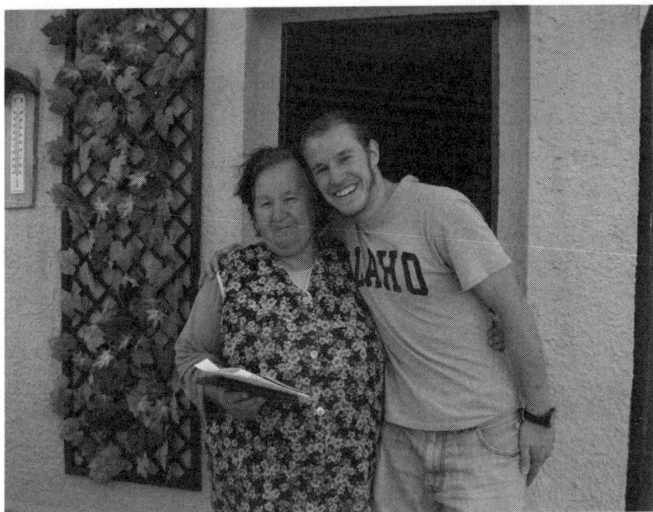

The Pact is fulfilled: Steve and Marie in Nepomuk

Steve and Anna in Nepomuk

ACKNOWLEDGMENTS

In writing *A Home Called Your Own*, I believe the most important people to thank are my ancestors who sacrificed years of their lives without knowing what the fruits of their labor would eventually build. To my great ancestor, Vaclav, who buried two of his wives and three of his children, and who at the end of his life could only say, "I am so lonely," and to the rest of my great ancestors who gathered around that table 125 years ago to make the original Pact, it was your act of love that made it possible for our home to be built. Without knowing it, your sacrifice set this story into motion and bound our family together across time. We will meet again.

I would also like to thank both the Hanna and Belohlavy families. While we haven't always gotten the concepts of family and home right (in fact we've probably missed the mark more than we've hit it), when we have gotten it right, it's felt so good that it aches. To Mom and Dad especially, I truly believe that you did build the Home Place. It feels so good to always have somewhere to come back to, even if that somewhere remains undefined at the moment. Adam and Paul, I'm so proud to call you brothers and first-hand partners in this story. Thank you for allowing me to tell it.

Special thanks also goes to Carmen, Anna, and Petra. For being a book about family, I didn't do a very good job at writing letters back to you in a timely fashion while I was writing this book. Please forgive me! There's a handwritten note headed your direction.

I would also like to thank everyone else who appears in the book. Your lives, quirks, and insights became a rich part of the story, and I am so blessed to have had the opportunity to share part of you with the world. It has been wonderful to get to know you as friends and family. Thank you for giving me the honor of chronicling a small piece of your life.

A deep sense of gratitude also goes out to my editor, Harvey Gover, who, like many of the seemingly unconnected events in this book, just happened to be sitting across from me at a luncheon one day and offered to read my manuscript. For the two and a half years since he read that first draft and offered to guide the project, I haven't been more honored to work with anyone else. I would also like to extend a warm thanks to Austin and Juliet Petersen who followed this book from concept to completion and read every draft along the way. Thank you for believing.

To everyone else who helped along the way, in no particular order: my mentor, Dr. Vincent Kituku, Darlene Anderson, Curtis Bower, Gus Simpson, Kim Barnes, Daniel Orozco, Lu Ullman, Daniel and Sabrina Grünhard, Gary Williams, Dan Bukvich, Steve Kunioka, Gary Engel, K.C. Neal, Dave Lakhani, Steve Vieira, Jack Cannon, Jodie Marie Fisher, Karthik Ram, Leah Schwisow Goede, Mark Olson, Scott Schuffield, Drew Cunningham, Austin Warren, Lisa Scott, the University of Idaho, the team at USAC study abroad, and my coworkers at Micron and Crucial who were just as excited about this book as I was.

And in terms of the final thanks, I would like to reserve that for you. Thank you for reading *A Home Called Your Own*. For an author, there truly is no greater honor.

Supporters

Just like the story of the Pact where my ancestors gathered around a table and pledged everything they owned to set one person free, I think it's particularly symbolic that over 125 years later, another group of people banded together and pledged their collective fortunes to make this book possible. I would like to thank the following 120 people for their support—this book wouldn't have happened without you.

Adam & Amanda Rupel
Adrian Escalante
Aiden & Alexis Rupel
Alice Maher
Alye Hannum
Amanda Turner
Arley & Bonnie Hanna
Austin & Juliet Petersen
Austin Warren
Bernie Druffel
Brady Paladichuk
Brayden Panttaja
Caitlin Eleanor Bond
Candice Adkins
Carly Pritchard
Caroline Riddle
Charlotte Hadlock
Chelsea Pidgeon
Christina Ginosar
Christoph Dally
Clay Berthelsen
Colin Baxter
Cordelle LaRoche
Cory Griffard
Craig Bourassa

Curtis Bower
Daniel Taylor
Darlene Anderson
Dave Lakhani
David Prinz
David Rosen
David Sukoff
Dea Skubitz
Diana Breeding
Don & Janet Hanna
Drew Cunningham
Dylan Rinker
Dylan Waterman
Ed Kowalczewski
Elaine Ambrose
Emily Hickman
Fazal Shariff
Gabe Flick
Garrett Holbrook
Gary Engel
Grace Chenal
Gus Simpson
Heather Wells
Jack Bynum
Jack Cannon

Jared Brickman

Jim Mundt

Jim Stroud

Jodi Marie Fisher

Jordan Hall

Jordan Ramsey

Josh Brunner

Josh Neill

Josh Snell

JP Schedin

Justin Knox

Kari Embree

Kasen & Jenn Christensen

Kathy Melamed

KC Neal

Kelby Wilson

Kelly Fluitt

Kelsey Breeding

Ken Hanna

Ken Rupel

Kim Barnes

Kim Ullman

Korey Gene Mitchell

Kristin Schmidt

Larry Hammons

Laurie Thornton

Lisa Schuette

Lisa Scott

Lori Ann

Lynn Berggren

Mark Olson

Matt Berggren

Mattea York

Meg Cropley

Melissa Leija

Michael Moreland

Michael Richardson

Michael VanLydegraf

Mike Hanna

Nate Eklund

Nate Hales

Nate Biggs

Neelima Dahal

Niki Braman

Paul Hanna

Paul Reni

Peter Clarke

Pia Schulze

Ranie Sternke

Richard Chung

Sarah Fivel Demoret

Sarah Reichman

Sarah Routh

Scott Shuffield

Seth Rathbun

Sophia Tsai

Spencer Oldemeyer

Steve Kunioka

Susan Escalante

Taryn Hoopes

Tasha Seal

Terry Katzer

Thomas Leija

Traci Glover

Trudy Mays

Tyler Flowers

Wayne Allan

Zach & Annie Stucky

Zach & Amanda Battles

Zane Jensen